E. G. Schlechtendahl (Ed.)

Specification of a CAD * I Neutral File for CAD Geometry

Wireframes, Surfaces, Solids
Version 3.2

Second, Revised and Enlarged Edition

Bayerische Motorenwerke AG
Cisigraph
Cranfield Institute of Technology
Danmarks Tekniske Højskole
Kernforschungszentrum Karlsruhe GmbH
NEH Consulting Engineers ApS
Universität Karlsruhe

Springer-Verlag
Berlin Heidelberg New York
London Paris Tokyo

Editors' addresses

I. Bey
E. G. Schlechtendahl

Kernforschungszentrum Karlsruhe GmbH
Postfach 3640, D-7500 Karlsruhe 1, Federal Republic of Germany

J. Leuridan
Leuven Measurement and Systems
Interleuvenlaan 65, B-3030 Heverlee, Belgium

ESPRIT Project 322: CAD * I (CAD Interfaces) belongs to the Research and Development area "Computer-Aided Design and Engineering (CAD/CAE)" within the Subprogramme 5 "Computer-Integrated Manufacturing (CIM)" of the ESPRIT Programme (European Strategic Programme for Research and Development in Information Technology) supported by the European Communities.

Direct exchange of data among different CAD systems is not feasible without difficulties but has been requested more and more frequently in practical application. The objectives pursued under this project consist in developing, testing, and providing efficient, supplier independent data exchange interfaces in the CAD environment.

Partners in the project are:
Bayerische Motorenwerke AG/FRG · CISIGRAPH/France · Cranfield Institute of Technology/UK · Danmarks Tekniske Højskole/Denmark · Estudios y Realizaciones en Diseño Informatizado SA (ERDISA) / Spain · Gesellschaft für Strukturanalyse (GfS) mbH/FRG · Katholieke Universiteit Leuven/Belgium · Kernforschungszentrum Karlsruhe GmbH/FRG · Leuven Measurement and Systems/Belgium · NEH Consulting Engineers ApS/Denmark · Rutherford Appleton Laboratory/UK · Universität Karlsruhe/FRG

This book is a revised and enlarged edition of "Specification of a CAD * I Neutral File for Solids" Version 2.1 which appeared in the same series.

ISBN 3-540-18397-3 Springer-Verlag Berlin Heidelberg New York
ISBN 0-387-18397-3 Springer-Verlag New York Berlin Heidelberg

Printed in Germany

Repro- u. Druckarbeiten: Weihert-Druck GmbH, Darmstadt
Bindearbeiten: Druckhaus Beltz, Hemsbach/Bergstraße
2145/3140 – 543210

ABSTRACT

One principal goal of the ESPRIT project CAD*I (CAD Interfaces) is to develop techniques for the exchange of CAD information between CAD systems.

This paper presents a proposal for a neutral file for CAD data: curves, surfaces, and solids. The proposal is based on a reference schema for CAD data bases and is defined informally with respect to its semantics and formally with respect to its syntax. The semantics is defined on three levels:

1. On the data structuring level the method for defining semantics is borrowed from the concepts of abstract data types: the effect of elementary operations on the data structure (creation, deletion, identification, navigation) is used.
2. On the reference model level semantics is defined textually supported by graphical representations and by mathematical formula.
3. For the interpretation of the neutral file semantics is defined on the basis of a finite state machine model of a post-processor: it is described in terms of the effect which the interpretation of the file will produce.

Syntax specifications appear in three forms:

1. The syntax of the HDSL (high level data specification language) is given in BNF notation.
2. The tokens on the neutral file are defined as a regular set of integers coded in one byte each.
3. The structure of the neutral file language (syntax) is defined in Backus-Naur form.

A general specification of the architecture of pre- and post-processors is also given.

CONTRIBUTORS

A. Assals, NEH - Consulting Engineers
N. Brändli, Kernforschungszentrum Karlsruhe
M. J. Chinnery, Cranfield Institute of Technology
H. Ferretti, Cisigraph
B. Frayssinet, Cisigraph
U. Gengenbach, Kernforschungszentrum Karlsruhe
C. Ghijs, Leuven Measurement and Systems
R. J. Goult, Cranfield Institute of Technology
L. Gungaard, Danmarks Tekniske Højskole
S. R. Hailstone, Cranfield Institute of Technology
P. B. Hansen, Danmarks Tekniske Højskole
N. E. Hansen, NEH - Consulting Engineers
H. Helpenstein, Gesellschaft für Strukturanalyse
F. Katz, Kernforschungszentrum Karlsruhe
R. Korff, Bayerische Motorenwerke AG
U. Kroszynski, Danmarks Tekniske Højskole
M. Lachance, Cranfield Institute of Technology
J. van Maanen, Rutherford Appleton Laboratory
M. Mittelstädt, Kernforschungszentrum Karlsruhe
Y. Moal, Cisigraph
B. Palstrøm, Danmarks Tekniske Højskole
S. G. Pavey, Cranfield Institute of Technology
M. Raflik, Cisigraph
W. Reichert, Kernforschungszentrum Karlsruhe
St. Rude, Universität Karlsruhe
B. Schilli, Universität Karlsruhe
E. G. Schlechtendahl, Kernforschungszentrum Karlsruhe
A. M. Spliid, NEH - Consulting Engineers
D. Thomas, Rutherford Appleton Laboratory
D. Trippner, Bayerische Motorenwerke AG
E. Trostmann, Danmarks Tekniske Højskole
W. Weick, Kernforschungszentrum Karlsruhe
D. Welner, Danmarks Tekniske Højskole

TABLE OF CONTENTS

LIST OF ILLUSTRATIONS

INTRODUCTION TO THE SPECIFICATION

1. INTRODUCTION

1.1 PURPOSE

The purpose of this paper is to document the results of Working Group 1 (wireframes), Working Group 2 (solids), and Working Group 3 (surfaces) of the ESPRIT project 322 CAD*I (CAD Interfaces). The goal of these working groups is:

1. Develop a neutral file format for transfer of CAD data (curves, surfaces, and solid models) between CAD systems, and from the CAD domain to CAA (computer aided analysis) and CAM (computer aided manufacturing).

2. Develop pre- and post-processors with a number of representative CAD systems for this neutral file format.

3. Develop representative test model files and perform cycle tests and inter-system tests for CAD model transfer.

4. Contribute to the standardization activities in the national standardization bodies and in ISO for the establishment of a neutral file format for CAD data.

This paper corresponds to a development stage as it was reached on July 6, 1987.

1.2 THE RELATION BETWEEN THIS PROPOSAL AND STEP

The International Standardisation Organisation (ISO) is presently developing a Standard/for Product Data Standard for Transfer of Product model data (STEP) in the ISO/TC184/SC4/WG1 committee. Members from the CAD*I project are involved in this effort, especially in the British and the German national delegations to the ISO committees. The CAD*I work has already influenced the STEP specification to a great deal. An important aspect is that the CAD*I project contributes to STEP the practical experience gained from processor implementations and actual tests of CAD model transfer. In order to be able to implement CAD*I processors the CAD*I specification must be established before the final and worldwide agreement on the STEP standard can be achieved. As a consequence, discrepancies between the present CAD*I specification and the present and future versions of still preliminary STEP documents are unavoidable.

At this time (mid 1987) most of the discrepancies between the CAD*I specification and the present STEP proposals are such that a one-to-one mapping is possible. However, certain essential features of the CAD*I specification do not yet have a corresponding and agreed-upon solution in STEP (e. g., the "scope" concept which was accepted by ISO/TC184/SC4/WG1 but not yet implemented). It is intended to translate the CAD*I specification into the corresponding STEP formulation as soon as the latter becomes both stable and powerful enough to represent all important elements of the CAD*I specification.

1.3 STRUCTURE OF THE DOCUMENT

This document contains three main sections:

1. "Introduction to the specification" on page 1 which describes the general approach and the basic concepts of the specification,

2. "Reference manual" on page 19 which is the main part of the specification,

3. "Implementation guidelines" on page 171 which provides information that may be useful for developing software on the basis of this specification.

2. APPROACH

The purpose of this chapter is to provide an overview of the needs and requirements, the environment, and assumptions used in the development of this specification.

The main requirement is to provide a means of transferring information contained in a CAD data base between any number of diverse CAD systems and from CAD systems into any other systems which may need such data. There is a need, therefore, for representing this information in a compact, machine-understandable form which captures the essence of the data without major loss of information or detail. A prerequisite to this is a knowledge of the range of structures used in CAD data bases, and the environment in which they were created. Furthermore, a methodology must be adopted to ensure that generation and interpretation, of a "neutral" representation of these structures, is performed in a consistent manner.

The transfer of CAD information must not be restricted to "complete" models only. A receiving CAD system must be able to continue with modifications and enhancement of the received product model. Hence, the specification must not only define data structures but also specify how certain operations which are common to all CAD systems work with that data structure.

It should be emphasized that we are dealing not just with a graphical or visual representation, but the complete representation of a product as stored in a data base. Existing standards for graphics and for drafting are well established (e.g. GKS, IGES) and are not the concern of this document.

This specification has developed from a combination of experiences with existing standards, a knowledge of geometric modeling processes, and an investigation of a wide range of CAD system environments. It is based on a view of the relationship between CAD data bases and a neutral transfer mechanism (Neutral File) as shown in Figure 1 on page 6.

In Figure 1 the first row of boxes indicates the overall concepts which the user must keep in mind: an interface implemented as a pair of pre- and post-processors performs the translation between the product data representations in CAD systems and the neutral file. The second row represents the formal specification contained in this book: the neutral file grammar which is specified in BNF productions, the semantical interpretation of a neutral file (defined as a finite state machine) in order to build a data structure which is compatible with the reference model specified. The last row shall indicate that validity of a neutral file requires conformance with the grammar, validity of the post-processor requires conformance with the semantic specification, and finally that CAD system data base contents can

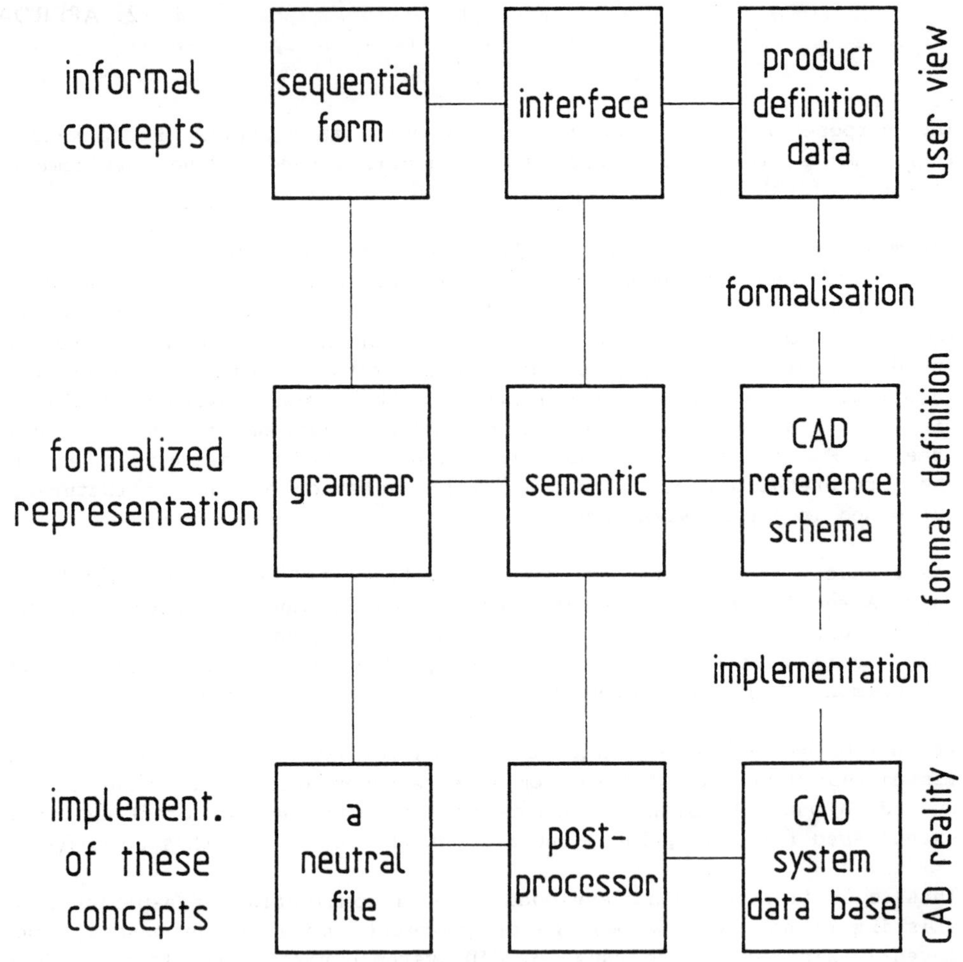

Figure 1. Relationships between neutral file and data base

be transported on the basis of this specification only to the extent that they conform to the reference schema.

In order to provide a rigorous specification, a number of formal concepts and systems are used to describe both the logical content of the information required, as well as a well-defined syntax (grammar) at the "physical" level. The logical definition of data structures is provided by a "data specification language" and is described fully in " 5. The CAD*I reference model specification in HDSL" on page 43. The syntax is defined using the Backus-Naur form (BNF) of notation, which is covered in " 7. The Physical Layer" on page 159 The division between "logical" and "physical" levels is an essential part of the specification. Although it is clearly necessary to mapping from one onto the other, the development of data structure definitions and the way in which the data is actually represented on a file should be produced independently. It is all too easy to confuse the requirements at a purely physical level with the actual data being transferred.

It was stated that there is a need to understand the contents of a CAD data base. However, the contents of a particular data base may only reflect, for example, the input of the user in creating a particular model. In the case of high level representation schemes, such as used in constructive solid geometry (CSG) modelers, this is a suitable method of transferring the information. This is not always the case, however, since many geometric model data bases contain purely geometric and other associated information. The point to be made here is that the neutral transfer mechanism must cater not only for high level representations, but also the very lowest level of data. A further point to be made is that the neutral file is not a copy of a particular data base. It contains all the relevant data in such a way that here is no loss of information.

The neutral file represents an intermediate stage of mapping one data base onto another. In that process, it is clearly necessary to map from a data base onto the neutral file, and from the neutral file onto other data bases. Clearly only two interfaces are required for a given system in order to achieve this. The consequences of this are that the processors must be very robust, and that, although the neutral file must be wide ranging enough to cope with as many systems as possible, it should also force any particular implementation to map onto the neutral schema.

A problem with some existing standards has been that implementors have used only parts of those specifications which suit their particular needs. The result is that the neutral file ceases to be a useful general transfer mechanism, since any other system interpreting files generated by such an implementation will have to provide extensive conversion facilities, thereby destroying the purpose of the neutral file. Clearly no single system will have a full implementation of the neutral schema, therefore, well defined subsets (implementation levels) of that schema need to be stated in the specification (this technique has been used successfully in the specification of the graphical kernel system GKS).

Although this specification relates to geometric modeling data, the underlying principles can be used to broaden its scope, such as to include the data requirements for complete product definition. In " 3. Basic principles" on page 9 these principles will be described in detail, however, it is necessary to describe the environment within which we are working. This requires a knowledge of the relationship between CAD systems and computer operating systems. We shall introduce some terms which are common to both environments:

1. The **universe** comprises the entire computing environment available at a particular CAD site.
2. The **world** corresponds to one or more data sets (files) which are used to store CAD data. The mechanism used to address such data is naming; within a particular CAD environment a single name may address one or more files which together represent a single product description.

The neutral file mechanism transfers a world between different universes. The world does not only represent a pure geometric structure, it also contains information relating to the environment of the sending system, when that particular world was created. This implies that it is not just pure data which needs to be transferred, but also a degree of functionality, e.g., a user in the receiving environment when selecting an object on the screen at his work station should obtain the same result as a user performing the same operation in the sending system.

Building a data structure that corresponds exactly to the received neutral file is the task of a post-processor program. In order to facilitate an incremental process for building such data structures in a way that each intermediate step is precisely defined, a generalized model of the post-processor is included in this document. The post-processor is defined as a finite state machine whose input is a sequence of statements on the neutral file and some user directives which guide the interpretation; its main output is the data structure which represents the received model. This technique has previously been used successfully for specifying computer graphics systems (GKS and PHIGS).

3. BASIC PRINCIPLES

This chapter describes the overall concepts underlying the specification of a neutral file for exchange of CAD models between CAD systems or a CAD system and other application areas.

3.1 USE OF FORMAL LANGUAGES

Formal languages are introduced in this specification on two levels:

1. On the logical layer, concerned with the data structures in CAD system data bases, a language similar to data structure declarations in Pascal is used.
2. on the physical layer, which is concerned with the representation on a sequential file, the formal syntax for the file is specified in BNF notation with the tokens being defined as regular expressions based on the alphabet.

This technique provides for consistency between the two layers if the file format definition is derived automatically from the formal schema specification. This principle has influenced the way in which the schema is formally specified.

3.2 INFORMAL DESCRIPTION OF THE CAD DATA SCHEMA

3.2.1 Entities and Attributes

Entities are the basic data structures of the schema. They are defined by structured collections of one or more data attributes. An attribute provides detail of part of an entity description. There are mainly two types of attribute, predefined and composite. Predefined attribute types include integer, real, logical, and string. Composite types are declared explicitly in the schema - for example, the attribute type REF_PART_LIBRARY which indicates a reference to an entity in a part library by grouping the three necessary attributes together will be defined as a composite attribute. Some collections of attributes may appear both as entities and as composite attributes, for example: 'POINT'.

3.2.2 References

An essential feature of entities is that they may be referenced. all relationships between entities are expressed by references. Two types of referencing mechanisms are provided, REFERENCE and REF_ONLY. These allow for either multiple references to the same entity (one - many), or only single references to an entity (one - one).

In principle, a relationship R(A,B) may be expressed either as a reference from A to B, or as a reference from B to A, or as a separate entity which refers to A as well as to B.

On the logical layer of data structuring the choice is determined by a certain anticipated behaviour of the entities. An entity which is being referenced by another entity cannot be deleted before the referencing entity is deleted.

On the physical layer, however, due to the requirements of sequentialising the neutral file, the referencing mechanism is restricted (see "The Physical Level" on page 15).

3.2.3 Properties

In some cases where entities may be used for transferring information between different applications (e.g. CAD and FEM), any application specific data (e.g. user-defined names) should not be embedded in those entities but should be associated via references. Data of this kind are defined as a "property".

Material properties are examples of properties which may be assigned to CAD geometric models. In order to allow geometric models to be defined independently from the relevant material properties in various application areas, the property "is_material_of" is not included in the geometric entity, but is implemented as a property associated to geometric entities.

The fundamental difference between a property and an entity is that entities can be referenced, while properties cannot. Properties must always refer to one or more entities.

3.2.4 Scope

A principle feature of the schema is that it supports scoping of entities, in a similar way to that used in some structured programming languages. The principle allows the "localised" definition of entities within some enclosing entity (see Figure 2 on page 12). A scoped entity enables a large collection of data to be addressed at a higher level as a single unit.

The main significance of this is in terms of functional behaviour of the data structure. Deletion of an entity which has other entities in its scope means that all the enclosed entities are deleted at once. Similarly, passing an entity with a scope to a modeling function means that this function has access to all the entities in that scope.

References are not allowed to entities defined within the scope of another entity. Consequently, entities which need to be "shared" (multiply referenced) by a number of scoped entities, need to be defined within a scope common to all these entities.

3.2.5 World

The world is the highest level entity in the schema. Within its scope are all other entities which together define the contents of a CAD database.

3.2.6 Assemblies and Components

Assemblies and components provide a means of grouping other entities together in a structured way. This structure is a tree which represents the 'consists_of' relationship. Although there is a clear correspondence with terms used in the mechanical products environment, the mechanism is intended to be more general. In this specification the components represent the objects to which geometric shapes are associated.

3.2.7 Geometry

The schema allows for varying levels of geometric complexity including 2D and 3D wireframe structures, surface models, and solid models. A given level implementation may provide for one or more of these.

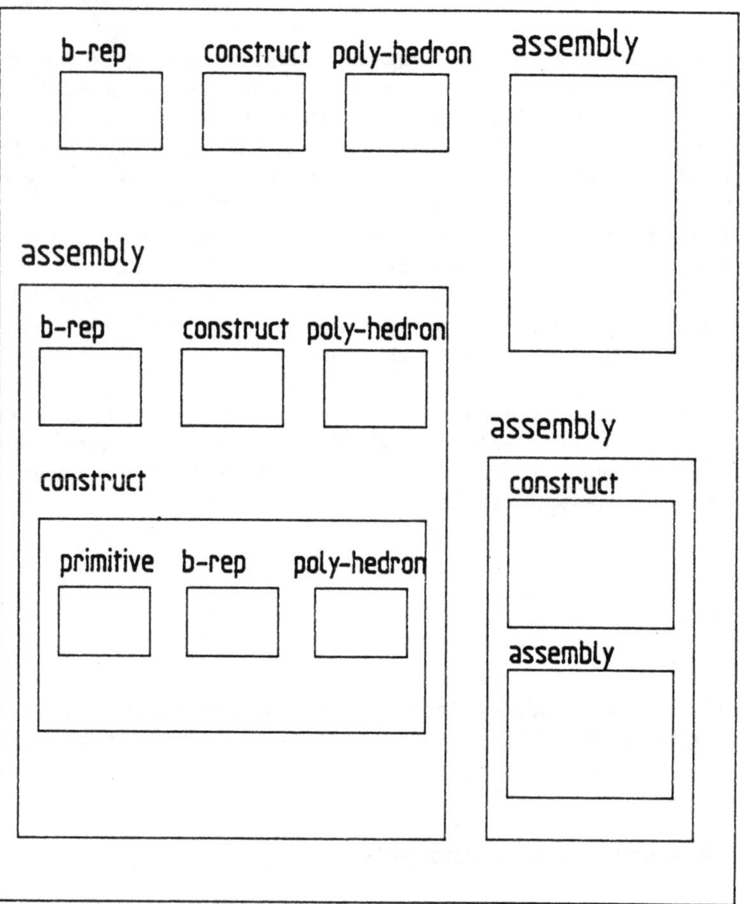

Figure 2. The scope aspect of the reference schema

3.2.7.1 Curves and Surfaces

The schema provides for regular conic curves (e.g. circle, ellipse, etc.), and quadric surfaces (e.g. cylinder, cone, etc.). Each of these has a specified parameterisation which must be adhered to when providing parameter values for other entities (e.g. trimmed curves). This is an attempt to exclude the idea of 'default parameterisation', the interpretation of which may differ from one implementation to another. In addition, parametric curves and surfaces are provided for by B-spline entities. These are specified by their control points, and may be rational or non-rational, uniform or non-uniform. Bezier representation of curves and surfaces is provided as a subset within B-spline entities. More complex entities such as trimmed, composite and offset curves and surfaces are also specified.

3.2.7.2 Solid Models

Two principal representations are supported, namely Boundary Representation (B-rep) and Constructive Solid Geometry (CSG).

CSG represents objects as combinations of well-defined primitive volumes (e.g. box, sphere, cylinder). The model is in the form of a tree structure in which the leaves are the primitives and the nodes are "boolean operations" to be performed (e.g. union, intersection). The schema provides for a comprehensive set of primitives, a mechanism for placing and orienting the primitives, and the CSG tree structure (referred to as a CONSTRUCT).

The **boundary representation**(B-rep) data structure comprises a topological structure (shell,face,loop,edge,vertex) together with associated geometric information. However, the reference schema also allows for polyhedral (facetted) representations of objects, by providing a simplified form of the general B-rep structure. In addition, an initial proposal provides for representing non-manifold B-rep objects, which caters for interior regions which require domains with different properties (e.g. composite materials).

3.2.7.3 Instancing and placement

Geometric entities may be positioned in identical form at various places. This is called instancing. An instance of an entity consists of a reference to that entity and information about how the instance is to be placed. Various forms of storing the placement information are available. Note that, although instances are independent entities and may be referenced, they are not copies of other entities.

3.2.8 User-defined name

In order to allow references to entities not only by interactively picking them at the workstation, but also by "user-defined names" in a textual form, provision is made for a special property called index entry. Each index entry will carry a unique user-defined name (unique in its environment) and a reference to the respective entity.

3.2.9 Libraries and External References

Most references in a world (neutral file) will be internal, that is to entities that are transferred on the same file. However, a complete product description often includes a number of individual database files as well as components taken from part libraries. In order to cater for this, "external" references are allowed to entities not transferred on the same file, but which are assumed to reside already in the receiving environment. User-defined names provide the basic means for passing external references. In addition, a special mechanism is provided for referencing entities in part libraries. These references will not be resolved until receiving system starts working with the world it has received.

3.2.9.1 Parametric Models and Macros

The term "parametric models" expresses the capability of certain CAD systems which allows the CAD system user to assign values to elementary data of some predefined type with the consequence that this will influence the CAD model in a certain way. A typical example is the length of some dimension in a model that is defined not as a constant but as a variable which has some value. Assignment of a new value to this length will cause a redefinition of all geometry that depends on this variable. The reference model allows the use of either constant values for predefined types, or references to entities of predefined type.

A macro is similar to a parametric model in that it contains references to entities which may be redefined by the CAD user with the effect of creating a new geometry dependent on such changes. However, while parametric models always have values assigned to their variables at the time of sending, and may constitute an integral part of some larger CAD model, macros have to be invoked explicitly by the user. The result of such invocation has to be built into the overall model by the user. This result will then no longer depend on the macro but will exist on its own in the CAD data base.

3.2.9.2 User records

User records are provided as a standard way for escaping from the restrictions of the schema when needed. User records are not semantically known in the reference model. They can be accommodated there as a means of storing information that is to be associated with entities, but that is to be interpreted only by special programs. User records may contain data of predefined type only. The record structure may be controlled by a special user-type record.

3.3 THE PHYSICAL LEVEL

3.3.1 Strictly sequential, free format, block structure

The physical layer represents a strictly sequential process that can build up the CAD data structure in the receiving system from a single parse of the neutral file. The consequence of this principle is that no forward references are allowed on the file. The reason for this principle is two-fold.

1. A strictly sequential file with no forward references is of linear complexity. The amount of work needed for binding (resolving references) is much reduced over the case where forward references are allowed. Together with the block structure principle, this solution minimizes the data management requirements for post-processing. Therefore the task of strictly sequentialising the data structure must be performed fully in the pre-processor. This is the best place to handle this task since (1) the pre-processor has all facilities of the sending system available to query the sending CAD system's data base, and (2) each neutral file is pre-processed once only while it may be post-processed many times.

2. The strictly sequential file can have a set of programs associated with it (the programming interface) where each statement of the neutral file corresponds to one subprogram (possibly a predefined sequence of calls). Such a one-to-one mapping would not be possible if forward references were permitted on the file. Hence, the work that has been done once in specifying the linearization of CAD data structures for the neutral file, has already performed a major step towards defining a standardized programming interface for writing into CAD data bases.

The file format supports the block structure that corresponds to the scope aspect of entities. The purpose of the block structure is to localize, on the file, all information which fully defines a certain entity. An effect of such localization is that the post processor, having found the end of the definition of an entity, may "forget" all information that was used to build up this entity. This principle allows minimisation of temporary data storage and data management that has to be performed by the post-processor. A second effect of this principle is that, in situations which require interpretation of only part of the neutral file, there is an obvious indication on the file where to start and to end with each entity. No search for information before the start or after the end is needed in order to completely define this entity.

3.3.2 Metafiles, Letters and Alphabets

All CAD*I neutral file follow the envelope concept. The beginning and the end of the neutral file is clearly marked inside a larger CAD*I metafile. The metafile may carry additional information such as letters, FORTRAN source code, even CAD information according to some other standard such as IGES, VDA-FS, or SET. No conflict arises between these different files even when they are transported as one sequential file on magnetic tape or computer network.

3.4 VALIDATION OF THE CAD MODEL TRANSFER

The purpose of transferring a CAD model from one system to another is to continue to use it in the receiving system. The transfer will be considered as correct if the same basic operations can be performed on the received data structures as could be applied in the sending system. The crucial question is:

- What is the set of basic operations which defines the correctness of a transfer?

We concentrate on three important aspects here which we consider as relevant to the correctness of CAD model transfer:

1. correctness of the operational model,
2. correctness of the geometry, and
3. correctness of graphical representation (which is not covered by the present specification).

3.4.1 Validation of the operational behaviour of the model

The correctness or incorrectness of the information structure will become apparent when a user operates on the received data structure interactively. He will generally want to

1. enter (the scope of) an entity in order to be able to operate on the entities in the scope of that entity
2. interrogate his environment with respect to what entities and properties of which type are available
3. identify entities in his environment by textual means (i.e. by typing in the user defined name of that entity

4. identify entities in his environment by non-textual means (i.e. by picking the corresponding graphical representation on the display screen
5. identify properties (or relations) by identifying the type of property and the related entity (entities)
6. create a new entity
7. create a new property (or relation)
8. delete an existing entity
9. delete an existing property and relation
10. modify the values of the attributes which constitute an entity or property result
11. perform modeling operations by invoking CAD system modeling functions and passing entities from his environment to these functions (the modeling functions change the data base content while the evaluating functions leave it unchanged).
12. evaluate his model by invoking evaluation CAD system functions and passing entities from his environment to these functions
13. perform linear transformations (these are a special and most often used modeling operation)

On the other hand, the CAD system user

- should not be able to address entities and properties which do not belong to his present environment.

The effect of the above operations on a data structure that conforms with this specification is described in more detail in "Semantics of reference models defined with HDSL" on page 37.

3.4.2 Validation of the geometry

The concept proposed here is that

1. all information needed to test the correctness of the geometrical information of a data base (neutral file) should be embedded in that data base (neutral file);

2. testing of geometrical accuracy should be based upon comparing points which are generated by intersecting the transferred geometric model with straight lines (or planes in the case of three-dimensional wireframes). It is assumed that points, straight lines, and planes are transmitted without any significant loss of accuracy;

3. the points to be tested are the result of a few well-defined operations which have been performed in the sending system and will have to be

repeated in the receiving system. These operations are intersections of entities with straight lines (in most cases);

4. the test relation should carry the maximum allowable distance between the intersection points generated by the sending and receiving systems.

    - For two-dimensional wireframe models a set of straight lines and an associated point set for each line is transmitted. For each transfer line the associated point set represents the intersection points of the line with the wireframe model.

    - For three-dimensional wireframe models intersection points between the curves of the model and test planes are to be used.

    - For surface models intersections between the surfaces and straight lines are used.

    - For solid models intersection between test lines and the surface of the solid are used.

REFERENCE MANUAL

4. THE HIGH LEVEL DATA SPECIFICATION LANGUAGE HDSL

4.1 TYPE DECLARATION

With reference to the algebraic specification of data types, the specification of a type T, defines a set (usually infinite) of constants (T-constants). Besides, certain T-specific properties (T-axioms) are valid for these constants (semantic of T). For example, the type NATURAL defines the set N=(0, 1, 2, 3, 4, 5 ...) of NATURAL constants, where the relation 2=SUC(SUC(0)) is one of the T-axioms (SUC denotes the successor function / SUC(X):=X+1).

The HDSL knows three different type classes

- ENTITY
- ATTRIBUTE
- PROPERTY

so that entities (see "Entities and Attributes" on page 9) are constants of an ENTITY type, attributes (see "Entities and Attributes" on page 9) are constants of an ATTRIBUTE type and properties ("Properties" on page 10) are constants of a PROPERTY type.

With type declarations one gives names to types.

An ENTITY- (ATTRIBUTE-, PROPERTY-) type declaration begins with the reserved word ENTITY (ATTRIBUTE, PROPERTY) and is followed by the (HDSL-)type name, the assignment character '=', and the (HDSL-)type. The type may be a predefined type (see "Predefined types" on page 22) a composite type (see "Composite types" on page 25) or a generic type (see "Generic types" on page 29). Two subsequent type declarations are delimited by a semicolon.

```
Syntax:   <type_declaration> ::= ENTITY <type_name> = <type> |
                                 ATTRIBUTE <type_name> = <type>  |
                                 PROPERTY  <type_name> = <type>

          <type_name> ::= <upper_alphanum>

          <type>      ::= <predefined> | <composite> | <generic>

          (*  <upper_alphanum> denotes all positive
              concatenations of capital letters and digits *)

Example:  ENTITY C     =  CLASS(TYPE1, TYPE2);
```

```
PROPERTY S   =  STRUCTURE
                 attr1 : REAL;
                 attr2 : LOGICAL;
                 attr3 : NAME;
                END;

ATTRIBUTE G  =  GENERIC(param : C)
                  STRUCTURE
                   attr1 : param;
                   attr2 : LOGICAL;
                   attr3 : NAME;
                  END;

ATTRIBUTE V  =  GENERIC(param : C)
                  STRUCTURE
                   attr1 : param;
                   CASE param OF
                     TYPE1 : (attr2 : LOGICAL);
                     TYPE2 : (attr3 : NAME);
                   END;
                  END;
```

4.2 PREDEFINED TYPES

It is not allowed to declare predefined types. They can be used to declare composite types (see "Composite types" on page 25) or generic types (see "Generic types" on page 29). Predefined types are members of the type class ATTRIBUTE. The predefined types of the HDSL are:

- INTEGER
- REAL
- LOGICAL
- STRING
- USER_DEFINED_NAME
- ARITHMETIC_EXPRESSION
- NIL
- D2
- D3

```
Syntax:   <predefined> ::= INTEGER | REAL | LOGICAL |
                           STRING | USER_DEFINED_NAME |
                           ARITHMETIC_EXPRESSION | NIL |
                           D2 | D3
```

4.2.1 The type INTEGER

Structure attributes (parameters) of type INTEGER have integers as values. The regular set integer (see "Tokens of the neutral file language" on page 160) formally defines the set of INTEGER constants.

Example: +2121 989000 -0000 +678686465 0

4.2.2 The type REAL

Structure attributes (parameters) of type REAL have fractions as values. The regular set real (see "Tokens of the neutral file language" on page 160) formally defines the set of REAL constants.

```
Example:  -12.321    2334.20434E-12  32344.   +12.313232
          .5         -.5             1.E6
```

4.2.3 The type LOGICAL

Structure attributes (parameters) of type LOGICAL are elements of the dual set (.T. .F.) where .T. and .F. denote the Boolean constants TRUE and FALSE. The regular set logical ("Tokens of the neutral file language" on page 160) formally defines the set of LOGICAL constants.

4.2.4 The type STRING

Structure attributes (parameters) of type STRING have character strings as values. The regular set string (see "Tokens of the neutral file language" on page 160) formally defines the set of STRING constants.

Example: 'asa' '123AAA' ' that''s a string'

4.2.5 The type USER_DEFINED_NAME

Structure attributes (parameters) of type USER_DEFINED_NAME have user-defined names (see "User-defined name" on page 13) as values. The regular set "user-defined name" (see "Tokens of the neutral file language" on page 160) formally defines the set of USER_DEFINED_NAME constants.

Example: "car" "TESTPART" "box11"

4.2.6 The type NIL

The constant set of NIL is empty. This implies that for example structure attributes (see "Fixed structure type" on page 25) of type NIL are useless in relation to the corresponding structure. In the example below, for entities of type POINT(D2) (two dimensional points) the third structure attribute dimz (z-dimension) has no meaning.

Example:
```
ATTRIBUTE DIM = ENUM(D2, D3)

ENTITY POINT = GENERIC(param : DIM)
                 STRUCTURE
                  dimx : REAL;
                  dimy : REAL;
                  CASE param OF
                    D2 : (dimz : NIL);
                    D3 : (dimz : REAL);
                  END;
                 END;
```

4.2.7 The constants D2, D3

The constant D2 (D3) denotes the "two-dimensional feature" ("three-dimensional feature") of any geometric entity.

4.2.8 The type ARITHMETIC_EXPRESSION

Structure attributes (parameters) of type ARITHMETIC_EXPRESSION have arithmetic expressions as values. The ARITHMETIC_EXPRESSION constants are defined in paragraph "Arithmetic expressions" on page 162.

4.3 COMPOSITE TYPES

A composite type is an enumeration type, a fixed structure type, a list type or a class type.

```
Syntax:     <composite> ::= <enum>  | <structure>  |  <list>  |
                            <class>
```

4.3.1 Enumeration types

An enumeration type is a finite enumeration of constants. The enumeration type is denoted by the sequence ENUM(e1, ...eN) where N denotes the cardinal number of the enumeration type and e1, ...eN denote the constant elements of the enumeration type. N has to be greater than 1. *Than a structure attribute (parameter) of enumeration type E has any constant element of E* as value. Enumeration type are members of the type class ATTRIBUTE.

```
Syntax:     <enum>    ::= ENUM ( <values> ) ;

            <values> ::= <upper_alphanum> , <values> |
                         <upper_alphanum>

            (*  <upper_alphanum> denotes all positive
                concatenations of capital letters and digits *)

Example:    ENTITY E = ENUM(value1, value2);
```

4.3.2 Fixed structure type

A constants of a fixed structure type (called fixed structures) is a finite collection of structure attributes, where the structure attributes can be of different type (In PASCAL, the analogue is the RECORD type) A fixed structure type is denoted by the sequence

```
STRUCTURE
 a1 : type1;
   ----
   ----
 aN : typeN;
END;
```

where a1, ...aN denote the structure attribute names, and type1, ...typeN denote the corresponding structure attributes types. A structure attribute type can be either a predefined type, or a composite type, or a type name, or a type instance. The sequences aJ : typeJ (J=1..N) are called the structure attribute definitions of the fixed structure.

In case of scoped entities (see "Scope" on page 11) the corresponding structure attribute definitions are enclosed by the reserved words SCOPE and END_SCOPE.

```
Syntax:   <structure> ::= STRUCTURE <attr_defs> END ;  |
                          STRUCTURE SCOPE; <attr_types> END_SCOPE;
                                    <attr_defs> END;

          <attr_defs> ::= <attr_name> : <attr_type> ; <attr_defs> |
                          <attr_name> : <attr_type> ;

          <attr_name> ::= <lower_alphanum>

          <attr_type> ::= <type_name> | <type_inst> |
                          <reference> | <structure> |
                          <list> | <class>

          (*  <lower_alphanum> denotes all positive
              concatenations of lower-case letters and digits *)

         <attr_types> ::= <attr_type> |
                          <attr_type> <attr_types>
```

Example:
```
ENTITY S1  =  STRUCTURE
               attr1 : REAL;
               attr2 : STRUCTURE
                        attr21 : REAL;
                        attr22 : LOGICAL;
                       END;
               attr3 : CLASS(REAL, INTEGER);
              END;
```

In this case, the value of a structure attribute (parameter) of type S1 is a (unscoped) structure, which consists of a REAL constant, a 2-element structure and a REAL- or an INTEGER constant.

```
ENTITY S2  =  STRUCTURE
               SCOPE;
                attr1 : REAL;
                attr2 : LOGICAL;
               END_SCOPE;
              attr3 : POINT(D2)
              END;
```

A structure attribute (parameter) of type S2 have entities with a scope as value. Besides, the scope consists of a REAL constant and a logical value. The structure attribute outside the scope has a 2-dimensional point as value (see "The type NIL" on page 24).

4.3.3 Lists

A constant of a list type (called list) is a finite collection of elements. In opposition to a fixed structure, the elements of a list have to be of the same type. The length of a list (i.e. the number of list elements) is arbitrary (but finite). The list type is a dynamic type. The sequence

```
LIST OF <type>
```

denotes a list type, and <type> denotes the domain of the list type.

Syntax: <list> ::= LIST OF <type>

Example:
```
ENTITY REAL_L1 = LIST OF REAL;

ENTITY REAL_L2 = LIST OF REAL_L1;
```

4.3.4 Classes

Analogous to the enumeration type definition (see "Enumeration types" on page 25) a class type is a finite enumeration of types. The sequence

```
CLASS(type1, ...typeN)
```

denotes a class type. Besides N is the cardinal number of the class type and the type elements type1, ...typeN are either predefined types, or any type names or any type instances. All type elements have to be of the same type class (see "Type declaration" on page 21). N denotes the length of the class type and is greater than 0. *Then a structure attribute (parameter) of class type C has any type element of C* as value.

```
Syntax:   <class>    ::= CLASS ( <cl_types> )

          <cl_types> ::= <cl_type> , <cl_types> | <cl_type>

          <cl_type>  ::= <predefined> | <type_name> | <type_inst> |
                         <reference>

Example:  ENTITY C = CLASS(LOGICAL, REAL, INTEGER, G(REAL));
```

The following example defines an illegal class type, because the second element of the class is neither a predefined type, nor a type name, nor type_instance:

```
ENTITY C1 = CLASS(LOGICAL, CLASS(REAL, INTEGER));
```

A correct and equivalent definition is:

```
ENTITY C2 = CLASS(REAL, INTEGER);

ENTITY C3 = CLASS(LOGICAL, C2);
```

One can verify, that C3 is equal to the class CLASS(LOGICAL, REAL, INTEGER).

4.4 THE TYPES REFERENCE, REF_ONLY

The type REFERENCE is a predefined generic type. For any ENTITY type E, the value of an structure attribute A of type REFERENCE(E) is a reference R to an entity ENT of type E (see "Entities and Attributes" on page 9). Sometimes it is necessary, that there is only one reference R to ENT. In this case A has to be of the type REF_ONLY(E). The parameter value of REFERENCE

(REF_ONLY) has to be the name of an ENTITY type or the instance of a generic ENTITY type.

The REFERENCE- (REF_ONLY-) constants are defined by the regular set 'name' (see "Tokens of the neutral file language" on page 160).

Syntax: <reference> ::= REFERENCE (<type_name>) |
REF_ONLY (<type_name>)

(* *<type_name> has to denote an ENTITY type* *)

4.5 GENERIC TYPES

There are generic structure types, generic enumeration types, generic class types and generic list types. A generic type is denoted by the sequence

GENERIC (param1: type1,...,paramN: typeN)
PARAMETRIC TYPE

where param1, ..paramN denote the parameters, type1, ...typeN denote the corresponding parameter types or parameter type names, and PARAMETRIC TYPE denotes a parametric composite type.

Syntax: <generic> ::= GENERIC (<par_dec>) <par_comp>

<par_dec> ::= <par_name> : <par_type> , <par_dec> |
<par_name> : par_type>

<par_name> ::= <lower_alphanum>

<par_type> ::= <par_enum> | <par_class> | <type_name>

<par_comp> ::= <par_enum> | <par_struc> | <par_list> |
<par_class>

A generic type declaration declares a set of types ST (in the example below, the generic entity type GEN1 denotes the type set (LIST OF INTEGER, LIST OF LOGICAL, LIST OF REAL)). To select one element of ST, one has to replace the parameters of PARAMETRIC TYPE by elements of the corresponding parameter types (parameter type names) type1, ...typeN. Such a selected type is called a type instance. Type instances are denoted by the sequence

gen_name(par_val1, ...par_valN)

where *gen_name has to be a generic type name* and par_valJ (J=1..N) has to be one of the corresponding value- or type elements. If S denotes a set of some of these value- (type-) elements par_valJ (J=1..N) then:

```
gen_name(S) :=  CLASS( gen_name(val1), ....., gen_name(valK) )
```

where K ≤ N and for each index J=1..K there exists an index I=1..N with valJ=par_valI.

In the example below, the type instance GEN4(REAL) denotes the list type LIST OF REAL and GEN4(C1) denotes the class CLASS(LIST OF INTEGER, LIST OF REAL, LIST OF LOGICAL).

```
Syntax:    <type_inst>  ::= <type_name> ( <par_values> )

           <par_values> ::= <par_value> , <par_values> |
                            <par_value>

           <par_value>  ::= <upper_alphanum>

           (* <upper_alphanum> denotes all positive
              concatenations of capital letters and digits *)

Example.:  ENTITY C1    =  CLASS(INTEGER, LOGICAL, REAL);

           ENTITY GEN1 = GENERIC(param : C1)
                           LIST OF param;

           ENTITY S1    =  STRUCTURE
                            attr1 : REAL;
                            attr2 : GEN1(INTEGER);
                           END
```

4.5.1 Parametric enumeration types

In contrast to a enumeration type (see "Enumeration types" on page 25), at least one of the value elements of a parametric enumeration type is a generic parameter.

```
Syntax:    <par_enum>   ::= ENUM ( <par_values> ) ;

           <par_values> ::= <par_value> , <par_values> |
                            <par-value>

           <par-value>  ::= <upper_alphanum> | <parameter>
```

```
<parameter>  ::= <upper_alphanum>

(*  <upper_alphanum> denotes all positive
    concatenations of capital letters and digits *)
```

4.5.2 Parametric structures

In contrast to a structure type (see "Fixed structure type" on page 25), at least one of the structure attribute types of a parametric structure type is a generic parameter.

```
Syntax:   <par_stru>   ::= STRUCTURE <par-attrs> END ;

          <par_attrs>  ::= <attr_name> : <par_type> ; <par_attrs> |
                           <attr_name> : <par_type> ;

          <attr_name>  ::= <lower_alphanum>

          <par_type>   ::= <type> | <type_name> | <parameter>

          <parameter>  ::= <lower_alphanum>

          (* <lower_alphanum> denotes all positive
             concatenations of lower-case letters and digits *)
```

4.5.3 Parametric lists

In contrast to a list type (see "Lists" on page 27), the domain of a parametric list type is a generic parameter.

```
Syntax:   <par_list>   ::= LIST OF <parameter>

          <parameter>  ::= <lower_alphanum>

          (*  <lower_alphanum> denotes all positive
              concatenations of lower-case letters and digits *)
```

4.5.4 Parametric classes

In contrast to a class type (see "Classes" on page 28), at least one of the type elements of the class type is a generic parameter.

```
Syntax:  <par_class>     ::= CLASS ( <par_cl_types> )

         <par_cl_types> ::= <par_cl_type> , <par_cl_types> |
                            <par_cl_type>

         <par_cl_type>  ::= <predefined> | <type_name> |
                            <parameter>

         <parameter> ::= <lower_alphanum>

         (*  <lower_alphanum> denotes all positive
             concatenations of lower case letters and digits *)
```

4.5.5 Variant structures

In fixed structures, as described in "Fixed structure type" on page 25, the sequence of the attribute definitions is fixed. In case of a variant structure type the structure attribute number and the structure attribute definitions of the structure type can be dependent on the value of variant parameters. A variant structure attribute definition is denoted by the sequence

CASE type OF
  v1: (a11 : type11;....a1k_1 : type1k_1);

    ----
  vN: (aN1 : typeN1;....aNk_N : typeNk_N);
END;

where va denotes the variant parameter. *The type of va has to be an enumeration type* and v1, ...vN denote some names of this enumeration type. Besides, v1, ..vN are disjunctive in pairs and N has to be equal or less than the cardinal number of va. A variant structure type contains at least one variant structure attribute definition.

4.5.6 Variant classes

In case of variant class types, the number and the names of the corresponding type elements (see "Classes" on page 28) can be dependent on the values of some variant parameters. A variant type element is denoted by the sequence

```
CASE va OF
  v1 : type11;....type1k₁;
    ---------
    ---------
  vN : typeN1;....typeNk_N;
END;
```

where va denote a variant parameter. *The type of va has to be an enumeration type* and v1, ...vN denote some names of this enumeration type. Besides, v1, ..vN are disjunctive in pairs and N has to be equal or less than the cardinal number of va. A variant class contains at least one variant type element.

4.5.7 Generic structures

In case of a generic structure, PARAMETRIC TYPE is either a parametric fixed structure or a variant structure. The parameter types have to be class types (see "Classes" on page 28) or, in case of a generic variant structure, enumeration types.

```
Example:  ENTITY C1   =  CLASS(LOGICAL, REAL, INTEGER);

          ENTITY E1   =  ENUM(value1, value2, value3);

          ENTITY GEN2 = GENERIC(param : C1)
                          STRUCTURE
                           attr1 : REAL;
                           attr2 : param;
                           attr3 : NAME;
                          END;
```

```
ENTITY GEN3 = GENERIC(param1 : C1, param2 : E1)
              STRUCTURE
               attr1 : param1;
               attr2 : GEN2(REAL);
               CASE param2 OF
                 value1 : (attr3 : INTEGER);
                 value2 : (attr4 : LOGICAL);
                 value3 : (attr5 : NAME);
               END;
              END;
```

In this case, a structure attribute (parameter) of type GEN3(REAL,value2) has a structure, consisting of a REAL constant, the 3-element structure GEN(REAL) and a LOGICAL constant as value.

4.5.8 Generic enumerations

In case of a generic enumeration type, PARAMETRIC TYPE is a parametric enumeration type. All the parameter types have to be enumeration types.

```
Exmaple: ENTITY E2   = ENUM(white, yellow);

         ENTITY GEN4 = GENERIC(param : E2)
                         ENUM(blue, red, black, param);
```

4.5.9 Generic classes

In case of a generic class type, PARAMETRIC TYPE is a parametric class type or a variant class type. All the parameter types have to be class types.

```
Example: ENTITY C1   = CLASS(INTEGER, LOGICAL, REAL);

         ENTITY E1   =  ENUM(value1, value2, value3);

         ENTITY GEN5 = GENERIC(param : C1)
                          CLASS(REAL, param);
```

```
ENTITY GEN6 = GENERIC(param : C1)
               CLASS(REAL, CASE param OF
                             value1 : INTEGER;
                             value2 : LOGICAL;
                             value3 : GEN5(REAL)
                           END);
```

In this case, a structure attribute (parameter) of type GEN6(value1) has a REAL- or an INTEGER constant and a structure attribute (parameter) of type GEN6(value3) has a REAL constant as value.

4.5.10 Generic lists

In case of a generic list type, PARAMETRIC TYPE is a parametric list type.

```
Example:  ENTITY C1   = CLASS(INTEGER, LOGICAL, REAL);

          ENTITY GEN7 = GENERIC( param : C1 )
                          LIST OF param;
```

4.6 THE PREDEFINED FUNCTION DIMENSION

The predefined function DIMENSION is defined on a subset of the set of all type instances (see "Generic types" on page 29). The range of DIMENSION is the 2-element set (D2, D3) (see "The constants D2, D3" on page 24) and for any type instance TI(p1, ..., pN), where pJ denotes the corresponding parameter values of the generic type TI (J=1..N), DIMENSION(TI(p1, ...pN)) is defined as follows:

DIMENSION(TI(p1, ..pN))=D2 : there exists an index J with J=1..N and pJ=D2, so that for all K with K=1..N and K≠J the value of pK is not equal to D2 or D3.

DIMENSION(TI(p1, ..pN))=D3 : there exists an index J with J=1..N and pJ=D3, so that for all K with K=1..N and K≠J the value of pK is not equal to D2 or D3.

Otherwise DIMENSION(TI(p1, ..pN)) is undefined.

Informally, the function DIMENSION computes for any "dimensioned" type D, the corresponding dimension feature.

Example:

```
ATTRIBUTE DIM = ENUM(D1, D2)

ENTITY POINT = GENERIC(param : DIM)
                  STRUCTURE
                   dimx : REAL;
                   dimy : REAL;
                   CASE param OF
                     D2 : (dimz : NIL);
                     D3 : (dimz : REAL);
                   END;
                  END;

ENTITY D2_POINT =  STRUCTURE
                     dimx : REAL;
                     dimy : REAL;
                   END;
```

Then DIMENSION(POINT(D2)) is equal to D2, DIMENSION(POINT(D3)) is equal to D3 and DIMENSION(D2_POINT) is undefined.

4.7 RULES APPLYING TO BUILDING A SCHEMA WITH HDSL

We will now define certain rules for building the reference schema from the specification elements defined above.

1. In a legal data structure no entity or property other than an entity of type WORLD (see below) may exist without being defined in the scope of another entity (no entity contains a LIST OF WORLD).

2. Entities may refer only to entities of their environment. If entity E1 is in the scope of E2, and E2 is in the scope of E3 and so on until WORLD, then all entities in the scope of E2 and E3 and so on until WORLD constitute the environment of E1.

3. No special ordering of entities and properties in the scope of another entity is required on the logical level. Such ordering will be introduced during the mapping from the logical data structure to the physical file to insure that no forward referencing occurs.

4. There are three basic forms of expressing a relationship between entities of type E1 and type E2.

a. referencing from E1 to E2
This form should be chosen when E2 entities may exist without being referred-to by an E1 entity, but not vice versa.

b. referencing from E2 to E1 (this represents the inverse relation)
This form should be chosen when E1 entities may exist without being referred-to by an E2 entity, but not vice versa. .treating E1 (or E2) as a property belonging to E2 (or E1)
This form should be chosen if the information grouped together in E1 (or E2, respectively) shall never exist on its own without belonging to an entity of type E2 (or E1).

c. introduce a separate property which refers to both E1 and E2.
This form should be chosen when both E1 entities and E2 entities may exist without a relation between them.

It is the task of the information modelers (the group of persons developing the specification) to choose among these possible versions. The consequence of the different choices will be that the information will behave differently according to the semantics model specified in "Semantics of reference models defined with HDSL".

4.8 SEMANTICS OF REFERENCE MODELS DEFINED WITH HDSL

All reference models that can be specified with HDSL have certain semantics in common. This common semantical behaviour is defined by the effect of the following operations on the data structure:

1. enter (the scope of) an entity in order to be able to operate on the entities in the scope of that entity
2. interrogate his environment with respect to what entities and properties of which type are available
3. identify entities in his environment by textual means (i.e. by typing in the user defined name of that entity
4. identify entities in his environment by non-textual means (i.e. by picking the corresponding graphical representation on the display screen
5. identify properties (or relations) by identifying the type of property and the related entity (entities)
6. create a new entity
7. create a new property (or relation)
8. delete an existing entity
9. delete an existing property and relation
10. modify the values of the attributes which constitute an entity or property result

11. perform modeling operations by invoking CAD system modeling functions and passing entities from his environment to these functions (the modeling functions change the data base content while the evaluating functions leave it unchanged).
12. evaluate his model by invoking evaluation CAD system functions and passing entities from his environment to these functions
13. perform linear transformations (these are a special and most often used modeling operation)

On the other hand, the CAD system user

- should not be able to address entities and properties which do not belong to his present environment.

4.8.1 Entering entities

The entity which comprises all others is a "world" (a CAD data base). From outside the world the user can delete the whole world completely or he may interrogate attributes of the world, but he cannot address individual entities inside the world. In order to do this, he will have to enter the world. Now he can operate on the entities in the world but not on entities which are enclosed in the scope of the entities which he can now reach. He may, however, continue to enter entities (those which have a scope) in order to go into more details. At any state, he can address entities in his actual environment, that are all entities in those scopes which he has entered and not yet left.

4.8.2 Interrogating the information content of the environment

The user is able to request a listing of all entities (possibly restricted to certain types) in the scopes of the entities he has entered and not yet left.

4.8.3 Identifying entities by textual means

He may address an entity in his environment by issuing its user-defined name. Within each scope, a user-defined name may exist only once. But in different scopes the same user defined name may appear. Uniqueness of the identification is achieved by searching the scope of the most recently opened entity first and if no match is found by searching backwards through the scopes of all entered entities.

4.8.4 Identifying entities by interactive picking

Any pickable element on the screen belongs to an entity of the actual environment. Example: If an edge of a boundary representation (B_REP) is picked inside the scope of the B_REP then the edge has been identified as an entity. If, however, the same edge is picked from outside the B_REP then the B_REP entity is identified. If the B_REP is part of an assembly which was displayed and not entered then picking the edge would identify the assembly rather than the B_REP or the edge alone.

4.8.5 Identifying properties

The same scoping rules apply to properties. Properties are identified by identifying the entity to which the property is attached and by the property type. Similarly, relations are identified by the entities to which they refer and the type of relation.

4.8.6 Creating a new entity

Creating a new entity implies that this entity becomes embedded in the scope of the most recently entered entity. The creation is possible only if that scope allows for entities of the requested type. Creating an entity will transform a valid CAD model into another valid CAD model.

4.8.7 Creating a new property or relation

A property or relation cannot be created on its own. It must be related to the entities to which it belongs. Properties and relations may be created only in the scope of an entity in which the referred-to entities are accessible.

4.8.8 Deleting an existing entity

Entities of the environment may be deleted. Deletion is possible only if no references exist to that entity.

4.8.9 Deleting an existing property or relation

Properties and relations may be deleted from the environment to which they belong.

4.8.10 Modifying values of attributes

Examples of such modifications are

- assigning a new coordinate to a point
- adding an instance of an entity to the list of entities which constitutes an assembly.

Such modifications are allowed by CAD system modeling functions only if the modification does not violate any of the constraints spelled out in this specification for the modified entity, nor for any other entity, property, or relation that refers to that entity.

As an example, if the specification allows a straight line segment to be defined by the reference to the two endpoints with the only constraint that the distance between these endpoints should not be less than some value, then modifying the coordinates of a point being referenced as endpoint of two lines (and by nothing else) would implicitly change the geometry of these two lines and would be legal unless the above constraint is violated for one of the line segments.

Similarly attribute values of properties and relations may be changed unless constraints specified for them are violated.

4.8.11 Invoking a modeling function

In any environment, the CAD system user may invoke a modeling and attribute operator that is accessible in this environment. We impose no other restrictions on the modeling operator but that it will install one or more new entities and properties in the present environment or delete entities from it in a way that the new model is consistent with the reference scheme.

4.8.12 Invoking evaluation functions

We impose no restriction on evaluation functions (including the function which displays entities) other than that they should not modify the present model. Graphical rendering of information is considered as one of the typical evaluation functions.

4.8.13 Linear transformations

Linear transformations may be applied to all entities which represent geometrical models and elementary geometric information:

1. assemblies
2. components
3. models of solid, surface. and wireframe type
4. elementary geometry like surface entities, curve entities, and points
5. instances of other geometric entities

These are treated in the following way:

1. Assemblies
   - For an assembly with a scope: the transformation is applied to all geometric entities in the scope of the assembly
   - For an assembly that is an instance of another assembly: the transformation definition in the instance is modified
2. Components
   - The transformation is applied to all geometric models associated to that component.
3. Solid models, surface models, and wireframe models
   - For a model with a scope: the transformation is applied to all geometric entities in the scope of the model
   - For a model that is an instance of another model: the transformation definition in the instance is modified

4. Elementary geometric entities

   - The transformation is applied to the geometric entity by changing appropriate coordinate values

5. Instances

   We have to distinguish between the following three different situations:

   a. The transformation is applied by the user to the instance itself: the placement information in the instance will be changed.
   b. The transformation was applied by the user to an entity which contained this such as it inherited the transformation as defined by the rule for transforming an entity with scope **and** the object referenced by the instance is **outside** the scope of the entity to which the user applied the transformation:
      the placement information in the instance will be changed.
   c. The transformation was applied by the user to an entity which contained this such as it inherited the transformation as defined by the rule for transforming an entity with scope **and** the object referenced by the instance is **inside** the scope of the entity to which the user applied the transformation:
      the placement information in the instance will **not** be changed as the referenced entity itself will already be transformed according to the above specified rules.

The following statements result from these rules as a consequence of the reference model as described in this document. Or else: any change to the reference model must be such that it does not conflict with the following statements:

- An entity B that is referenced by an entity A is **not** subject to a linear transformation simply because it is referenced.
- No entity is transformed twice as a consequence of a single user command
- Entities with parametric coordinate representation (a variable instead of a constant value) cannot be treated by linear transformation but require remodeling.

5. THE CAD*I REFERENCE MODEL SPECIFICATION

This specification is set up such that for each entity, property, or attribute we define in sequence

1. **the data structure** formally in HDSL,
2. **the BNF productions** which define the representation on the neutral file,
3. **the semantic description** in textual form (sometimes with illustrations). The attribute names used in the HDSL definition are used in the text and in the illustrations.

NOTE the symbol convention for vector notations used in this document is:

> **vectors** are typed in **boldface** letters
> \+ denotes scalar and vector addition
> \- denotes scalar and vector subtraction
> . or no sign between symbols denotes multiplication with a scalar
> ***** denotes the vector (cross) product
> • denotes the scalar product of vectors
> **r** denotes a vector quantity
> a denotes a scalar quantity

For each entity, class, property, relation, and attribute type in the formal schema definition (HDSL) we will now give an informal description of their meaning. This will be done by describing the individual attributes of the respective data structures.

5.1 ATTRIBUTE TYPES FOR GENERAL USE

5.1.1 ANY

```
ATTRIBUTE ANY = GENERIC (type: CLASS( REAL , INTEGER, LINE(D2),
                LINE(D3), POINT(D2), POINT(D3), PLACEMENT(D2),
                PLACEMENT(D3), DIRECTION(D2), DIRECTION(D3),
                ROTATION(D2), ROTATION(D3), POINT_ON_SURFACE,
                DIRECTION_ON_SURFACE ))
            CLASS( type, REF_ANY(type) );
```

For the predefined data types REAL and INTEGER the syntax is:

```
<any(real)>    ::= real | <ref_any>
<any(integer)> ::= integer | <ref_any>
```

The syntax for the other forms is given in conjunction with the respective entities.

This is a class of attribute types which indicates that data is given in elementary form or as reference to an entity of the corresponding type. All entities which can appear in this form as attributes have two syntactical representations: one with a name as the first argument indicating that an entity of that type is to be created, and one without the name argument indicating that the data is to be treated as a structured attribute.

5.1.2 DIM

```
ATTRIBUTE DIM = ENUM( D2, D3 ) ;
```

This information does not appear explicitly on the neutral file. It is recognised from the fact that either three or two coordinates are given.

This attribute indicates two- and three-dimensional features.

5.1.3 TYPE_ID

```
ATTRIBUTE TYPE_ID = ENUM( ASSEMBLY, COMPONENT, CURVE(D2), CURVE(D3),
                          INTEGER, LOGICAL, POINT(D2), POINT(D3),
                          REAL, SOLID_MODEL, STRING, SURFACE,
                          SURFACE_MODEL, USER_DEFINED_NAME,
                          WIREFRAME_MODEL(D2), WIREFRAME_MODEL(D3) );

<type_id> ::= ASSEMBLY | COMPONENT | CURVE(D2) | CURVE(D3) |
              INTEGER | LOGICAL | POINT(D2) | POINT(D3) |
              REAL | SOLID_MODEL | STRING | SURFACE |
              SURFACE_MODEL | USER_DEFINED_NAME |
              WIREFRAME_MODEL(D2) | WIREFRAME_MODEL(D3)
```

The TYPE_ID is an enumeration data type that indicates to application programs the type of certain entities or attributes. TYPE_ID values LOGICAL, STRING, and USER_DEFINED_NAME are permitted only as descriptors for RECORD_TYPE. All TYPE_IDs for geometric data types are not permitted as RECORD_TYPE descriptors.

5.1.4 UPDATE

```
ATTRIBUTE UPDATE = ENUM( UPON_MODIFICATION, UPON_EVALUATION,
                         BY_USER_COMMAND ) ;
```

```
<update> ::= UPON_MODIFICATION | UPON_EVALUATION |
             BY_USER_COMMAND
```

This is an enumeration type attribute used in entities of type HYBRID_SOLID, INTEGER, and REAL. Its values indicate when the value attribute of the corresponding entity is to be updated. The possibilities are:

1. Update the value immediately when the expression is modified. This updating mode will guarantee that the the value and the expression are always consistent. The consistency attribute will always be .T..

2. Update the value only when some application attempts to access the value and the consistency is .F.. Together with the updating the consistency attribute will be set to .T.. Any modification of the expression will not cause immediate updating but will only set consistency to .F.. This mode of operation will minimize the number of evaluations of the expression but nevertheless guarantees that the application always uses a value that is consistent with the expression.

3. Updating may be done only upon explicit user request. In this mode, modification will set consistency to .F., updating will set it to .T.. Applications may still use a value that is not consistent with the expression.

5.1.5 LIST OF predefined values

The attribute types LIST OF REFERENCE and LIST OF REF_ONLY are translated to the neutral file as:

```
<name_list> ::= ( [name [, name]* ] )
```

The attribute type LIST OF INTEGER is translated to the neutral file as:

```
<integer_list> ::= ( [integer [, integer]* ] )
```

The attribute type LIST OF LOGICAL is translated to the neutral file as:

```
<logical_list> ::= ( [logical [, logical]* ] )
```

The attribute type LIST OF REAL is translated to the neutral file as:

```
<real_list> ::= ( [real [, real]* ] )
```

5.2 GENERAL DATA BASE STRUCTURE

5.2.1 WORLD

```
ATTRIBUTE WORLD_HEADER = STRUCTURE
            length_unit_factor   : REAL;
            angle_unit           : REAL;
            world_size           : REAL;
            distance_test_value  : REAL;
            angle_test_value     : REAL;
            curvature_test_value : REAL;
                         END;

<world_header> ::= WORLD_HEADER ( real , real , real ,
                                  real , real , real ) ;

ENTITY WORLD = STRUCTURE
           header  : WORLD_HEADER
           SCOPE;
                 PART_LIBRARY;
                 ROUTINE_LIBRARY;
                 ASPECT;
                 ASSEMBLY_SCOPE_ENTITY;
                 RECORD;
                 MATERIAL;
                 GEOMETRY_ASSOCIATION;
                 INDEX_ENTRY;
           END_SCOPE;
         END;
```

```
<world> ::=  WORLD ( name : OPEN ) ;
                <world_header>
             SCOPE;
                 [<part_library> <routine_library> | <aspect> |
                  <assembly_scope_entity> | <record> | <material> |
                  <geometry_association> |
                  <index_entry>]*
             END_SCOPE;
              WORLD ( name , CLOSE ) ;
```

The WORLD represents a complete CAD data base. It is characterized by a number of attributes that apply to the whole data base (and, consequently, also to the whole neutral file) as well as all the entities and attributes constituting the world scope.

The world header attributes are:

- the length unit given by the length_unit_factor, such that the length unit corresponding to a real value of 1.0 is length_unit_factor times one meter. If centimeters are used the value of this attribute would be 0.01.
- the angle_unit such that a real value corresponds to angle_unit times one radian.
- the world_size which limits the maximum coordinate in terms of the length units defined by length_unit_factor.
- the minimal allowable distance value indicates that points closer to each other than this value are considered to coincide, and that circles with a lesser radius are to be considered as points only. This value is also used for testing the continuity of curves which should join continuously.
- the angle_test_value which indicates the allowable angle between curves which should join with continuous tangency condition.
- the curvature_test_value which indicates the allowable curvature difference (in reciprocal length units) between curves which should join with continuous curvature condition.

The world is the only entity that provides for libraries. Hence, only the world can establish relationships to information not stored in the same world.

The world has a name on the neutral file even though this name is not used for any purpose in this specification. The name is included only for the sake of generality of the translation from the HDSL description to the neutral file format.

5.2.2 ASSEMBLY

```
ENTITY ASSEMBLY = STRUCTURE
          SCOPE;
               ASPECT;
               ASSEMBLY_SCOPE_ENTITY;
               RECORD;
               MATERIAL;
               GEOMETRY_ASSOCIATION;
               INDEX_ENTRY;
          END_SCOPE;
                  result : LIST OF CLASS( REFERENCE(ASSEMBLY),
                                          REFERENCE(COMPONENT) );
                END;

<assembly> ::= ASSEMBLY ( name : OPEN ) ;
          SCOPE;
              [<aspect> | <assembly_scope_entity> | <record> |
               <material> | <geometry_association> |
                                     *
               <index_entry>]
          END_SCOPE;
               ASSEMBLY_RESULT <name_list> ;
             ASSEMBLY ( name , CLOSE ) ;

ENTITY ASSEMBLY_SCOPE_ENTITY = CLASS( INTEGER, REAL,
                                      SURFACE_SCOPE_ENTITY,
                                      DIRECTION(DIM), PLACEMENT(DIM),
                                      SOLID_MODEL, COMPONENT, ROUTINE,
                                      ASSEMBLY, MACRO,
                                      RECORD_TYPE,
                                      INSTANCE(ASSEMBLY_SCOPE_ENTITY) );

<assembly_scope_entity> ::= <integer> | <real> |
              <surface_scope_entity> | <direction(dim)> |
              <placement(dim)> | <solid_model> | <component> |
              <routine> | <assembly> | <macro> | <record_type> |
              <instance>
```

An assembly (see Figure 3 on page 49) is an entity that has a scope. The scope of an assembly is the same as the scope of a world. Hence, a whole world may be transferred to become an assembly in the receiving system. In this

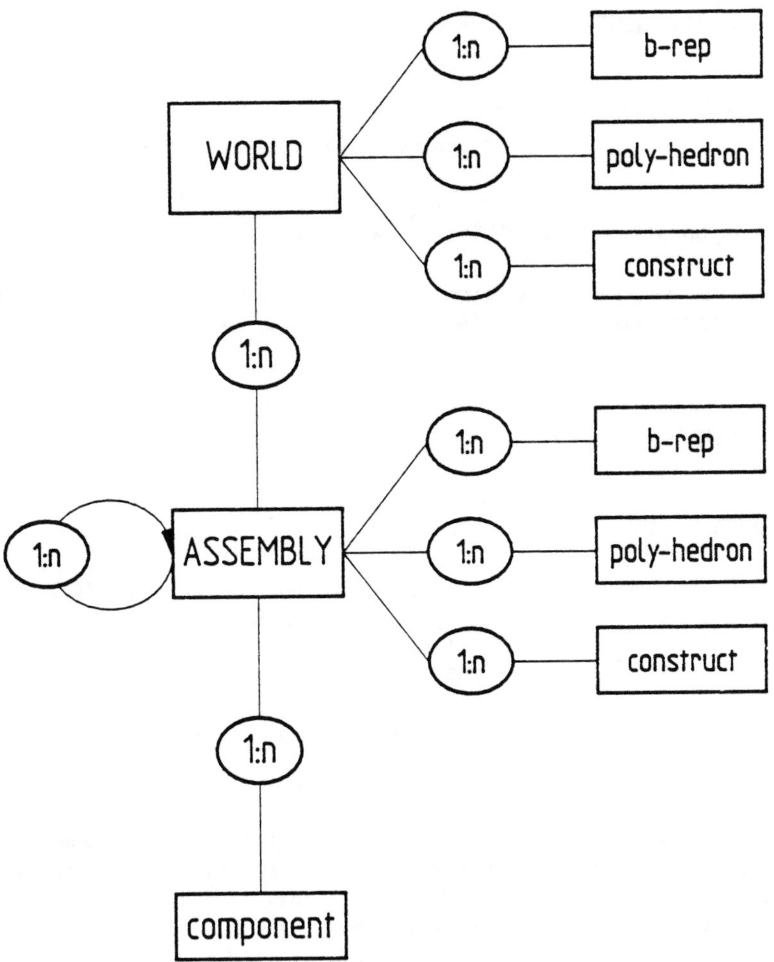

Figure 3. The assembly structure in the reference schema

respect, an assembly has a similar function as the directory of data sets in a number of operating systems.

In addition to providing a scope for other data, an assembly has a result called "result". The result is a list of instances of components or, recursively, assemblies. Whenever an operation such as display, evaluate volume, or other is applied to an assembly, it is meant to apply to all the entities of "result".

5.2.3 COMPONENT

```
ENTITY COMPONENT = STRUCTURE
                     (* component has no attributes *)
                   END;

<component> ::= COMPONENT ( name : ) ;
```

A component is the elementary constituent of an assembly. Components may have geometric models associated via a GEOMETRY_ASSOCIATION.

5.2.4 PART_LIBRARY

```
ENTITY PART_LIBRARY = STRUCTURE
                        description : STRING;
                        (* when in use the PART_LIBRARY
                           will be bound to a list of worlds *)
                        library     : LIST OF REF_EXTERNAL;
                      END;

<part_library> ::= PART_LIBRARY ( name : string , ( [<ref_external>
                                                              *
                     [, <ref_external>] ]  ) ) ;
```

A part_library is a world that contains entities (e.g., standard parts) which may be referenced from entities in another world. On the neutral file, the part_library is characterized by some descriptive text string. During actual use of the CAD system, each part_library will be bound to a list of worlds so that the references can be resolved.

5.2.5 ROUTINE_LIBRARY

```
ENTITY ROUTINE_LIBRARY = STRUCTURE
                           description : STRING;
                         END;

<routine_library> ::=  ROUTINE_LIBRARY ( name : string ) ;
```

A routine library is an operating system data set (or a list of them) that contains executable modules of routines. Such routines may be called from the CAD system during an application. They behave similar to macros in that they produce an entity as a result which may be stored in the data base.

5.3 REFERENCING MECHANISMS

The CAD*I reference model knows the following types of referencing mechanisms:

1. internal references
   These references are built into the HDSL as the REFERENCE and REF_ONLY data types (see "The types REFERENCE, REF_ONLY" on page 28). These references are to entities which are transferred in the same neutral file and are to be bound (resolved) by the post-processor.

2. external references
   These references are also to be bound by the post-processor. However, the referred-to entities are not transferred on the same neutral file but are assumed to exist already in the receiving system. They may have been transferred previous on a CAD*I neutral file or with some other data format, or they may have been created in the receiving system independently. Such references are expressed by user-defined names, INDEX_ENTRY properties, and REF_EXTERNAL attributes.

3. references to entities in other data bases
   These references are to be bound not by the post-processor but by the receiving system at a later time, namely when the transferred information is actually used. The referred entities may have been transferred previous on a CAD*I neutral file (or with some other data format), or they may have been created in the receiving system independently. Such references are expressed by user-defined names, INDEX_ENTRY properties, and REF_PART_LIBRARY attributes.

5.3.1 INDEX_ENTRY

```
PROPERTY INDEX_ENTRY = STRUCTURE
                        user_def : USER_DEFINED_NAME;
                        object   : REF_ONLY( CLASS( REAL, INTEGER,
                                     GEOMETRIC, ASPECT, FACE,
                                     PLACEMENT, MACRO, ROUTINE,
                                     RECORD_TYPE) );
                        END;
```

```
<index_entry> ::= INDEX_ENTRY ( user_defined_name , name ) ;
```

Entities of the classes specified in the schema may have a user-defined name associated. This user-defined name may be used to identify the entities whenever an interactive identification (by picking on the workstation monitor) is not possible. In particular, when sequences of commands to the CAD system are input on the keyboard or read from a text file, user-defined names serve for identifying entities.

User-defined names must be unique in each scope.

5.3.2 REF_EXTERNAL

```
ATTRIBUTE REF_EXTERNAL = STRUCTURE
                           user_def   : USER_DEFINED_NAME;
                           descriptor : TYPE_ID;
                         END;
```

```
<ref_external> ::= REF_EXTERNAL ( user_defined_name , <type_id> ) ;
```

This is a reference to an entity in the receiving environment. It is characterized by the user-defined name of the entity which is to searched for in the receiving environment, and a type identification for this entity to ensure that the binding will be performed only to entities of this type.

Binding of external references occurs during post_processing. The receiving world will contain REFERENCE(TYPE) instead of REF_EXTERNAL(TYPE).

5.3.3 REF_PART_LIBRARY

```
ATTRIBUTE REF_PART_LIBRARY = STRUCTURE
                              library    : REFERENCE(PART_LIBRARY);
                              user_def   : USER_DEFINED_NAME;
                              descriptor : TYPE_ID;
                             END;

<ref_part_library> ::= REF_PART_LIBRARY  ( name ,
                               user_defined_name , <type_id> ) ;
```

This is a reference to an entity in a part library. It is characterized by a reference to the part-library, the user-defined name of the entity which is to be searched for in the part library, and a type identification for this entity to ensure that the binding will be performed only to entities of this type.

Binding of library references occurs during the application (not at post-processing time).

5.3.4 REF_ANY

```
ATTRIBUTE REF_ANY = GENERIC (type: CLASS( PREDEFINED_ENTITY,
                                          GEOMETRIC,
                                          DIRECTION(DIM) ))
                         CLASS( REFERENCE(type),
                                REFERENCE(FORMAL_PARAMETER),
                                REF_PART_LIBRARY,
                                REF_EXTERNAL );

<ref_any> ::= name | <ref_part_library> | <ref_external>
```

This is a class of reference types for referencing geometric and predefined entities. Such references may be either internal (e.g., to entities transferred on the same file), references to entities in a library (with binding taking place at the time of application), external references (references to entities already existing in the receiving environment with binding taking place at pre-processing time) References to formal parameters are allowed only within macros.

5.4 GEOMETRIC MODEL ENTITIES

5.4.1 GEOMETRIC_MODEL

```
ENTITY GEOMETRIC_MODEL = CLASS( WIREFRAME_MODEL(DIM),
                                SURFACE_MODEL,
                                SOLID_MODEL
                                INSTANCE(GEOMETRIC_MODEL) );

<geometric_model> ::= <wireframe_model> | <surface_model> |
                      <solid_model> | <instance>
```

The GEOMETRIC_MODEL is a class representing entities according to the geometric modeling techniques WIREFRAME_MODEL (two-dimensional and three-dimensional) SURFACE_MODEL, and SOLID_MODEL.

5.4.2 WIREFRAME_MODEL

```
ENTITY WIREFRAME_MODEL = GENERIC (d : DIM)
                          STRUCTURE
            SCOPE;
                  WIREFRAME_SCOPE_ENTITY;
                  INDEX_ENTRY;
            END_SCOPE;
                     result : LIST OF REF_ONLY(BOUNDED_CURVE(d));
                   END;

<wireframe_model> ::= WIREFRAME_MODEL ( name : OPEN ) ;
            SCOPE;
                 [<wireframe_scope_entity> |
                  <index_entry>]*
            END_SCOPE;
                      WIREFRAME_MODEL_RESULT <name_list> ;
                      WIREFRAME_MODEL ( name , CLOSE ) ;
```

```
ENTITY WIREFRAME_SCOPE_ENTITY =
                CLASS( POINT(DIM),
                       SURFACE, CURVE(DIM)
                       INSTANCE(WIREFRAME_SCOPE_ENTITY) );

<wireframe_scope_entity ::= <point(dim)> | <surface> | <curve(dim)> |
                            <instance>
```

A WIREFRAME_MODEL is an entity that has a scope. A WIREFRAME_MODEL may have a material property associated with it. Surface entities are required in wireframe models which contain geometry defined on surfaces (see "Geometry on surfaces" on page 93). The result is a list of references to bounded curves only.

5.4.3 SURFACE_MODEL

```
ENTITY SURFACE_MODEL = STRUCTURE
         SCOPE;
                SURFACE_SCOPE_ENTITY;
                INDEX_ENTRY;
         END_SCOPE;
                    result : LIST OF REF_ONLY(BOUNDED_SURFACE);
                  END;

<surface_model> ::=  SURFACE_MODEL ( name : OPEN ) ;
         SCOPE;
             [<surface_scope_entity> | <index_entry>]*
         END_SCOPE;
                 SURFACE_MODEL_RESULT <name_list> ;
                 SURFACE_MODEL ( name , CLOSE ) ;

ENTITY SURFACE_SCOPE_ENTITY = CLASS( POINT(DIM),
                                     SURFACE, CURVE(DIM),
                                     INSTANCE(SURFACE_SCOPE_ENTITY) );

<surface_scope_entity> ::= <point(dim)> | <surface> | <curve(dim)> |
                           <instance>                              ;
```

A SURFACE_MODEL is an entity that has a scope. A SURFACE_MODEL may have a material property associated with it. The result is a list of references to bounded surfaces only.

5.4.4 SOLID_MODEL

```
ENTITY SOLID_MODEL = CLASS( POLY_HEDRON, B_REP,
                            COMPOUND_B_REP, CONSTRUCT,
                            HYBRID_SOLID,
                            INSTANCE(SOLID_MODEL) );

<solid_model> ::= <poly_hedron> | <b_rep> | <compound_b_rep> |
                  <construct> | <hybrid_solid> | <instance>
```

A solid may be a B_REP, a CONSTRUCT, a POLY_HEDRON, a HYBRID_SOLID, or a COMPOUND_B_REP.

5.5 POINTS AND CURVES

5.5.1 Attribute types related to curves

5.5.1.1 CURVE_TRANSITION_CODE

```
ATTRIBUTE CURVE_TRANSITION_CODE =
                        ENUM( CONTINUOUS,
                              CONT_SAME_GRADIENT,
                              CONT_SAME_GRADIENT_SAME_CURVATURE );

<curve_transition_code>  ::=  CONTINUOUS | CONT_SAME_GRADIENT |
                              CONT_SAME_GRADIENT_SAME_CURVATURE
```

The curve transition code indicates whether two consecutive segments of a composite curve are considered to join such that they are continuous, with the same gradient, or with the same curvature. This condition takes priority over the actual geometric definition of the curve segments (see "COMPOSITE_CURVE" on page 77).

5.5.2 DIRECTION

```
ENTITY DIRECTION = GENERIC (d : DIM)
                     STRUCTURE
                       x : ANY(REAL);
                       y : ANY(REAL);
                       CASE d OF
                         D3: (z : ANY(REAL));
                         D2: (z : NIL);
                       END;
                     END;

<direction(dim)> ::= <direction(d2)> | <direction(d3)>

<direction(d2)> ::=  DIRECTION ( name : <any(real)> , <any(real)> ) ;

<any(direction(dim))> ::= <any(direction(d2))> | <any(direction(d3))>

<any(direction(d2))> ::= <ref_any> |
                     DIRECTION ( <any(real)> , <any(real)> )

<direction(d3)> ::=  DIRECTION ( name : <any(real)> ,
                                 <any(real)> , <any(real)> );

<any(direction(d3))> ::= <ref_any> |
                DIRECTION ( <any(real)> , <any(real)> , <any(real)> )
```

The DIRECTION entity defines the x-, y-, and z-components of a direction vector. For two-dimensional directions the z-component is implied to be zero. The direction vector in the reference schema is normalized. On the neutral file, however, the direction vector needs not to be normalized. The receiving system has to derive the normalized direction vector from the data received on the file by the following algorithm:

$$length = SQRT(x\_received^2 + y\_received^2 + z\_received^2)$$

Obviously the condition length > 0 has to apply. Then we obtain finally:

x = x_received/length
y = y_received/length
z = z_received/length

5.5.3 POINT

```
ENTITY POINT= GENERIC (d : DIM)
                STRUCTURE
                  x : ANY(REAL);
                  y : ANY(REAL);
                  CASE d OF
                    D3: (z : ANY(REAL));
                    D2: (z : NIL);
                  END;
                END;

<point(dim)> ::= <point(d2)> | <point(d3)>

<point(d2)> ::=  POINT ( name : <any(real)> , <any(real)> ) ;

<any(point(dim))> ::= <any(point(d2))> | <any(point(d3))>

<any(point(d2))> ::=  <ref_any> |
                      POINT ( <any(real)> , <any(real)> )

<point(d3)> ::=  POINT ( name : <any(real)> ,
                         <any(real)> , <any(real)> ) ;

<any(point(d3))> ::=  <ref_any> |
                      POINT ( <any(real)> , <any(real)> , <any(real)> )
```

A POINT may identifies a location in two- or three-dimensional Cartesian space by giving the coordinate values: x, y, and (for three-dimensional points) z.

5.5.4 Curve classes

5.5.4.1 CURVE

```
ENTITY CURVE = GENERIC (d : DIM)
                CLASS( ELEMENTARY_CURVE(d),
                       TRIMMED_CURVE(d),
                       COMPOSITE_CURVE(d),
                       INSTANCE(CURVE(d)),
                       CASE d OF
                         D2: OFFSET_CURVE;
                         D3: SURFACE_CURVE;
                       END );
```

```
<curve(dim)> ::= <curve(d2)> | <curve(d3)>

<curve(d2)> ::= <elementary_curve(d2)> | <trimmed_curve(d2)> |
                <composite_curve(d2)> | <instance> | <offset_curve>

<curve(d3)> ::= <elementary_curve(d3)> | <trimmed_curve(d3)> |
                <composite_curve(d3)> | <instance> | <surface_curve>
```

This is the class of elementary, trimmed, and composite curves.

5.5.4.2 ELEMENTARY_CURVE

```
ENTITY ELEMENTARY_CURVE = GENERIC (d : DIM)
                 CLASS( LINE(d), LINE_SEGMENT(d), POLYGON(d),
                 CIRCLE(d), ELLIPSE(d), PARABOLA(d), HYPERBOLA(d),
                 POLY_CURVE(d), B_SPLINE_CURVE(d),
                 INSTANCE(ELEMENTARY_CURVE(d)) );

<elementary_curve(dim)> ::= <elementary_curve(d2)> |
                            <elementary_curve(d3)>

<elementary_curve(d2)> ::= <line(d2) | <line_segment(d2)> |
                           <polygon(d2)> | <circle(d2)> |
                           <ellipse(d2)> | <parabola(d2)> |
                           <hyperbola(d2)> | <poly_curve(d2)> |
                           <b_spline_curve(d2)> | <instance>

<elementary_curve(d3)> ::= <line(d3) | <line_segment(d3)> |
                           <polygon(d3)> | <circle(d3)> |
                           <ellipse(d3)> | <parabola(d3)> |
                           <hyperbola(d3)> | <poly_curve(d3)> |
                           <b_spline_curve(d3)> | <instance>
```

5.5.4.3 BOUNDED_CURVE

```
ENTITY BOUNDED_CURVE = GENERIC (d : DIM)
                 CLASS( CIRCLE(d), ELLIPSE(d), B_SPLINE_CURVE(d),
                 LINE_SEGMENT(d), POLYGON(d) TRIMMED_CURVE(d),
                 COMPOSITE_CURVE(d), INSTANCE(BOUNDED_CURVE(d)),
                     CASE d OF
                       D2: NIL;
                       D3: SURFACE_CURVE;
                     END );

(* The surface curves only if they are of trimmed or composite type *)
```

```
<bounded_curve(dim)> ::= <bounded_curve(d2)> |
                          <bounded_curve(d3)>

<bounded_curve(d2)> ::= <circle(d2)> | <ellipse(d2)> |
                        <b_spline_curve(d2)> | <line_segment(d2)> |
                        <polygon(d2> | <trimmed_curve(d2)> |
                        <composite_curve(d2)> | <instance> |

<bounded_curve(d3)> ::= <circle(d3)> | <ellipse(d3)> |
                        <b_spline_curve(d3)> | <line_segment(d3)> |
                        <polygon(d3)> | <trimmed_curve(d3)> |
                        <composite_curve(d3)> | <instance> |
                        <surface_curve>
```

This entity type represents all bounded curves. It consists of the trimmed curves and those conics that are bounded by their geometric definition. The purpose of introducing this entity type is to guarantee that the result of a wireframe model is always bounded.

5.5.4.4 CLOSED_CURVE

```
ENTITY CLOSED_CURVE = GENERIC (d : DIM)
                  CLASS( CIRCLE(d), ELLIPSE(d), B_SPLINE_CURVE(d),
                  COMPOSITE_CURVE(d), (* See "COMPOSITE_CURVE" on page 77 *
                  INSTANCE(CLOSED_CURVE(d)),
                       CASE d OF
                         D2: NIL;
                         D3: SURFACE_CURVE
                       END );

(* The surface curves only if they are geometrical closed *)

<closed_curve(dim)> ::= <closed_curve(d2)> |
                        <closed_curve(d3)>

<closed_curve(d2)> ::= <circle(d2)> | <ellipse(d2)> |
                       <b_spline_curve(d2)> |
                       <composite_curve(d2)> | <instance> |

<closed_curve(d3)> ::= <circle(d3)> | <ellipse(d3)> |
                       <b_spline_curve(d3)> |
                       <composite_curve(d3)> | <instance> |
                       <surface_curve>
```

A CLOSED_CURVE is a class of curves consisting of

1. CIRCLE

2. ELLIPSE
3. B_SPLINE_CURVE, provided that the form number is CIRCLE or ELLIPSE and the actual geometry passes the test that the points corresponding to the maximum and minimum parameter range have the same coordinates with the accuracy specified in the appropriate world attribute.
4. COMPOSITE_CURVE provided that point_1 of the first TRIMMED_CURVE and point_2 of the last TRIMMED_CURVE representing the first and last segment of the composite curve are references to the same point entity (represented by the same name on the neutral file).
5. The above rules apply correspondingly to curves on surfaces.

The entity ELEMENTARY_CURVE consists of a class of curves that constitutes the basic geometry definitions for wireframe entities.

5.5.5 Elementary curves

5.5.5.1 LINE

```
ENTITY LINE = GENERIC (d : DIM)
                  STRUCTURE
                    point     : ANY(POINT(d));
                    direction : ANY(DIRECTION(d));
                  END;

<line(dim)> ::= <line(d2)> | <line(d3)>

<line(d2)> ::= LINE ( name : <any(point(d2))> ,
                             <any(direction(d2))> ) ;

<any(line(dim))> ::= <any(line(d2))> | <any(line(d3))>

<any(line(d2))> ::=  <ref_any> |
                     LINE ( <any(point(d2))> , <any(direction(d2))> )

<line(d3)> ::= LINE ( name : <any(point(d3))> ,
                             <any(direction(d3))> ) ;

<any(line(d3))> ::=  <ref_any> |
                     LINE ( <any(point(d3))> , <any(direction(d3))> )
```

The LINE is a geometrical entity defined as an elementary straight line going through the specified point with the specified direction. The point may be defined locally or be represented by a reference to a point entity. The same applies to the direction. The line, as all elementary curves, has an implied curve parameter. The parameterisation is:

r(u) = **point** + **direction** * u

NOTE that direction is normalized.

If several lines refer the same point they will always go through the same point even when that point is moved interactively. Similarly, if several lines refer the same direction entity they will always be parallel.

5.5.5.2 LINE_SEGMENT

```
ENTITY LINE_SEGMENT = GENERIC (d : DIM)
                        STRUCTURE
                          first_point : ANY(POINT(d));
                          last_point  : ANY(POINT(d));
                        END;
```

```
<line_segment(dim)> ::= <line_segment(d2)> | <line_segment(d2)>

<line_segment(d2)> ::= LINE_SEGMENT ( name : <any(point(d2))> ,
                                             <any(point(d2))> ) ;

<line_segment(d3)> ::= LINE_SEGMENT ( name : <any(point(d3))> ,
                                             <any(point(d3))> ) ;
```

The LINE_SEGMENT is a geometrical entity defined as an elementary straight line going through the specified point with the specified direction. The point may be defined locally or be represented by a reference to a point entity. The same applies to the direction. The line, as all elementary curves, has an implied curve parameter. The parameterisation is:

r(u) = **first_point***(1-u) + **last_point***u

The parameter range is $0 \leq u \leq 1$.

5.5.5.3 CIRCLE

```
ENTITY CIRCLE = GENERIC (d : DIM)
                  STRUCTURE
                    radius          : ANY(REAL); (* positive *)
                    center          : ANY(POINT(d));
                    CASE d OF
                      D3: (normal : ANY(DIRECTION(d)));
                      D2: (normal : NIL);
                    END;
                    reference_point : ANY(POINT(d)) ;
                  END;

<circle(dim)> ::= <circle(d2)> | <circle(d3)>

<circle(d2)> ::= CIRCLE ( name : <any(real)> , <any(point(d2))> ,
                          <any(point(d2))> ) ;

<circle(d3)> ::= CIRCLE ( name : <any(real)> , <any(point(d3))> ,
                          <any(direction(d3))> , <any(point(d3))> ) ;
```

The interpretation of this data is as follows (see Figure 4)

$$\text{dir} = \text{reference\_point} - \text{centre} - ((\text{reference\_point} - \text{centre}) \cdot \text{normal})\text{normal}$$

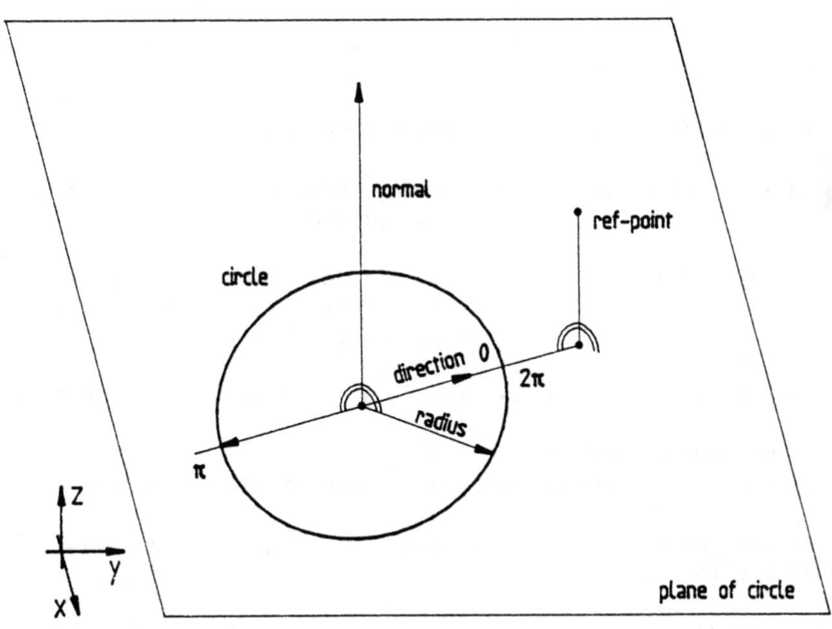

Figure 4. The CIRCLE

This is then normalised to produce **a**, the circle is then defined for values of u from 0 to 2π.

$\mathbf{r}(u) = \mathbf{centre} + \text{radius}\ (\ \mathbf{a}\cos(u) + (\mathbf{normal} * \mathbf{a})\sin(u))$

1. the reference point should be, but may not be a) on the circle b) in the plane of the circle.
2. If the reference point is irrelevant in a particular model, it must nevertheless be supplied by the sending system. Any point that makes **dir** not vanish represents a valid default value for reference point.
3. In the case of DIM=D2, ie 2D circle, the axis of the circle is $[0,0,1]^T$

5.5.5.4 ELLIPSE

```
ENTITY ELLIPSE = GENERIC (d : DIM)
                   STRUCTURE
                     semi_major       : ANY(REAL); (* positive *)
                     semi_minor       : ANY(REAL); (* positive *)
                     center           : ANY(POINT(d);
                     CASE d OF
                       D3: (normal : ANY(DIRECTION(D3)));
                       D2: (normal : NIL);
                     END;
                     reference_point : ANY(POINT(d)) ;
                   END;
```

```
<ellipse(dim)> ::= <ellipse(d2)> | <ellipse(d3)>

<ellipse(d2)> ::= ELLIPSE ( name : <any(real)> , <any(real)> ,
                            <any(point(d2))> , <any(point(d2))> ) ;

<ellipse(d3)> ::= ELLIPSE ( name : <any(real)> , <any(real)> ,
                            <any(point(d3))> , <any(direction(d3))> ,
                            <any(point(d3))> ) ;
```

This represents a curve parameterised as follows (see Figure 5 on page 65):

$$\mathbf{dir} = \mathbf{reference\_point} - \mathbf{centre} - ((\mathbf{reference\_point} - \mathbf{centre})\bullet\mathbf{normal})\mathbf{normal}$$

This is then normalised to produce **a**, the ellipse is then defined for values of u from 0 to 2π:

$\mathbf{r}(u) = \mathbf{centre} + \text{semi\_major}\ \mathbf{a}\cos(u) + \text{semi\_minor}\ (\mathbf{n}*\mathbf{a})\sin(u)$

5.5.5.5 HYPERBOLA

```
ENTITY HYPERBOLA = GENERIC (d : DIM)
                    STRUCTURE
                     semi_axis       : ANY(REAL); (* positive *)
                     semi_imag_axis  : ANY(REAL); (* positive *)
                     center          : ANY(POINT(d));
                     CASE d OF
                       D3: (normal : ANY(DIRECTION(D3)));
                       D2: (normal : NIL);
                     END;
                     reference_point : ANY(POINT(d)) ;
                    END;
```

```
<hyperbola(dim)> ::= <hyperbola(d2)> | <hyperbola(d3)>

<hyperbola(d2)> ::= HYPERBOLA ( name : <any(real)> , <any(real)> ,
                              <any(point(d2))> , <any(point(d2))> ) ;
```

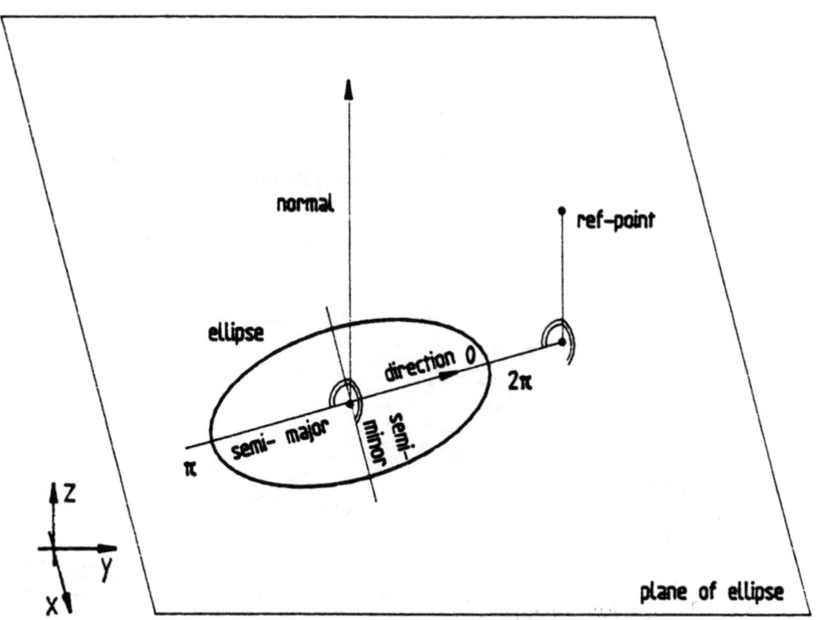

Figure 5. The ELLIPSE

```
<hyperbola(d3)> ::= HYPERBOLA ( name : <any(real)> , <any(real)> ,
                              <any(point(d3))> , <any(direction(d3))> ,
                              <any(point(d3))> ) ;
```

This represents a curve parameterised as follows (see Figure 6):

dir = **reference_point**
 - **centre** - ((**reference_point** - **centre**)•**normal**)**normal**

This is then normalised to produce **a**, the hyperbola is then defined for any real values of u:

r(u) = **centre** + semi_axis **a** cosh u + semi_imag_axis(**n*a**)sinh u

The reference point is approximately a vertex position, used to define a major axis direction on the chosen branch of the hyperbola. The parameter range is infinite.

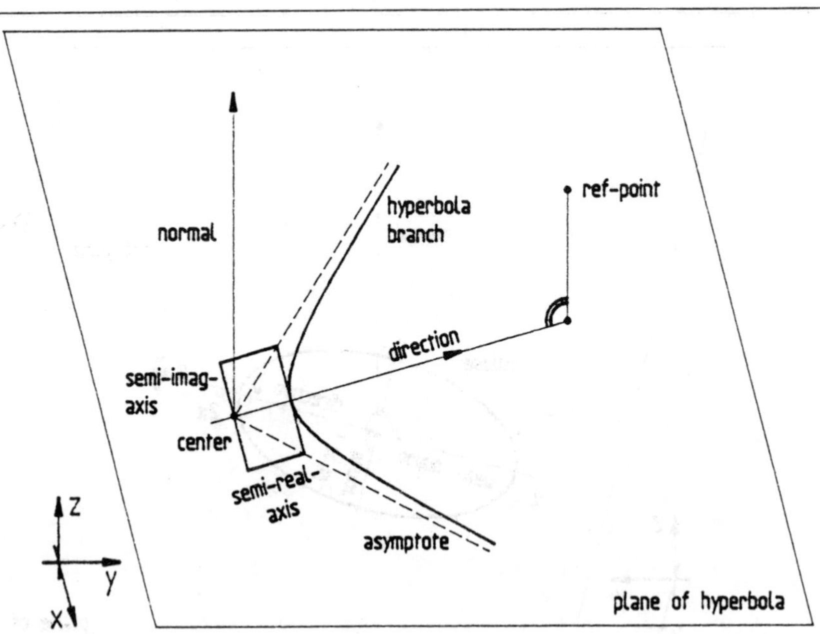

Figure 6. The HYPERBOLA

5.5.5.6 PARABOLA

```
ENTITY PARABOLA = GENERIC (d : DIM)
                    STRUCTURE
                      focal_distance  : ANY(REAL); (* positive *)
                      vertex          : ANY(POINT(d));
                      CASE d OF
                        D3: (normal : ANY(DIRECTION(d)));
                        D2: (normal : NIL);
                      END;
                      reference_point : ANY(POINT(d)) ;
                    END;
```

```
<parabola(dim)> ::= <parabola(d2)> | <parabola(d3)>

<parabola(d2)> ::= PARABOLA ( name : <any(real)> , <any(point(d2))> ,
                         <any(point(d2))> ) ;

<parabola(d3)> ::= PARABOLA ( name : <any(real)> , <any(point(d3))> ,
                         <any(direction(d3))> , <any(point(d3))> ) ;
```

This represents a curve parameterised as follows (see Figure 7 on page 68):

$$\mathbf{dir} = \mathbf{reference\_point} - \mathbf{vertex} - ((\mathbf{reference\_point} - \mathbf{vertex}) \bullet \mathbf{normal})\mathbf{normal}$$

This is then normalised to produce **a**, the parabola is then defined for any real values of u:

$$\mathbf{r}(u) = \mathbf{vertex} + focal\_distance\ \mathbf{a}\ u^2 + 2\ focal\_distance\ \mathbf{normal} * \mathbf{a}\ u$$

5.5.5.7 POLYGON

```
ENTITY POLYGON= GENERIC (d : DIM)
                  STRUCTURE
                    point-list : LIST OF ANY(POINT(d));
                  END;
```

```
<polygon(dim)> ::= <polygon(d2)> | <polygon(d3)>

<polygon(d2)> ::= POLYGON ( name : ( [<any(point(d2))>
                  [ , <any(point(d2))>]* ] ) ) ;

<polygon(d3)> ::= POLYGON ( name : ( [<any(point(d3))>
                  [ , <any(point(d3))>]* ] ) ) ;
```

The polygon defines a connected sequence of straight line segments. The line segments are given by the ordered list of (at least two) points. The number of segments is implicitly defined as being one less than the number of points in the point list. A closed polygon is indicated by the first and last reference in the list being identical.

5.5.5.8 B_SPLINE_CURVE

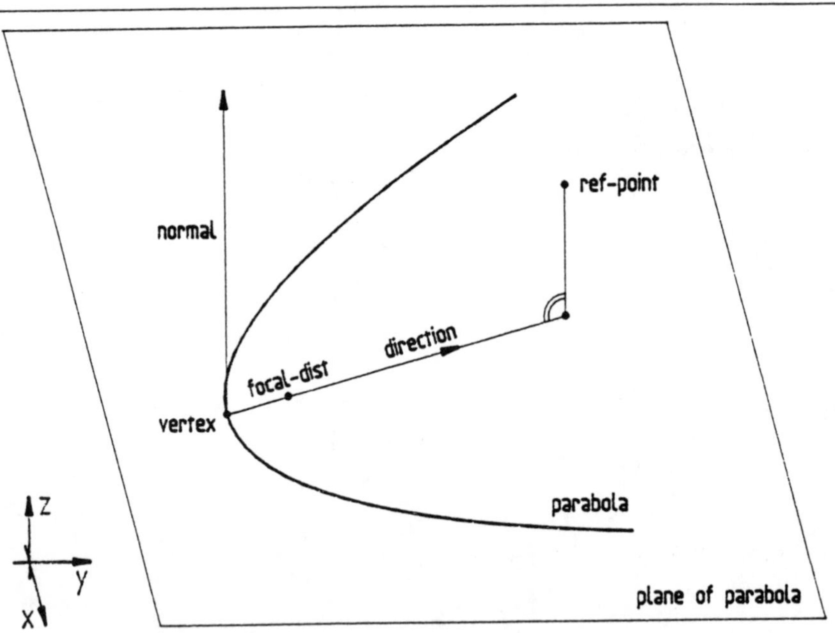

Figure 7. The PARABOLA

```
ENTITY B_SPLINE_CURVE = GENERIC (d : DIM)
       STRUCTURE
        rational                         : LOGICAL;
        uniform                          : LOGICAL;
        bezier                           : LOGICAL
        degree                           : INTEGER;
        upper_index_on_control_points    : INTEGER;
        control_points                   : LIST OF ANY(POINT(d));
                                           (* 0..K *)
        knot_multiplicities              : LIST OF INTEGER;
                                           (* 1..L *)
        knots                            : [LIST OF REAL];
                                           (* 1..L *)
        weights                          : [LIST OF REAL];
                                           (* 0..K *)
        form_number                      : [INTEGER];
       END;

<b_spline_curve(dim)> ::= <b_spline_curve(d2)> | <b_spline_curve(d3)>

<b_spline_curve(d2)> ::= B_SPLINE_CURVE  ( name :  logical , logical ,
                           logical , integer , integer ,
                           ( [<any(point(d2))> [,
                           <any(point(d2))>]*  ]  ) ,
                           <integer_list> , [<real_list>]  ,
                           [<real_list>] , [integer] ) ;

<B_spline_curve(d3)> ::= B_SPLINE_CURVE ( name :      logical ,
                             logical , logical , integer , integer ,
                             ( [<any(point(d3))> [ ,
                             <any(point(d3))>]*  ] ) ,
                             <integer_list> , [<real_list>] ,
                             [<real_list>] , [integer] ) ;
```

The attribute upper_index_on_control_points has the value K, that is the number of spans between the control points (control_points-1).
The attribute control_points contains the $\mathbf{r}_i$ with the indices $i = 0$ to K.

The attribute knot_multiplicities contains values m_i (see remark below).

The attribute knots contains the u_i for $i = 1..L$.

The attribute weights contains the w_i for $i = 0..K$.

1. If rational=.T. then all values of weights must be positive and the curve is given by:

$$\mathbf{r}(u) = \frac{\sum_{i=0}^{K} w_i \, \mathbf{r}_i \, N_i(u)}{\sum_{i=0}^{K} w_i \, N_i(u)}$$

$N_i(u)$ are the normalised B-spline basis functions defined on the knot set:

$$u_{i\text{-degree}}, \ldots, u_{i+1} \text{ with } u_{j+1} \geq u_j \text{ (ie non decreasing)}$$

They are determined by the degree and the chosen parameter values u_i and are zero for $u < u_{i\text{-degree}}$ or $u > u_{i+1}$.

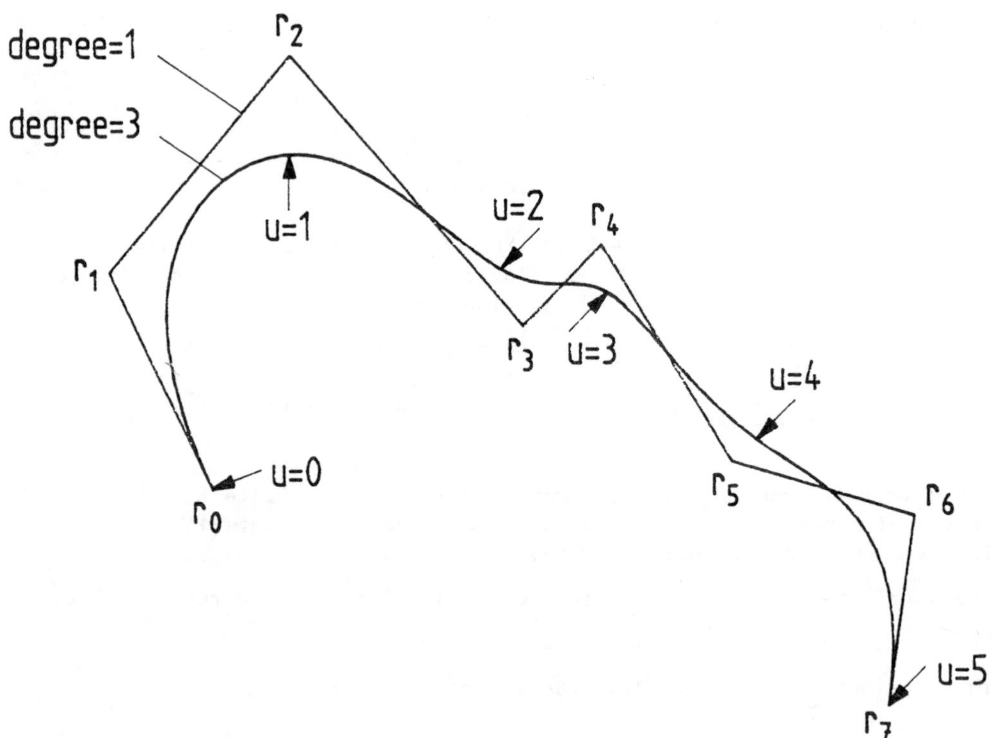

Figure 8. A B_SPLINE_CURVE example for degrees 1 and 3.

2. The knot_multiplicities m_i should all be in the range (1..degree+1) and should satisfy:

$$\sum_{i=1}^{L} m_i = \text{degree} + K + 2$$

In evaluating the basis functions a knot u_j of, for example, multiplicity 3 is interpreted as a sequence u_j, u_j, u_j in the knot set.

3. If uniform=.T. it will be enough to give u_0 because the knots satisfy: $u_{j+1} - u_j = 1$, or 0 for multiple knots.

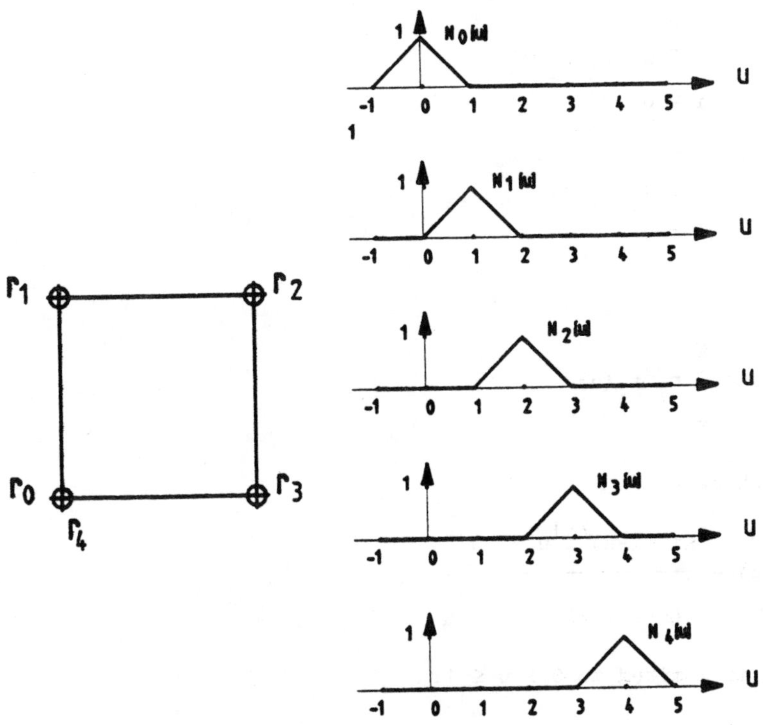

Figure 9. A B_SPLINE_CURVE example for a closed polygon: The four corner points are represented as references in the B-spline data structure to the effect that the shape of the polygon changes immediately with a translation of the points.

4. If rational=.F., then the weight list is empty indicating that the denominator is 1. The above becomes:

$$\mathbf{r}(u) = \sum_{i=0}^{K} \mathbf{r}_i N_i(u)$$

In this case the weight values are not included, implicitly all weights are 1.0.

5. If Bezier = .T. the curve represented is a single segment Bezier curve. The knot set will not be included explicitly. The curve can be represented either as a B-spline curve with multiple knots (0,0,...,0,1,1, ... 1) each value 0 or 1 being repeated degree + 1 times, or directly as a Bezier curve:

$$\mathbf{r}(u) = \frac{\sum_{i=0}^{K} w_i \mathbf{r}_i f_i(u)}{\sum_{i=0}^{K} w_i f_i(u)}$$

or

$$\mathbf{r}(u) = \sum_{i=0}^{K} \mathbf{r}_i f_i(u)$$

in each case

$$f_i(u) = \frac{K!\ (i-u)^{K-1} u^i}{(K-i)!\ i!}$$

and u is limited to $0 \le u \le 1$.

It should be noted that every Bezier curve has an equivalent representation as a B-spline curve but not every B-spline curve can be represented as a single Bezier curve.

6. The form number is optional. When present, it is used to identify special cases of conic curves as in the IGES 3.0 specification. The receiving

system will have to check whether the received B_SPLINE_CURVE geometry actually conforms with this shape within an accuracy to be specified as a directive to the post-processor. If the test fails it means that the received entity is invalid. The default value is UNDEFINED.

The form number has the following meaning:

form number	intended geometric form
1	UNDEFINED
2	POLYLINE
3	CIRCLE
4	CIRCULAR_ARC
5	ELLIPTIC_ARC
6	PARABOLIC_ARC
7	HYPERBOLIC_ARC

7. A simple polygon is represented as a B_SPLINE_CURVE of degree 1.

8. A B-spline which connects individual points in a functional way such that the geometry of the curve changes automatically when the knot points are moved, will contain references to these knot points rather than the points in form of attribute types.

EXAMPLE 1

Figure 8 on page 70 shows examples of B-spline curves of degree one and three. The B-spline curve of degree 1 represents a polyline. The description of the other spline is as following:

```
B_SPLINE_CURVE :
        rational                      : .F.
        uniform                       : .T.
        bezier                        : .F.
        degree                        :  3
        upper_index_on_control_points :  7
        control_points                : -12.0   -6.0  0.0
                                        -16.0    2.0  0.0
                                         -9.0   10.0  0.0
                                          0.0    0.0  0.0
                                          3.0    3.0  0.0
                                          8.0   -5.0  0.0
                                         15.0   -7.0  0.0
                                         14.0  -14.0  0.0
        knot_multiplicities           :  4 1 1 1 1 4
        knot indices                  :  0 1 2 3 4 5
        form number                   :  UNDEFINED
```

EXAMPLE 2

Figure 9 on page 71 shows an example of a closed B-spline curve of degree 1 representing a polygon with four corners. The attributes of this entity are:

rational : has the value .F.
uniform : has the value .T.
bezier : has the value .F.
degree : has the value 1
upper_index_on_control_points: has the value 4
control_points: is a list of references to the first, second, third, fourth, and again to the first point in this order those are $P_0, P_1, P_2, P_3, P_4 (=P_0)$
knot_multiplicities: is a list of five times 1
knots : is a list of 7 u_i values
because uniform = .T. it could also be the value u_0
weights : is missing since rational = .F.
form number : is missing

For degree = 1, Figure 9 on page 71 shows the base functions $N_i(u)$.

This implies a linear interpolation between

r_0 and r_1 (u from 0 to 1)

r_1 and r_2 (u from 1 to 2)

r_2 and r_3 (u from 2 to 3)

r_3 and r_4 (u from 3 to 4)

The knot set for $N_i(u)$ is $u_{i\text{-degree}}$ to u_{i+1}, and for i = 0 to K and degree = 1, we get

knot 1:	u_{-1} u_0 u_1	for $N_0(u)$
knot 2:	u_0 u_1 u_2	for $N_1(u)$
knot 3:	u_1 u_2 u_3	for $N_2(u)$
knot 4:	u_2 u_3 u_4	for $N_3(u)$
knot L:	u_3 u_4 u_5	for $N_4(u)$

multiplicities: 1 1 1 1 1 1 1

$$\Sigma m_i = \text{degree} + K + 2 = 1 + 4 + 2 = 7$$

Instead of specifying all the knots, with multiplicity = 1, the list can be shortened if several of the u values are equal. In our example

$$u_{-1} = u_0 \text{ and } u_4 = u_5$$

(Note, that in the special case of a closed polygon we also have $u_5 = u_0$, but that is irrelevant in this context.) Hence, the number of multiplicities becomes L = 5 with

m1 = 2 for (u_{-1}, u_0)

m2 = 1 for u_1

m3 = 1 for u_2

m4 = 1 for u_3

m5 = 2 for (u_4, u_5)

$$\Sigma m_i = 2 + 1 + 1 + 1 + 2 = 7$$

5.5.6 Derived curve entities

5.5.6.1 TRIMMED_CURVE

```
ENTITY TRIMMED_CURVE = GENERIC (d : DIM)
                  STRUCTURE;
                    curve       : REF_ANY(CURVE(d);
                    parameter_1 : REAL;
                    parameter_2 : REAL;
                    sense       : LOGICAL;
                    point_1     : [REF_ANY(POINT(d))];
                    point_2     : [REF_ANY(POINT(d))];
                  END;
```

```
<trimmed_curve> ::= TRIMMED_CURVE ( name :  name , real , real ,
                                     logical , [ name ] ,
                                     [ name ] ) ;
```

1. The TRIMMED_CURVE entity defines a section out of the definition range of the elementary curve referenced. The curve is to be evaluated between the parameter values starting at parameter_1 and going to parameter_2.

2. If sense is .T. then we distinguish

   a. If parameter_1 < parameter_2 then the trimmed curve is defined in the same sense of increasing parameter values as the referenced curve.
   b. If parameter_2 > parameter_1 then the trimmed curve is defined in the sense of increasing parameter values from parameter_1 to the upper limit of the parameter range of the referenced curve and then continued from the lower limit of the parameter range of the referenced curve up to parameter_2. This definition is valid only if the referenced curve is a CLOSED_CURVE (see "CLOSED_CURVE" on page 60).

3. If sense is .F. then we distinguish

   a. If parameter_2 > parameter_1 then the trimmed curve is defined in the sense of decreasing parameter values opposite to the sense of the referenced curve.
   b. If parameter_2 < parameter_1 then the trimmed curve is defined in the sense of decreasing parameter values from parameter_1 to the lower limit of the parameter range of the referenced curve and then continued from the upper limit of the parameter range of the refer-

enced curve down to parameter_2. This definition is valid only if the referenced curve is a CLOSED_CURVE (see "CLOSED_CURVE" on page 60).

4. For curves whose parameter is an angle (CIRCLE etc.) the parameter values given as parameter_1 and parameter_2 are also angles. Their unit is defined by the appropriate value in the world attributes.

5. If a TRIMMED_CURVE has the attributes point_1 (corresponding to parameter_1 if sense is .T. and corresponding to parameter_2 of sense is .F.) and point_2 (corresponding to parameter_2 if sense is .T. and corresponding to parameter_1 of sense is .F.) it is considered to to start and terminated exactly in the points referenced. The receiving system will have to check whether the parametric representation satisfies this condition within the accuracy requirement as specified in the corresponding world attribute.

5.5.6.2 COMPOSITE_CURVE

```
ENTITY COMPOSITE_CURVE = GENERIC (d : DIM)
         STRUCTURE
           no_of_segments : INTEGER;
           segments       : LIST OF REF_ANY(CURVE(d));
           senses         : LIST OF LOGICAL;
           transitions    : LIST OF CURVE_TRANSITION_CODE;
           param_range    : [LIST OF REAL] ;
         END;
```

```
<composite_curve> ::= COMPOSITE_CURVE ( name :  integer , <name_list> ,
                      <logical_list> , ( [<curve_transition_code>
                      [, <curve_transition_code>]* ] ) ,
                      <real_list> ) ;
```

1. The COMPOSITE_CURVE is a sequence of no_of_segments segments each of which is represented by a TRIMMED_CURVE. The TRIMMED_CURVE entities when used in this context must have the point_1 and point_2 attributes. Furthermore, the point_2 attribute for each segment must be a reference to the same point entity as the point_1 attribute of the subsequent segment. If the COMPOSITE_CURVE is to be considered as a CLOSED_CURVE the point_2 attribute of the last segment and the point_1 attribute of the first segment must refer the same point entity.

2. For closed curves the no_of_segments entries in the list of the transitions attribute represent the continuity condition of the end-points of the corresponding segment. If the curve is not closed the number of transitions is (no_of_segments-1) as the last segment has continuation.

3. The parameter range defines the parameter values assigned to the curve transition points, each constituent curve receives a 'rescale parameter'. This ensures that the transmitted composite curve is subject to a simple linear reparameterisation. The values of the (no_of_segments+1) entries in this list must be increasing from the first to the last.

4. The list of senses is used to denote whether or not the sense of a component curve is the same or is opposite to its originally defined sense.

5.5.7 Curves with functional dependency

5.5.7.1 OFFSET_CURVE

```
ENTITY OFFSET_CURVE = STRUCTURE
                          curve : REF_ANY(CURVE(D2));
                       distance : ANY(REAL);
                        END;
```

```
<offset_curve> ::= OFFSET_CURVE ( name : name , <any(real)> ) ;
```

This defines a simple plane offset curve by offsetting a two-dimensional curve in its plane a distance distance along the normal to the curve. The normal to the curve is defined such that the cross product of the normal to the plane in which the curve is defined multiplied with the sense of increasing curve parameter is parallel to the curve normal. distance may be positive or negative. It is the responsibility of the generating system to ensure that the resulting curve is well-defined.

5.6 SURFACES

5.6.1 Surface classes

5.6.1.1 SURFACE

```
ENTITY SURFACE = CLASS( RECTANGULAR_SURFACE,
                        CURVE_BOUNDED_SURFACE );

<surface> ::= <rectangular_surface> | <curve_bounded_surface>
```

This is the class of all surfaces, both the RECTANGULAR ones and those which have irregular outer and possibly internal boundaries.

5.6.1.2 RECTANGULAR_SURFACE

```
ENTITY RECTANGULAR_SURFACE =  CLASS( ELEMENTARY_SURFACE,
                                     RECTANGULAR_TRIMMED_SURFACE,
                                     RECTANGULAR_COMPOSITE_SURFACE,
                                     OFFSET_SURFACE );

<rectangular_surface> ::=  <elementary_surface> |
                           <rectangular_trimmed_surface> |
                           <rectangular_composite_surface> |
                           <offset_surface>
```

This is the class of all surfaces that are defined on a rectangular region of their two-dimensional (u,v)-parameter space.

5.6.1.3 ELEMENTARY_SURFACE

```
ENTITY ELEMENTARY_SURFACE = CLASS( SPHERICAL_SURFACE,
                                   CYLINDRICAL_SURFACE,
                                   CONICAL_SURFACE,
                                   TOROIDAL_SURFACE,
                                   PLANAR_SURFACE,
                                   SURFACE_OF_REVOLUTION(DIM),
                                   SURFACE_OF_TRANSLATION(DIM),
                                   B_SPLINE_SURFACE );
```

```
<elementary_surface> ::= <spherical_surface> | <cylindrical_surface> |
                         <conical_surface> | <toroidal_surface> |
                         <planar_surface> |
                         <surface_of_revolution(dim)> |
                         <surface_of_translation(dim)> |
                         <b_spline_surface>
```

The elementary surface entity represents a parametric surface in Cartesian space with the parameter ranges in (u,v) limited to constant upper and lower values.

5.6.2 PLANAR_SURFACE

```
ENTITY PLANAR_SURFACE = STRUCTURE
                          point           : ANY(POINT(D3));
                          normal          : ANY(DIRECTION(D3));
                          reference_point : ANY(POINT(D3)) ;
                        END;

<planar_surface> ::= PLANAR_SURFACE ( name :  <any(point(d3))> ,
                     <any(direction(d3))> , <any(point(d3))> ) ;
```

The surface is parameterised as:

dir = (**reference_point** - **point**) - ((**reference_point** - **point**)•**normal**)**normal**
dir is then normalised to define **a**
r(u,v) = **point** + **a** u + (**normal*a**)v

for arbitrary real values of u and v.

1. **point** is a point in the plane located at u=v=o.
2. The reference point **reference_point** should be approximately in the plane and is used to define an axis **a** in the plane for parameterisation. The definition is unambiguous provided

   (**reference_point** - **point**) * **normal** is non zero.

   If the reference point is not given an arbitrary point satisfying the above condition may be used.

5.6.3 SPHERICAL_SURFACE

```
ENTITY SPHERICAL_SURFACE = STRUCTURE
                              centre          : ANY(POINT(D3));
                              radius          : ANY(REAL);
                              axis:           : [ANY(DIRECTION(D3))];
                              reference_point : ANY(POINT(D3));
                            END;
```

```
<spherical_surface> ::= SPHERICAL_SURFACE ( name :  <any(point(d3))> ,
                          <any(real)> , [<any(direction(d3))>] ,
                          <any(point(d3))> ) ;
```

This represents a curve parameterised as follows:

dir = (**reference_point** - **centre**) - (**reference_point** - **centre**)•**axis**)**axis**

dir is normalised to define **a**

r(u,v) = centre + radius **a** cos(v) cos(u) +
radius (**axis*****a**) cos(v) sin(u) + radius **axis** sin(v)

1. The **reference_point** is not essential for the geometric definition of **axis** spherical surface but it is essential for the unique parameterisation.

   The **reference_point** should lie approximately on the plane through the centre normal to **axis**.

   The parametric ranges are $0 \le u < 2\pi$, $-\pi/2 \le v < \pi/2$, for complete sphere.

5.6.4 CONICAL_SURFACE

```
ENTITY CONICAL_SURFACE = STRUCTURE
                            point           : ANY(POINT(D3));
                            axis            : ANY(DIRECTION(D3));
                            radius          : ANY(REAL);
                            semi_angle      : ANY(REAL);
                            reference_point : ANY(POINT(D3)) ;
                          END;
```

```
<conical_surface> ::= CONICAL_SURFACE ( name : <any(point(d3))> ,
                        <any(direction(d3))> , <any(real)> ,
                        <any(real)> , <any(point(d3))> ) ;
```

The surface is parameterised as:

dir = (**reference_point** - **point**)
- ((**reference_point** - **point**)•**axis**)**axis**

dir is then normalised to define **a**

r(u,v) = **point** + v **axis** + v tan(semi_angle) **a** cos(u)
+ v tan(semi_angle) (**axis*a**) sin(u)

1. semi_angle defines the semi_vertical angle of the cone measured in the valid angle unit with $0 < \text{semi\_angle} < \pi/2$ for a valid definition.
2. **point** is any point on the axis from which the cone has the specified radius. In particular, for radius=0 the point becomes the vertex of the cone.
3. **reference_point** is used to define the parameterisation and should lie approximately on the plane through **point** normal to **a**.
4. The parametric range for u is $0 \le u < 2\pi$, v is arbitrary real.

5.6.5 CYLINDRICAL_SURFACE

```
ENTITY CYLINDRICAL_SURFACE =
                 STRUCTURE
                   point_on_axis    : ANY(POINT(D3));
                   axis_direction   : ANY(DIRECTION(D3));
                   radius           : ANY(REAL); (* positive *)
                   reference_point  : ANY(POINT(D3)) ;
                 END;
```

```
<cylindrical_surface> ::= CYLINDRICAL_SURFACE ( name :
                     <any(point(d3))> , <any(direction(d3))> ,
                     <any(real)> , <any(point(d3))> ) ;
```

The surface is parameterised as:

dir = (**reference_point** - **axis_point**) - ((**reference_point** - **axis_point**)•**axis**)**axis**

dir is then normalised to define **a**

r(u,v) = **axis_point** + radius **a** cos(u) + radius (**axis*a**) sin(u) + v **a**

1. The reference point p is not essential for the geometric definition of **axis** cylindrical surface but it is essential for the unique parameterisation.
2. **reference_point** should be distinct from **axis_point** and should lie approximately in the plane through **point** normal to **a**.
3. Parametric range for u is $0 \le u < 2\pi$

5.6.6 TOROIDAL_SURFACE

```
ENTITY TOROIDAL_SURFACE =  STRUCTURE
                             centre          : ANY(POINT(D3));
                             axis            : ANY(DIRECTION(D3));
                             major_radius    : ANY(REAL);
                             minor_radius    : ANY(REAL);
                             reference_point : ANY(POINT(D3)) ;
                           END;
```

```
<toroidal_surface> ::= TOROIDAL_SURFACE ( name :  <any(point(d3))> ,
                         <any(direction(d3))> , <any(real)> ,
                         <any(real)> , <any(point(d3))> ) ;
```

The torus is parameterised as:

dir = (**reference_point** - **centre**) - (**reference_point** - **centre**)•**axis**)**axis**

dir is normalised to define **a**

r(u,v) = **centre** + minor_radius **a** sin(u) +
(major_radius + minor_radius cos(u))**a** cos(v) -
(major_radius + minor_radius cos(u))(**axis*a**) sin(v)

1. The axis, centre and radii are essential for the geometric definition

2. The reference point defines the parameterisation. The reference point must not lie on the central axis and should ideally be approximately at the centre of one of the minor circular sections of the torus.
3. For a complete torus the parametric ranges are $0 \le u < 2\pi$, $0 \le v < 2\pi$.

5.6.7 B_SPLINE_SURFACE

```
ENTITY B_SPLINE_SURFACE =
        STRUCTURE
         u_rational                         : LOGICAL;
         v_rational                         : LOGICAL;
         uniform_u                          : LOGICAL;
         uniform_v                          : LOGICAL;
         bezier                             : LOGICAL;
         u_degree                           : INTEGER;
         v_degree                           : INTEGER;
         upper_index_on_u_control_points : INTEGER; (* K1 *)
         upper_index_on_v_control_points : INTEGER; (* K2 *)
         control_points                     : LIST OF ANY(POINT(D3));
                                              (* 0..K1,0..K2 *)
         u_multiplicities                   : LIST OF INTEGER;
                                              (* 1..L1 *)
         u_knots                            : [LIST OF REAL;]
                                              (* 1..L1 *)
         v_multiplicities                   : LIST OF INTEGER;
                                              (* 1..L2 *)
         v_knots                            : [LIST OF REAL;]
                                              (* 1..L2 *)
         weights                            : [LIST OF REAL;]
                                              (* 0..K1,0..K2 *)
         form_number                        : [INTEGER;]
        END;
```

```
<B_spline_surface> ::=    B_SPLINE_SURFACE ( name :  logical ,
                 logical , logical , logical , logical , integer ,
                 integer , integer , integer ,
                 ( [<any(point(d3))> [,
                 <any(point(d3))>]* ] ) ,
                 <integer_list> , <real_list> , <integer_list> ,
                 <real_list> , <real_list> , [integer] );
```

The attribute upper_index_on_u_control_points has the value K1
The attribute upper_index_on_v_control_points has the value K2
The attribute control_points contains the $\mathbf{r}_{i,\,j}$ for i = 0..K1 and j = 0..K2 where the i-index changes first.
The attribute u_knots contains the u_i for i = 1..L1.
The attribute v_knots contains the v_j for j = 1..L2.
The attribute weights contains the $w_{i,\,j}$ for i = 0..K1 and j = 0..K2 where the i-index changes first.

1. If either u_rational = .T. or v_rational = .T. then the surface is given by:

$$\mathbf{r}(u,v) = \frac{\sum_{i=0}^{K1} \sum_{j=0}^{K2} w_{i,\,j}\, \mathbf{r}_{i,\,j}\, N_i(u)\, N_j(v)}{\sum_{i=0}^{K1} \sum_{j=0}^{K2} w_{i,\,j}\, N_i(u)\, N_j(v)}$$

2. If only u_rational = .T. (and v_rational =.F.) the weights will depend on i only and the dimension of weights becomes (0..L1).

3. If only v_rational = .T. (and u_rational =.F.) the weights will depend on j only and the dimension of weights becomes (0..L2).

4. If rational = .F. and v_rational = .F. then the surface is given by:

$$\mathbf{r}(u,v) = \sum_{i=0}^{K1} \sum_{j=0}^{K2} \mathbf{r}_{i,\,j}\, N_i(u)\, N_j(v)$$

   In this case the weights are omitted, implicitly $w_{i,\,j}=1.0$

5. The restrictions on knot_multiplicities and the interpretation of multiple knots are defined as for B_SPLINE_CURVE.

6. $N_i(u)$ and $N_j(v)$ are the normalised B-spline basis functions defined on the knot sets:

   $u_{i-d1}, \dots, u_{i+1}$ with $u_{k+1} \geq u_k$ (ie non decreasing)

   $v_{j-d2}, \dots, v_{j+1}$ with $v_{k+1} \geq v_k$ (ie non decreasing)

7. The control points and weights are ordered as $\mathbf{r}_{0,0}, \mathbf{r}_{1,0}, \mathbf{r}_{2,0}, \ldots, \mathbf{r}_{(K1-1),K2}, \mathbf{r}_{K1,K2}$

8. If uniform=.T., the knots satisfy: $u_{k+1} - u_k = 1$, or 0 for a multiple knot.

9. If rational=.F., then the weights are omitted and implicitly defined as 1.0.

10. If Bezier=.T., the surface is defined as a single Bezier patch. The knot lists are empty and the knots implicitly take the repeated values 0 and 1 as for the Bezier curve. In this case the surface can also be defined directly as a Bezier surface:

$$\mathbf{r}(u,v) = \frac{\sum_{i=0}^{K1} \sum_{j=0}^{K2} w_{i,j} \mathbf{r}_{i,j} f_i(u) f_j(v)}{\sum_{i=0}^{K1} \sum_{j=0}^{K2} w_{i,j} f_i(u) f_j(v)}$$

or, if also rational=.F.

$$\mathbf{r}(u,v) = \sum_{i=0}^{K1} \sum_{j=0}^{K2} w_{i,j} r_{i,j} f_i(u) f_j(v)$$

where $f_i(u)$, $f_j(v)$ are Bezier basis functions as defined as follows:

$$f_i(u) = \frac{K1!(1-u)^{K1-i} u^i}{(1-K1!)(i)!} \quad \text{with } 0 \le u \le 1$$

$$f_j(v) = \frac{K2!(1-v)^{K2-j} vu^j}{(1-K2!)(j)!} \quad \text{with } 0 \le v \le 1$$

11. The form number is optional. When present, it it used to identify special cases of quadric surfaces of degree 2, ruled surfaces, or surfaces of revolution. The receiving system will have to check whether the received B_SPLINE_SURFACE geometry actually conforms with this shape within an accuracy to be specified as a directive to the post-processor. If the

test fails it means that the received entity is invalid. The default value is UNDEFINED.

The form number has the following meaning:

form number	intended geometric form
1	UNDEFINED
2	PLANAR_SURFACE
3	CYLINDRICAL_SURFACE
4	CONICAL_SURFACE
5	SPHERICAL_SURFACE
6	TOROIDAL_SURFACE
7	SURFACE_OF_REVOLUTION
8	RULED_SURFACE
9	QUADRIC

5.6.8 SURFACE_OF_REVOLUTION

```
ENTITY SURFACE_OF_REVOLUTION = GENERIC (d : DIM)
                    STRUCTURE
                      CASE d OF
                        D2: (curve           : REF_ANY(CURVE(D2));
                             reference_point : ANY(POINT(D3));
                        D3: (curve           : REF_ANY(CURVE(D3)));
                      END;
                      axis_point     : ANY(POINT(D3));
                      axis_direction : ANY(DIRECTION(D3));
                    END;
```

```
<surface_of_revolution(dim)> ::=  <surface_of_revolution(d2)> |
                                   <surface_of_revolution(d3)>

<surface_of_revolution(d2)> ::= SURFACE_OF_REVOLUTION ( name :
                         name , <any(point(d3))> , <any(point(d3))> ,
                         <any(direction(d3))> ) ;

<surface_of_revolution(d3)> ::= SURFACE_OF_REVOLUTION ( name :  name ,
                         <any(point(d3))> , <any(direction(d3))> ) ;
```

The surface is parameterised as:

r(u,v) = **axis_point** + (**curve**(u) - **axis_point**) cos(v)
+ (**curve**(u) - **axis_point•axis**)**axis** (1-cos(v))
+ **axis** * (**curve**(u)- **axis_point**) sin(v)

curve has parameterisation **curve**(u).

1. The curve may be either two-dimensional or three-dimensional. If the curve is two-dimensional the following rules apply:

   a. The curve is defined in a local (xy)-coordinate system to be placed in space such that the x-coordinate coincides with the r-coordinate, and the y-coordinate with the z'-coordinate used below.
   b. The curve will be placed in space such that the curve plane coincides with the plane defined by the point, the axis direction and the reference point. The origin of the local coordinate system is in **point**. The two-dimensional y-axis (z'-axis of the local r,ϕ,z'_system) coincides with the direction specified. The reference point lies in the xy-plane of the two-dimensional coordinate system (rz'-plane of the local r,ϕ,z'-system).
   c. The curve must not be intersect itself.
   d. The parameter value v=0 corresponds to points in the rz'-plane.

2. If the curve is three-dimensional the following rules apply:

   a. In order to produce a single valued surface with a complete revolution the curve should be such that when expressed in a cylindrical coordinate system (r,ϕ,z) centred at **axis_point** with axis **axis** no two distinct parametric points on the curve should have the same values for (r,z').

3. For a complete surface of revolution the parametric range is $0 \leq v < 2\pi$.

4. The parameter range for u is defined with the referenced curve.

5. The geometric form of the surface is not dependent upon the curve parameterisation.

5.6.9 SURFACE_OF_TRANSLATION

```
ENTITY SURFACE_OF_TRANSLATION = GENERIC (d : DIM)
                STRUCTURE
                  curve          : REF_ANY(CURVE(d);
                  axis_direction : ANY(DIRECTION(D3));
                  CASE d OF
                    D2: (axis_point      : any(point(d3));
                         reference_point : any(point(d3)));
                    D3: (axis_point      : NIL;
                         reference_point : NIL);
                  END;
                END;
```

```
<surface_of_translation(dim)> ::=  <surface_of_translation(d2)> |
                                   <surface_of_translation(d3)>

<surface_of_translation(d2)> ::= SURFACE_OF_TRANSLATION ( name :
                      name , <any(direction(d3))> ,
                      <any(point(d3))> , <any(point(d3))> ) ;

<surface_of_translation(d3)> ::= SURFACE_OF_TRANSLATION ( name :
                      name , <any(direction(d3))> ) ;
```

The surface is parameterised as:

r(u,v) = **curve**(u) + **axis** v
curve has parameterisation **curve**(u).

Note: This is a simple swept surface or generalised cylinder obtained by sweeping the curve in direction **axis**.

1. The curve may be either two-dimensional or three-dimensional. If the curve is two-dimensional the following rules apply:

   a. The curve is defined in a local (x'y')-coordinate system to be placed in space such that the normal to the two-dimensional (x'y')-plane coincides with the axis_direction specified.
   b. The origin of the local (x'y') coordinate system is in axis_point. The two-dimensional x'-axis points to the reference point.
   c. The curve must not be intersect itself.
   d. The parameter value v=0 corresponds to points in the x'y'-plane .

2. If the curve is three-dimensional the following rules apply:

   a. The translation of the curve should not produce a surface that overlaps or or intersects itself.

3. For a complete surface of revolution the parametric range is $0 \le v < 2\pi$.

4. The parameter range for u is defined with the referenced curve.

5. The geometric form of the surface is not dependent upon the curve parameterisation.

5.6.10 RECTANGULAR_TRIMMED_SURFACE

```
ENTITY RECTANGULAR_TRIMMED_SURFACE =
                       STRUCTURE
                         surface : REF_ANY(RECTANGULAR_SURFACE);
                         umin    : ANY(REAL);
                         umax    : ANY(REAL);
                         vmin    : ANY(REAL);
                         vmax    : ANY(REAL);
                       END;
```

```
<rectangular_trimmed_surface> ::=
            RECTANGULAR_TRIMMED_SURFACE ( name :  name , <any(real)> ,
            <any(real)> , <any(real)> , <any(real)> ) ;
```

1. The trimmed surface is a simple bounded surface in which the bounding parameter values are constant parametric lines u=umin, u=umax, v=vmin, and v=vmax. All these values must lie within the parametric range of the referenced surface with umin<umax and vmin<vmax.
2. For those surfaces (eg. SPHERICAL_SURFACE) whose parametric range is in angle units the bounding parameter values are in the same angle units as specified for the neutral file.
3. If any of the bounding parameter values is beyond the parametric range of the surface a default value equal to the natural surface boundary is to be assumed. The post-processor should give a warning in this case.
4. The optional curves_on_surfaces correspond to the bounding parameter values. They are the best available approximations. The receiving system will have to check whether they can be used immediately or whether they have to be enhanced.

5.6.11 RECTANGULAR_COMPOSITE_SURFACE

```
ENTITY RECTANGULAR_COMPOSITE_SURFACE =
        STRUCTURE
          n_u      : INTEGER;
          n_v      : INTEGER;
          surfaces : LIST OF REF_ANY(RECTANGULAR_TRIMMED_SURFACE);
          u_sense  : LIST OF LOGICAL; (* 1..n_u*n_v *)
          v_sense  : LIST OF LOGICAL; (* 1..n_u*n_v *)
        END;
```

```
<rectangular_composite_curve> ::=
        RECTANGULAR_COMPOSITE_SURFACE ( name :  integer , integer ,
        <name_list> , <logical_list> , <logical_list> ) ;
```

1. This is a composite surface having a simple rectangular topology with n_u patches in u direction and n_v patches in v direction. Each composite surface must be bounded and topological rectangular and therefore be either a B_SPLINE_SURFACE or a RECTANGULAR_TRIMMED_SURFACE. It is required that there is at least positional continuity between the adjacent patches.

2. The lists of surfaces and senses are ordered as [1,1] [2,1] ... [n_u,n_v]. If every sense = .T. adjacent patches in the u direction are adjoined such that the u-high boundary of the first patch coincides with the u-low boundary of the second patch. A u_sense = .F. for a patch would result in adjoining its u-low boundary to the u-low boundary of the next patch in sequence. Similar considerations apply to the v_sense flag.

3. Each patch is, if necessary, reparameterised from 0 to 1 and the resulting composite surface has a parametric range from 0 to n_u and from 0 to n_v.

5.6.12 CURVE_BOUNDED_SURFACE

```
ENTITY CURVE_BOUNDED_SURFACE =
        STRUCTURE
          surface    : REF_ANY(RECTANGULAR_SURFACE);
          boundaries : LIST OF REF_ANY(COMPOSITE_CURVE_ON_SURFACE) ;
        END;
```

```
<curve_bounded_surface> ::= CURVE_BOUNDED_SURFACE ( name :  name ,
                            <name_list> ) ;
```

1. Each boundary is a closed composite curve on the same surface (attribute closed=.T.)
2. The first entry in the list represents the outer boundary.
3. Any parts of the natural surface boundary (constant curve parameter value) constitute part of the boundary. They should nevertheless be included explicitly in the composite curve.
4. The inner boundaries must be disjoint with each other and with the outer boundary.
5. The interior of the bounded surface is defined to be **n** * **t** from any point on the boundary, where **n** is the surface normal and **t** the boundary curve tangent vector at this point. The region so defined must be simply connected.

5.6.13 OFFSET_SURFACE

```
ENTITY OFFSET_SURFACE = STRUCTURE
                          surface : REF_ANY(RECTANGULAR_SURFACE>);
                         distance : ANY(REAL);
                        END;

 <offset_surface> ::= OFFSET_SURFACE ( name :  name , <any(real)> ) ;
```

This is a procedural definition of a simple offset surface at a normal distance distance from the originating surface. The attribute distance may be positive or negative to indicate the preferred side of the surface, the positive side being defined by the cross product of the the direction vectors of increasing u-parameter with increasing v-parameter.

The offset distance must be less than the smallest radius of curvature of the referenced surface.

5.7 GEOMETRY ON SURFACES

5.7.1 SURFACE_CURVE

```
ENTITY SURFACE_CURVE =
         STRUCTURE
          SCOPE;
               SURFACE_CURVE_SCOPE_ENTITY;
          END_SCOPE;
           curve : REFERENCE(CURVE_ON_SURFACE);
         END;

<surface_curve> ::= SURFACE_CURVE ( name : OPEN ) ;
          SCOPE ;
                                             *
               [<surface_curve_scope_entity>]
          END_SCOPE ;
                  SURFACE_CURVE_RESULT ( name ) ;
                  SURFACE_CURVE ( name , CLOSE ) ;

ENTITY SURFACE_CURVE_SCOPE_ENTITY = CLASS( POINT(DIM),
                                           SURFACE, CURVE(DIM),
                                           POINT_ON_SURFACE,
                                           CURVE_ON_SURFACE );

<surface_curve_scope_entity> ::= <point(dim)> | <surface> |
                                 <curve(dim)> | <point_on_surface> |
                                 <curve_on_surface>
```

The surface curve is a single scoped entity which contains in its scope the complete data structure that defines the curve geometry. hence, in wireframe models the surface-curve behaves as a single three-dimensional curve entity (see "Points and curves" on page 56 and "Geometry on surfaces"). The curve attribute refers to the top of that data structure. The surface entities which are referred from within the curve_on_surface entities may lie within the scope of the same surface-curve or outside.

5.7.2 Classes of curves on surfaces

5.7.2.1 CURVE_ON_SURFACE

```
ENTITY CURVE_ON_SURFACE = CLASS( ELEMENTARY_CURVE_ON_SURFACE,
                                 TRIMMED_CURVE_ON_SURFACE,
                                 COMPOSITE_CURVE_ON_SURFACE
                                 INTERSECTION_CURVE );

<curve_on_surface> ::=  <elementary_curve_on_surface> |
                        <trimmed_curve_on_surface> |
                        <composite_curve_on_surface> |
                        <intersection_curve>)
```

This is the class of elementary, trimmed, and composite curves on surfaces.

5.7.3 POINT_ON_SURFACE

```
ENTITY POINT_ON_SURFACE = STRUCTURE
                            surface : REF_ANY(RECTANGULAR_SURFACE);
                            u       : ANY(REAL);
                            v       : ANY(REAL);
                          END;

<point_on_surface> ::= POINT_ON_SURFACE ( name :  name , <any(real)> ,
                        <any(real)> ) ;

<any(point_on_surface)> ::= <ref_any> |
                    POINT_ON_SURFACE ( name , <any(real)> , <any(real)> )
```

The POINT_ON_SURFACE is an entity that defines the location of a point by giving the (u,v) parameters to be used in the parametric representation of the referenced surface.

5.7.4 Curves on surfaces

These entities represent any curves on a surface. The curves are represented in exactly the same way as two-dimensional curves in the xy-plane. This means that the algorithms described for the evaluation of two-dimensional curves in "Points and curves" on page 56 apply here as well. However, the curve points are all defined in the two-dimensional parameter space associated with the referenced surface. Hence, after application of the curve evaluation algorithm the resulting (x,y) values have to be treated as (u,v) coordinates in the parameter space of the referenced surface.

5.7.5 Elementary curves on surface

5.7.5.1 ELEMENTARY_CURVE_ON_SURFACE

```
ENTITY ELEMENTARY_CURVE_ON_SURFACE = CLASS( LINESEGMENT_ON_SURFACE,
                                            B_SPLINE_CURVE_ON_SURFACE );

<elementary_curve_on_surface> ::= <line_segment_on_surface> |
                                  <b_spline_curve_on_surface>
```

The class of elementary curves on surfaces corresponds to the class of elementary curves. The difference is that the "on_surface"-curves are defined in the (uv)-space spanned by the (uv)-parameters of the surface to which these curves belong.

5.7.5.2 LINE_SEGMENT_ON_SURFACE

```
ENTITY LINE_SEGMENT_ON_SURFACE =
          STRUCTURE
            surface     : REF_ANY(RECTANGULAR_SURFACE);
            first_point : ANY(POINT_ON_SURFACE);
            last_point  : ANY(POINT_ON_SURFACE);
          END;

<line_segment_on_surface> ::=
          LINE_SEGMENT_ON_SURFACE ( name :  name ,
          <any(point_on_surface)> , <any(point_on_surface)> ) ;
```

5.7.5.3 B_SPLINE_CURVE_ON_SURFACE

```
ENTITY B_SPLINE_CURVE_ON_SURFACE =
                STRUCTURE
                  surface        : REF_ANY(RECTANGULAR_SURFACE);
                  rational       : LOGICAL;
                  uniform        : LOGICAL;
                  bezier         : LOGICAL;
                  degree         : INTEGER;
                  upper_index_on_control_points : INTEGER;
                  control_points : LIST OF ANY(POINT(D2));
                                      (* 0..K *)
                  knot_multiplicities : LIST OF INTEGER;
                                      (* 1..L *)
                  knots               : [ LIST OF REAL];
                                      (* 1..L *)
                  weights             : [ LIST OF REAL];
                                      (* 0..K *)
                END;
```

```
<b_spline_curve_on_surface> ::=
         B_SPLINE_CURVE_ON_SURFACE ( name :  name , logical ,
         logical , logical , integer , integer ,
         ( [<any(point(d2))> [,
         <any(point(d2))>]* ] ) , <integer_list> ,
         <real_list> , <real_list> ) ;
```

5.7.6 INTERSECTION_CURVE

```
ENTITY INTERSECTION_CURVE =
       STRUCTURE
         curve     : REF_ANY(CURVE(D3));
                     (* may not refer to an intersection curve *)
         curve_s1  : [REF_ANY(CURVE_ON_SURFACE)] ;
         curve_s2  : [REF_ANY(CURVE_ON_SURFACE)] ;
         surface1  : REF_ANY(RECTANGULAR_SURFACE);
         surface2  : REF_ANY(RECTANGULAR_SURFACE);
         priority  : [ENUM(1,2,3)] ;
       END;
```

```
<intersection_curve> ::= INTERSECTION_CURVE ( name :  name ,
                    [name] , [name] , name , name ,
                    integer ) ;
```

1. This entity defines a curve as the intersection of the two referenced surfaces. curve is the three-dimensional curve representation. curve_s1 and curve_s2 are representations in the two-dimensional parametric space of the surface1 and surface2 respectively.

2. master_representation is an integer indicating whether the three-dimensional curve (1), curve_s1 (2), or curve_s2 (3) are considered to be the reference if the receiving system detects that the redundant representation do not agree within the desired accuracy.

3. All three curve representations (curve, curve_s1, and curve_s2) are merely the best available approximations of the intersection. The receiving system will have to insure that the approximations are good enough.

5.7.7 Derived curves on surfaces

5.7.7.1 TRIMMED_CURVE_ON_SURFACE

```
ENTITY TRIMMED_CURVE_ON_SURFACE =
              STRUCTURE
                surface      : REF_ANY(RECTANGULAR_SURFACE);
                curve        : REF_ANY(B_SPLINE_CURVE_ON_SURFACE);
                parameter_1  : REAL;
                parameter_2  : REAL;
                sense        : LOGICAL;
                point_1      : [REF_ANY(POINT_ON_SURFACE)];
                point_2      : [REF_ANY(POINT_ON_SURFACE)];
              END;
```

```
<trimmed_curve_on_surface> ::=
        TRIMMED_CURVE_ON_SURFACE ( name :  name , name , real , real ,
        logical , [name] , [name] ) ;
```

5.7.7.2 COMPOSITE_CURVE_ON_SURFACE

```
ENTITY COMPOSITE_CURVE_ON_SURFACE =
        STRUCTURE
          surface     : REF_ANY(RECTANGULAR_SURFACE);
          no_of_arcs  : INTEGER;
          segments    : LIST OF REF_ANY(TRIMMED_CURVE_ON_SURFACE);
                        (* 1..n_of_arcs *)
          transitions : LIST OF CURVE_TRANSITION_CODE;
                        (* 1..no_of_arcs *) or (* 1..no_of_arcs-1 *)
        END;
```

```
<composite_curve_on_surface> ::=
      COMPOSITE_CURVE_ON_SURFACE ( name : name , integer ,
      <name_list> , ( [<curve_transition_code>
      [,<curve_transition_code>]* ] ) ) ;
```

5.8 BOUNDARY REPRESENTATIONS

5.8.1 Standard boundary representation

5.8.1.1 B_REP

```
ENTITY B_REP =  STRUCTURE
           SCOPE;
                 B_REP_SCOPE_ENTITY;
                 INDEX_ENTRY;
           END_SCOPE;
                  result     : LIST OF REF_ONLY(SHELL);
                END;
```

```
<b_rep> ::= B_REP ( name : OPEN ) ;
           SCOPE;
                [<b_rep_scope> |
                 <index_entry>]*
           END_SCOPE;
              B_REP_RESULT ( <name_list> ) ;
            B_REP ( name , CLOSE ) ;
```

```
ENTITY B_REP_SCOPE_ENTITY = CLASS( POINT(D3),
                                   DIRECTION(D3), VERTEX,
                                   EDGE_CURVE,
                                   EDGE, LOOP, FACE,
                                   SHELL,INDEX_ENTRY);

<b_rep_scope> ::=  <point(d3)> | <direction(d3)> | <vertex> |
                   <edge_curve> | <edge> | <loop> | <face> | <shell> |
                   <index_entry>
```

A B_REP is an entity that has a scope. A B_REP may have a material property associated with it. The B_REP is a 'self-contained' entity in the sense that no entity in the B_REP may refer to an entity outside the scope of the B_REP. All referenced entities must be within the B_REP scope itself. The scope of a B_REP contains both topological and geometrical entities. Geometry is represented by lists of the entities POINT, DIRECTION, EDGE_CURVE and FACE_SURFACE which are referenced by the topological entities defined subsequently. Topology is represented by lists of the entities, VERTEX, EDGE, LOOP, FACE and SHELL in that order so that no entity is referenced before it is defined.

The B_REP data structure comprises both topological and geometrical entities (see Figure 10 on page 100). Though checks for consistency of a model are assumed to be the responsibility of the receiving CAD system the object has to be

1. a two manifold and

2. the topological structure has to fulfill the Euler formula.

$$V - E + 2F - L - 2(S - G) = 0$$

V: Number of vertices
E: Number of edges
F: Number of faces
L: Number of loops
S: Number of shells
G: Genus of the solid object
i.e. number of through holes
or number of " handles" (= number of "tunnels")

This formula still allows for different valid topological structures for the same object.

The objectives for creating a topological structure for a given object on the basis of the Euler formula are, therefore,

- to avoid artifact edges and to
- use the minimal topological structure.

The topological structures for cylinder, cone, sphere and torus that fulfill those requirements are presented in (see Figure 11 on page 101 and Figure 12 on page 102).

- A B_REP must have one and only one peripheral SHELL
- A B_REP may have zero or more interior void SHELL entities
- The result attribute of a B_REP consists of an ordered list of references to SHELL entities. The first entry in that list is a reference to the SHELL that represents the outer boundary of the B_REP.

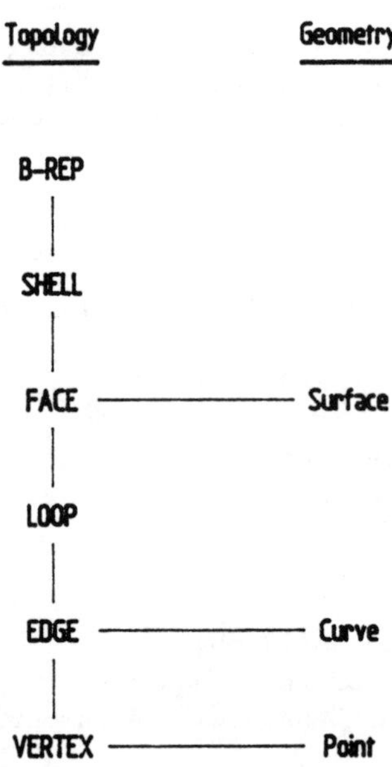

Figure 10. The topological and geometrical entities of a B_REP

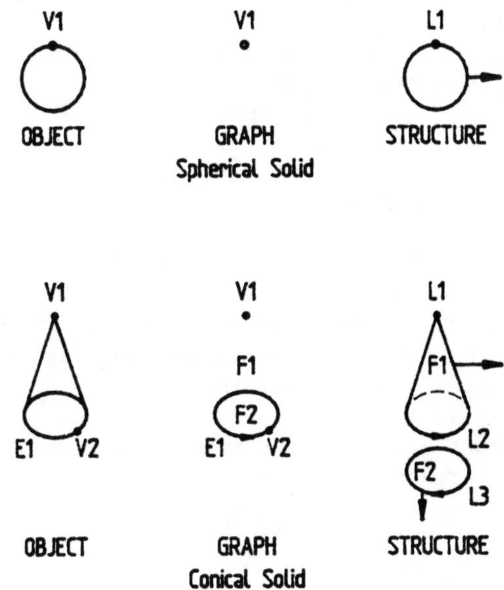

Figure 11. Examples of allowable B_REP topologies: These are topologies of solid model representations for a sphere and a cone.

5.8.1.2 SHELL

```
ENTITY SHELL = STRUCTURE
                 shell : LIST OF REFERENCE(FACE);
               END;

<shell> ::= SHELL ( name : <name_list> ) ;
```

A shell is a topological entity defined within the scope of a B_REP. It is defined by a list of references to its bounding faces. The order of the list is arbitrary but the faces must be connected and form a continuous surface which divides the three-dimensional space into two distinct regions.

- Every SHELL is either the external boundary of a B_REP or an internal void within a B_REP.
- Every SHELL consists of one or more references to FACE entities

5.8.1.3 FACE

```
ENTITY FACE = STRUCTURE
                surface_ref : REF_ANY(FACE_SURFACE);
                orientation : LOGICAL;
                loop        : LIST OF REF_ONLY(LOOP);
              END;!

<face> ::=  FACE ( name :  name , logical , <name_list> ) ;
```

A FACE is a topological entity defined within the scope of a B_REP. It is defined in terms of a set of bounding LOOP entities, the underlying surface geometry, and an orientation.

- A FACE must belong to one and only one shell.
- A FACE must have as its geometry one and only one FACE_SURFACE.

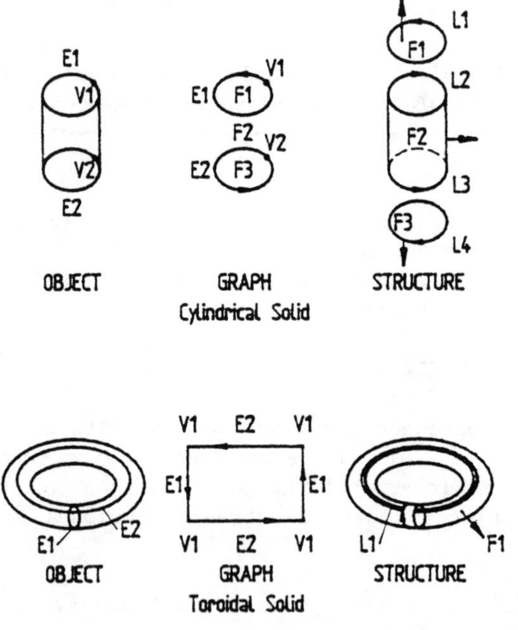

Figure 12. Examples of allowable B_REP topologies: These are topologies of solid model representations for a cylinder and a torus.

- The ORIENTATION flag of the FACE indicates whether the normal direction of the FACE agrees with the normal direction of the underlying surface geometry. ORIENTATION is .T. if the normal directions agree otherwise it is .F..

  Intuitively that means whether the solid_to_void direction at any point on the associated surface agrees (.T.) or not (.F.) with the implied normal the surface at that point.

  In the case of a PLANAR_SURFACE, ORIENTATION is .T. if the normal points from solid to void. In cylinders, cones, spheres and torus surfaces, ORIENTATION is .T. if the solid is on the inside, i.e. on the side of the axis, center and center of the minor circle respectively.

  In other u,v parametric surfaces, ORIENTATION is .T. if the normal at point **P** (u,v) computed as

  $$\mathbf{n} = \partial \mathbf{P}/\partial u * \partial \mathbf{P}/\partial v$$

  points from solid to void
- A FACE must be bound by one or more loops, understood in the sense that for an EDGE_LOOP the associated surface is bounded by the closed contours built by the edge curves associated to its edges.
- Every EDGE_LOOP bounding a FACE must be oriented such that the following inequality holds:

  $$(\text{FACE\_ORIENTATION} * \text{LOOP\_ORIENTATION}) \cdot \text{FACE\_SIDE} > 0$$

  At a given point on a edge curve of the LOOP the vectors are defined as follows:

  FACE_ORIENTATION : pointing from solid to void
  LOOP_ORIENTATION : pointing in the direction of the edge curve
  FACE_SIDE : tangent to the surface associated to the face and pointing from the edge curve into the face

  Intuitively that means that an observer standing on the surface on the void side and walking along the LOOP has the finite part of the surface on his left.

5.8.1.4 FACE_SURFACE

```
ENTITY FACE_SURFACE = CLASS( SPHERICAL_SURFACE, CYLINDRICAL_SURFACE,
                             CONICAL_SURFACE, TORUS_SURFACE,
                             PLANAR_SURFACE,
                             SURFACE_OF_REVOLUTION(D2),
                             SURFACE_OF_TRANSLATION(D2),
                             POLY_SURFACE, B_SPLINE_SURFACE );
```

```
<face_surface> ::= <spherical_surface> | <cylindrical_surface> |
                   <conical_surface> | <torus_surface> |
                   <planar_surface> | <surface_of_revolution(d2)> |
                   <poly_surface> | <b_spline_surface>
                   <surface_of_translation(d2)> |
```

The entity FACE_SURFACE consists of a class of surfaces that may be referenced by the topological entity FACE in a B_REP.

5.8.1.5 LOOP

```
ENTITY LOOP = CLASS ( EDGE_LOOP, VERTEX_LOOP );

<loop> ::=  <edge_loop> | <vertex_loop>
```

A loop is a topological entity defined within the scope of a B_REP or a COMPOUND_B_REP.

- A loop must be part or all the boundary of one and only one FACE.
- A loop must be either a VERTEX_LOOP or an EDGE_LOOP.
- Every EDGE_LOOP consists of an ordered list of unique references to one or more EDGE entities. The list of edges should define a continuous path in an anti-clockwise sense when viewed from void to solid. Adjacent EDGE entities in the EDGE_LOOP have a common VERTEX as do the first and last EDGE entities.
- Every reference to an EDGE in an EDGE_LOOP has an ORIENTATION flag associated with it, to indicate whether the sense of the EDGE in the LOOP coincides with the sense of the LOOP. The ORIENTATION flag is .T. if the senses coincide otherwise its .F..
- A VERTEX_LOOP is a reference to one and only one VERTEX

See Figure 13 on page 105.

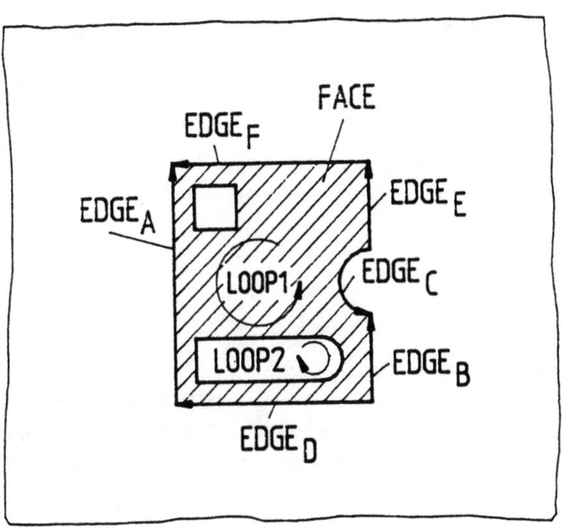

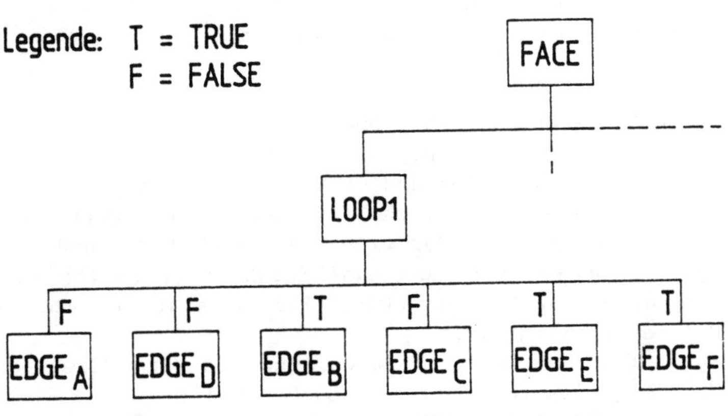

Figure 13. Loop and edge orientation in B_REP entities

5.8.1.6 EDGE_LOOP

```
ENTITY EDGE_LOOP = STRUCTURE
                     loop : LIST OF STRUCTURE
                                edge_ref    : REFERENCE(EDGE);
                                edge_orient : LOGICAL;
                              END;
                   END;
```

```
<edge_loop> ::= EDGE_LOOP ( name : ( [( name , logical )
                [, ( name , logical )]* ] ) );
```

An EDGE_LOOP contains an ordered list of references to edges together with the indication whether the orientation of the edge in this loop is as the orientation of the edge itself or inverted (.F.). See also "FACE" on page 102.

5.8.1.7 EDGE

```
ENTITY EDGE  =  STRUCTURE
                  curve        : REFERENCE(EDGE_CURVE);
                  start_vertex : REFERENCE(VERTEX);
                  end_vertex   : REFERENCE(VERTEX);
                END;
```

```
<edge> ::=  EDGE ( name : name , name , name ) ;
```

An EDGE is a topological entity defined within the scope of a B_REP. It is defined in terms of its bounding vertices and its underlying EDGE_CURVE geometry.

- Every EDGE has one and only one start VERTEX.
- Every EDGE has one and only one end VERTEX.
- Every EDGE refers to one and only one underlying EDGE_CURVE.
- Every EDGE is defined by the sequence of its start - and end VERTEX in that way that it coincides with the sense of the underlying EDGE_CURVE.
- Every EDGE whose start and end VERTEX refer to the same point has a closed curve as underlying EDGE_CURVE. In that case the sense of the EDGE is defined arbitrarily.
- Every EDGE occurs exactly twice, once in each direction, in the lists of EDGE entities referenced by LOOP entities.
- An artifact EDGE is an EDGE that has only one FACE associated with it. That means that the same FACE lies on both sides of the EDGE.

The geometry associated with the EDGE is defined as a curve that is common to the surfaces which are associated to all FACES adjacent to that EDGE. In most cases, this will be the intersection of the two surfaces. However, tangent connection is also allowed. The curve attribute of an EDGE refers to a curve representation which, when received on a neutral file, is the the best available approximation to that common curve. The receiving system must check whether it should iteratively improve the curve representation in order to achieve the desired accuracy. This process may be controlled by directives to the post-processor.

5.8.1.8 EDGE_CURVE

```
ENTITY EDGE_CURVE = CLASS ( LINE(D3), CIRCLE(D3), ELLIPSE(D3),
                            PARABOLA(D3), HYPERBOLA(D3),
                            B_SPLINE_CURVE(D3) );

<edge_curve> ::= <line(d3)> | <circle(d3)> | <ellipse(d3)> |
                 <parabola(d3)> | <hyperbola(d3)> |
                 <b_spline_curve(d3>
```

The entity EDGE_CURVE consists of a class of elementary curves that may be referenced by the topological entity EDGE in a B_REP. The FACE_SURFACE geometry in a B_REP has the highest priority in defining the B_REP geometry. That means that the EDGE_CURVE geometry associated to the EDGE is considered to be the best approximation available of the curve that is common to the two surfaces associated to adjacent faces.

5.8.1.9 VERTEX_LOOP

```
ENTITY VERTEX_LOOP = STRUCTURE
                       vertex : REFERENCE(VERTEX);
                     END;

<vertex_loop> ::= VERTEX_LOOP ( name : name ) ;
```

see description of LOOP in this chapter.

5.8.1.10 VERTEX

```
ENTITY VERTEX = STRUCTURE
                  point_ref : REFERENCE(POINT(D3));
                END;

<vertex> ::= VERTEX ( name : name ) ;
```

A vertex is a topological entity defined within the scope of a B_REP.

- Every VERTEX consists of a reference to one and only one point

- A VERTEX may be referenced from one and only one VERTEX_LOOP
- A VERTEX may be referenced from one or more EDGE entities
- The FACE_SURFACE geometry in a B_REP has the highest priority in defining the geometry of a B_REP. That means that the POINT geometry associated to the VERTEX is considered to be the best approximation available of the point that is common to all surfaces associated with the faces that meet at the particular VERTEX.
  The receiving system will have to check whether all surfaces of the adjacent faces join close enough to the point received on the neutral file or whether an iterative improvement is required. This process may be controlled by directives given to the post-processor.

5.8.2 The POLYHEDRON: a boundary representation with planar faces

5.8.2.1 POLY_HEDRON

```
ENTITY POLYHEDRON = STRUCTURE
        SCOPE;
              POLYHEDRON_SCOPE_ENTITY;
        END_SCOPE;
                   result      : LIST OF REF_ONLY(POLY_SHELL);
                 END;

<polyhedron> ::=  POLYHEDRON ( name : OPEN ) ;
        SCOPE;
             [<polyhedron_scope>]* ]
        END_SCOPE;
              POLYHEDRON_RESULT ( <name_list> ) ;
              POLYHEDRON ( name , CLOSE ) ;

<polyhedron_scope> = <point(d3)> | <poly_loop> |
                 <poly_face> | <poly_shell>
```

The POLY_HEDRON has been introduced in order to support the large number of systems that allow boundary type solids representations with PLANAR_SURFACE entities only. POLY_HEDRON entities may be represented by B_REP entities, but their representation on the neutral file as POLY_HEDRON will be more compact. A POLY_HEDRON is an entity that has a scope. A POLY_HEDRON may have a material property associated with it. Within the scope of a POLY_HEDRON there are both topological and geometrical entities. Geometry is represented by lists of point entities which are referenced by the topological POLY_VERTEX entities.

The POLY_HEDRON is a 'self-contained' entity in the sense that no entity in the POLY_HEDRON may refer to an entity outside the scope of the POLY_HEDRON. All referenced entities must be within the POLY_HEDRON scope itself.

- A POLY_HEDRON consists of a list of references to one or more POLY_SHELL entities where the first entry in the list is the peripheral POLY_SHELL

- The result of the POLY_HEDRON consists of a list of references to one or more POLY_SHELL entities. The first reference indicates the outermost shell, the others indicate interior voids.

5.8.2.2 POLY_SHELL

```
ENTITY POLY_SHELL = STRUCTURE
                      shell : LIST OF REFERENCE(POLY_FACE);
                    END;
```

```
<poly_shell> ::=  POLY_SHELL ( name : <name_list> ) ;
```

A POLY_SHELL is a topological entity defined within the scope of a POLY_HEDRON.

- Every POLY_SHELL is either the external boundary of a POLY_HEDRON or an internal void within a POLY_HEDRON.

- Every POLY_SHELL consists of a list of references to POLY_FACE entities.

5.8.2.3 POLY_FACE

```
ENTITY POLY_FACE = STRUCTURE
                     loop_list : LIST OF REF_ONLY(POLY_LOOP);
                   END;
```

```
<poly_face> ::= POLY_FACE ( name : <name_list ) ;
```

A POLY_FACE is a topological entity defined within the scope of a POLY_HEDRON. The geometry of the POLY_FACE is implied to be planar.

- Every POLY_FACE must belong to one and only one POLY_SHELL

- Every POLY_FACE must be bound by one or more POLY_LOOP entities lying in the same plane where the first entry in the POLY_LOOP list is the peripheral POLY_LOOP.

5.8.2.4 POLY_LOOP

```
ENTITY POLY_LOOP = STRUCTURE
                      point_list : LIST OF ANY(POINT(D3));
                    END;
```

```
<poly_loop> ::=  POLY_LOOP ( name : ( [<any(point(d3))>
                                                        *
                             [, <any(point(d3))>]  ] ) ) ;
```

A POLY_LOOP is a topological entity defined within the scope of a POLY_HEDRON.

- Every POLY_LOOP is part or all the boundary of one POLY_FACE

- Every POLY_LOOP consists of an ordered list of unique references to three or more POINT entities. The list is ordered such that the sense of the POLY_LOOP is anti-clockwise when viewed from void to solid.

5.8.3 An experimental compound boundary representation

5.8.3.1 COMPOUND_B_REP

```
ENTITY COMPOUND_B_REP =
                STRUCTURE
           SCOPE;
                 B_REP_SCOPE_ENTITY;
                 REGION;
                 INDEX_ENTRY;
                 MATERIAL;
           END_SCOPE;
                  regions          : LIST OF REF_ONLY(REGION);
                END;
```

```
<compound_b_rep> ::=  COMPOUND_B_REP ( name : OPEN ) ;
          SCOPE;
               [<b_rep_scope> | <region> | <index_entry> |
                <material>]*
          END_SCOPE;
                         COMPOUND_B_REP_RESULT ( <name_list> ) ;
                         COMPOUND_B_REP ( name , OPEN ) ;
```

The COMPOUND_B_REP is included in this specification as an 'experimental' entity. Most CAD systems are presently unable to deal with such kind of models. The entity has been included in order to demonstrate that the present neutral file proposal is capable of handling models that are yet to be implemented in future CAD systems.

The COMPOUND_B_REP is a generalization of the B_REP solids model and has been introduced to cope with the needs of applications (such as finite element analysis) in which adjacent regions inside a solids model have different properties (material, e.g.) associated. The B_REP model allows voids only but does not provide for faces being shared by adjacent shells.

A COMPOUND_B_REP is an entity that has a scope. Within the scope of a COMPOUND_B_REP there are both topological and geometrical entities. Geometry is represented by lists of the entities point, curve and surface which are referenced by the topological entities defined subsequently. Topology is represented by lists of the entities, vertex, edge, loop, face and shell in that order so that no entity is referenced before it is defined. Each shell may have a material property associated (while a B_REP has such properties only as a whole). The COMPOUND_B_REP is constituted by a list of regions which each may be considered as a model similar to a B_REP which means that each region is a list of shells ordered such that the first shell is assumed to be the 'peripheral' shell and all others are interior (voids or fully enclosed shells with other properties). The basic difference between B_REP and COMPOUND_B_REP is that in the first a face may be referenced by one shell only, while in the latter this applies to the the periphery of the whole COMPOUND_B_REP only. Internal faces are shared (referenced by) two shells and are characterized in these two shells by opposite direction indicators.

The COMPOUND_B_REP is a 'self-contained' entity in the sense that no entity in the COMPOUND_B_REP may refer to an entity outside the scope of the COMPOUND_B_REP. All referenced entities must be within the COMPOUND_B_REP scope itself.

5.8.3.2 REGION

```
ENTITY REGION = STRUCTURE
                  shells : LIST OF REF_ONLY(SHELL);
                END;

<region> ::= REGION ( name : <name_list> ) ;
```

This is an entity similar to a B_REP in the scope of a COMPOUND_B_REP. It allows to model boundary representations of solids with different attributes associated to each shell.

5.9 CONSTRUCTIVE SOLID GEOMETRY

5.9.1 CONSTRUCT

```
ENTITY CONSTRUCT =
            STRUCTURE
           SCOPE;
                CONSTRUCT_SCOPE_ENTITY;
                INDEX_ENTRY;
           END_SCOPE;
              result     : REFERENCE (BOOL_OPERAND,PRIMITIVE));
            END;

<construct> ::= CONSTRUCT ( name : OPEN ) ;
           SCOPE;
               [<construct_scope> |
                                   *
                <index_entry>]
           END_SCOPE;
                 CONSTRUCT_RESULT ( name ) ;
               CONSTRUCT ( name , CLOSE ) ;

ENTITY CONSTRUCT_SCOPE_ENTITY = CLASS( POINT(D3),EDGE_CURVE,
                                       DIRECTION(D3), PLACEMENT(DIM),
                                       PRIMITIVE, POLY_HEDRON,
                                       B_REP, BOOLEAN );
```

```
<construct_scope> ::= <point(d3)> | <edge_curve> |
                      <direction(d3)> | <placement(dim)> |
                      <primitive> | <poly_hedron> |
                      <b_rep> | <boolean>
```

A CONSTRUCT is an entity that has a scope. The data structure of a construct represents a three-dimensional geometrical shape. Certain domains of this shape may have material properties associated with them. A construct is not an elementary solid model but defines a function which -when evaluated- will produce a solid. The function operators are BOOLEAN, the operands are of type BOOL_OPERAND. The elementary operands which are called PRIMITIVE entities exist in the scope of the CONSTRUCT only. However, POLYHEDRON models and B_REP entities may exist in the construct scope and may be used as operands to boolean operations (if the CAD system provides this capability). The attribute result is an instance of the BOOLEAN which represents the root of the boolean tree or simply of a PRIMITIVE, B_REP, POLYHEDRON, or another CONSTRUCT.

(For an example, see Figure 14 on page 114).

5.9.2 BOOLEAN

```
ENTITY BOOLEAN = STRUCTURE
                   operator       : BOOL_OPERATOR;
                   first_operand  : REFERENCE(BOOL_OPERAND);
                   second_operand : REFERENCE(BOOL_OPERAND);
                 END;

<boolean> ::= BOOLEAN ( name : <bool_operator> , name , name ) ;
```

This is the data structure representation of a boolean operation (see Figure 14 on page 114). Depending on the operator the second operand is subtracted from, intersected or united with the first operand.

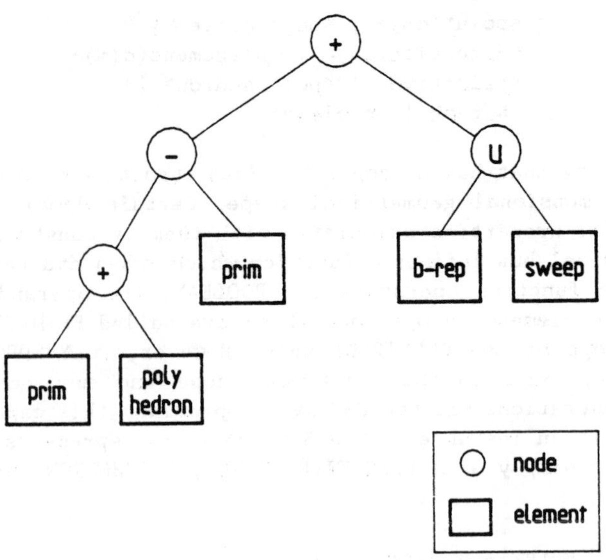

Figure 14. Example of a boolean tree in a CONSTRUCT

5.9.3 BOOL_OPERAND

```
ENTITY BOOL_OPERAND = CLASS( BOOLEAN,
                             PRIMITIVE,
                             POLYHEDRON,
                             B_REP,
                             COMPOUND_B_REP,
                             INSTANCE(BOOL_OPERAND),
                             CONSTRUCT );
```

```
<bool_operand> ::= <boolean> | <primitive> | <polyhedron> | <b_rep> |
                   <compound_b_rep> | <instance> <construct>
```

BOOL_OPERAND is a class of entities which can occur as an operand to a BOOLEAN operation using regularized boolean operators (see e.g. A.A.G.Requicha and H.B.Voelcker, Solid Modeling, in IEEE Computer Graphics and Applications, Vol.2, No.2, Mar. 1982, pp.9-24)

5.9.4 BOOL_OPERATOR

```
ATTRIBUTE BOOL_OPERATOR = ENUM( DIFFERENCE , UNION , INTERSECTION );

<bool_operator> ::= DIFFERENCE | UNION | INTERSECTION
```

BOOL_OPERATOR is an attribute that defines whether the two operands of a boolean expression are to be combined as a difference (first operand minus second operand), union, or intersection.

Any properties, such as material, associated with the first operand will dominate over properties associated with the second operand in the intersecting volume.

5.9.5 PRIMITIVE

```
ENTITY PRIMITIVE = CLASS( BOX,
                          SOLID_SPHERE,
                          SOLID_CYLINDER,
                          TRUNCATED_CONE,
                          TRUNCATED_PYRAMID,
                          REGULAR_PRISM,
                          SOLID_TORUS,
                          LINEAR_SWEEP,
                          ROTATIONAL_SWEEP,
                          PLANAR_HALFSPACE );

<primitive> ::=  <box> | <solid_sphere> | <solid_cylinder> |
                 <truncated_cone> | <truncated_pyramid> |
                 <regular_prism> | <solid_torus> | <linear_sweep> |
                 <rotational_sweep> | <planar_halfspace>
```

This is a class of entities that can exist only in the scope of a CONSTRUCT entity. They are used as operands in boolean expressions. The attribute list of a PRIMITIVE entity consists of

- shape information i.e. the dimensions of the primitive and

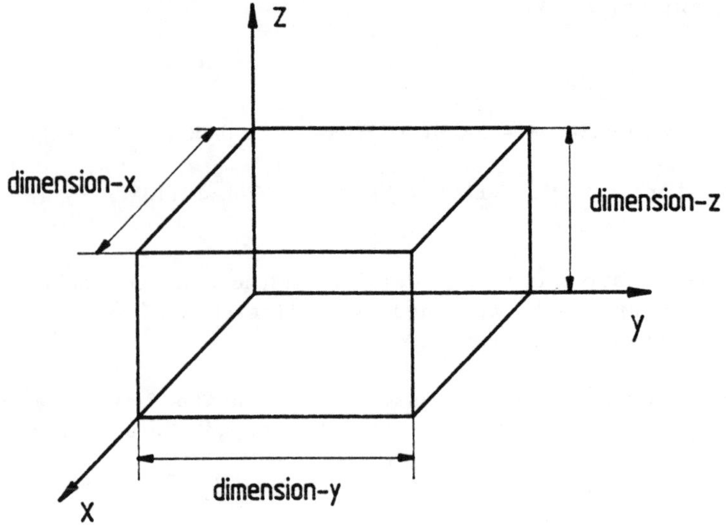

Figure 15. The BOX primitive

- placement information i.e. the description of the local coordinate system of the primitive.

5.9.6 Primitives for constructive solid geometry

5.9.6.1 PLANAR_HALFSPACE

```
ENTITY PLANAR_HALFSPACE = STRUCTURE
                            point  : ANY(POINT(D3));
                            normal : ANY(DIRECTION(D3));
                          END;

<planar_halfspace> ::=  PLANAR_HALFSPACE ( name :
                        <any(point(d3))> , <any(direction(d3))> ) ;
```

A PLANAR_HALFSPACE (see Figure 16 on page 117) is a CSG primitive. The planar boundary of the PLANAR_HALFSPACE is implied to be the xy-plane. The material lies in the direction of the normal i.e. in positive z-direction.

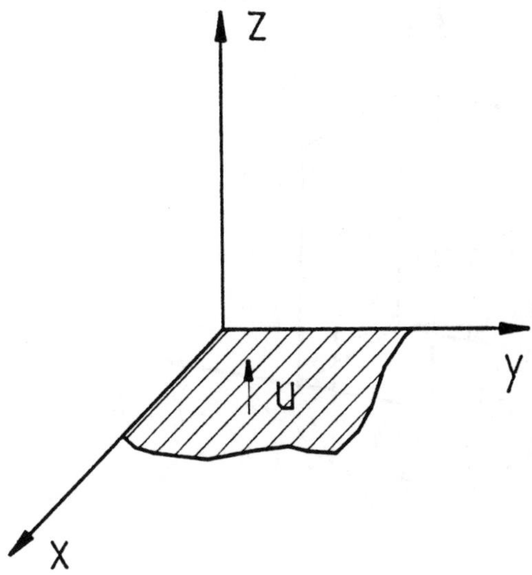

Figure 16. The PLANAR_HALFSPACE primitive

The placement information consists of the origin of the local coordinate system and the local z-axis.

The boolean operations in a construct which contains a PLANAR_HALFSPACE must guarantee that the construct is bounded even though the primitive itself is unbounded.

5.9.6.2 REGULAR_PRISM

```
ENTITY REGULAR_PRISM = STRUCTURE
                         origin  : ANY(POINT(D3));
                         dir_x   : ANY(DIRECTION(D3));
                         dir_xz  : ANY(DIRECTION(D3));
                         radius  : ANY(REAL);
                         height  : ANY(REAL);
                         corners : ANY(INTEGER);
                       END;

<regular_prism> ::=  REGULAR_PRISM ( name :  <any(point(d3))> ,
               <any(direction(d3))> , <any(direction(d3))> ,
               <any(real)> , <any(real)> , <any(integer)> ) ;
```

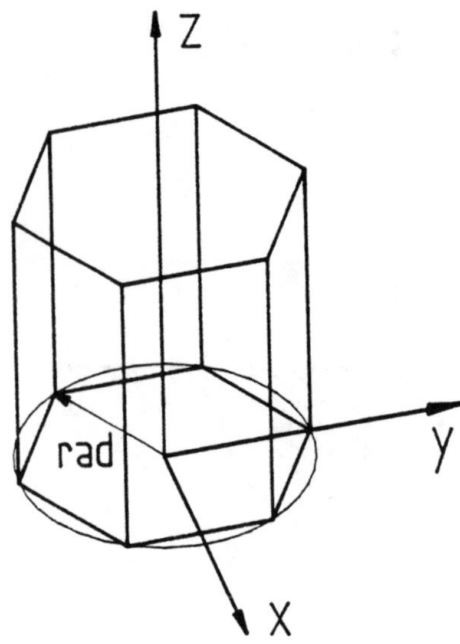

Figure 17. The REGULAR_PRISM primitive

A REGULAR_PRISM (see Figure 17 on page 118) is a construct primitive. Its shape is defined by the right circular cylinder within which it is inscribed. The cylinder is described by its radius and height. An integer, three or greater, defines the number of sides. The axis of the REGULAR_PRISM coincides with the positive z-axis. The base lies in the xy-plane with its center located at the **origin**. The REGULAR_PRISM is oriented relative to the z-axis so that one of its vertices lies on the positive x-axis.

The placement information consists of the attributes

- **origin** to indicate the origin of the local coordinate system
- **dir_x** to define the local x-axis and
- **dir_xz** lying in the xz-plane

The local y-axis is calculated by **dir_y** = **dir_xz** * **dir_x** and subsequently the local z-axis by **dir_z** = **dir_x** * **dir_y**.

Material is assumed to be inside the REGULAR_PRISM.

5.9.6.3 BOX

```
ENTITY BOX = STRUCTURE
               origin      : ANY(POINT(D3));
               dir_x       : ANY(DIRECTION(D3));
               dir_xz      : ANY(DIRECTION(D3));
               dimension_x : ANY(REAL);
               dimension_y : ANY(REAL);
               dimension_z : ANY(REAL);
             END;

<box> ::=  BOX ( name :  <any(point(d3))> , <any(direction(d3))> ,
                 <any(direction(d3))> , <any(real)> , <any(real)> ,
                 <any(real)> ) ;
```

A BOX (see Figure 15 on page 116) is a construct primitive. Its shape is a rectangular parallelepiped, placed in the +X, +Y, +Z octant with one vertex at the **origin** and the three edges respectively lying along the +X, +Y, +Z axis. The dimensions of the BOX are given by "dimension_x", "dimension_y" and "dimension_z".

The placement information consists of the attributes

- **origin** to indicate the origin of the local coordinate system,
- **dir_x** to define the local x-axis and
- **dir_xz** lying in the local xz-plane

The local y-axis is calculated by **dir_y** = **dir_xz** * **dir_x** and subsequently the local z-axis by **dir_z** = **dir_x** * **dir_y**. Material is assumed to be inside the BOX.

5.9.6.4 SOLID_CYLINDER

```
ENTITY SOLID_CYLINDER = STRUCTURE
                          origin : ANY(POINT(D3));
                          dir_z  : ANY(DIRECTION(D3));
                          radius : ANY(REAL);
                          height : ANY(REAL);
                        END;
```

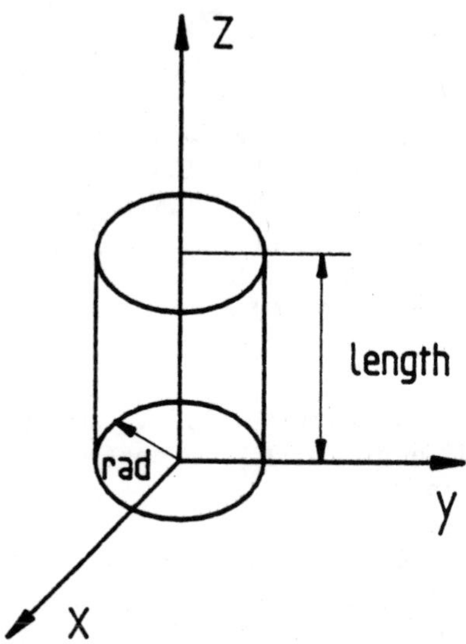

Figure 18. The SOLID_CYLINDER primitive

```
<solid_cylinder> ::= SOLID_CYLINDER ( name :
                     <any(point(d3))> , <any(direction(d3))> ,
                     <any(real)> , <any(real)> ) ;
```

The SOLID_CYLINDER (see Figure 18) is a construct primitive. Its shape is defined by its radius and its height. The axis of the SOLID_CYLINDER is colinear to the positive z-axis and its base is lying in the xy-plane.

The placement information of the SOLID_CYLINDER consists of the local origin and the local z-axis.

Material is assumed to be inside the SOLID_CYLINDER.

5.9.6.5 SOLID_SPHERE

The SOLID_SPHERE (see Figure 19 on page 121)

```
ENTITY SOLID_SPHERE = STRUCTURE
                          center : ANY(POINT(D3));
                          radius : ANY(REAL);
                      END;
```

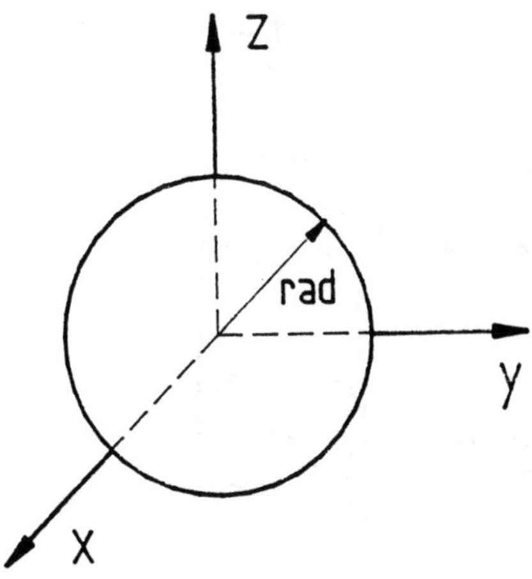

Figure 19. The SOLID_SPHERE primitive

```
<solid_sphere> ::= SOLID_SPHERE ( name :  <any(point(d3)) , <any(real) ) ;
```

is a construct primitive. It is defined by its radius and a point for its center. Material is assumed to be inside the SOLID_SPHERE.

5.9.6.6 TRUNCATED_CONE

```
ENTITY TRUNCATED_CONE = STRUCTURE
                           origin   : ANY(POINT(D3));
                           dir_z    : ANY(DIRECTION(D3));
                           radius1  : ANY(REAL);
                           radius2  : ANY(REAL);
                           height   : ANY(REAL);
                        END;
```

```
<truncated_cone> ::=  TRUNCATED_CONE ( name :  <any(point(d3))> ,
                 <any(direction(d3))> , <any(real)> , <any(real)> ,
                 <any(real)> ) ;
```

The TRUNCATED_CONE (see Figure 20 on page 122) is a construct primitive. Its shape is defined by its base radius radius1 and top radius radius2 and

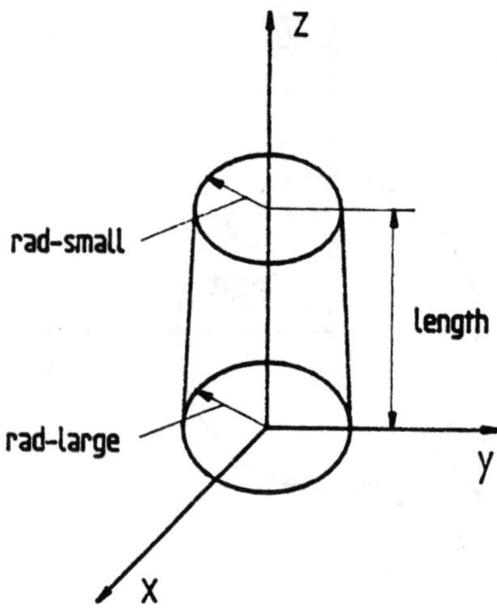

Figure 20. The TRUNCATED_CONE primitive

the height. The axis of the TRUNCATED_CONE is colinear to the positive z-axis and the base lies in the xy-plane.

The placement information of the SOLID_CYLINDER consists of the local origin and the local z-axis.

Material is assumed to be inside the TRUNCATED_CONE.

5.9.6.7 TRUNCATED_PYRAMID

```
ENTITY TRUNCATED_PYRAMID = STRUCTURE
                             origin   : ANY(POINT(D3));
                             dir_x    : ANY(DIRECTION(D3));
                             dir_xz   : ANY(DIRECTION(D3));
                             radius1  : ANY(REAL);
                             radius2  : ANY(REAL);
                             height   : ANY(REAL);
                             corners  : ANY(INTEGER);
                           END;
```

```
<truncated_pyramid> ::= TRUNCATED_PYRAMID ( name : <any(point(d3))> ,
                <any(direction(d3))> , <any(direction(d3))> ,
                <any(real)> , <any(real)> , <any(real)> ,
                <any(integer)> ) ;
```

A TRUNCATED_PYRAMID (see Figure 21 on page 124) is a construct primitive. Its shape is defined by the right circular cone within which it is inscribed. The cone is described as for the TRUNCATED_CONE. An integer, three or greater, defines the number of sides. The axis of the TRUNCATED_PYRAMID lies along the positive z-axis, with its base in the xy-plane. The TRUNCATED_PYRAMID is oriented relative to the z-axis so that one of its vertices lies on the positive x-axis.

The placement information consists of the attributes

- **origin** to indicate the origin of the local coordinate system,
- **dir_x** to define the local x-axis and
- **dir_xz** lying in the local xz-plane

The local y-axis is calculated by **dir_y** = **dir_xz** * **dir_x** and subsequently the local z-axis by **dir_z** = **dir_x** * **dir_y**.

Material is assumed to be inside the TRUNCATED_PYRAMID.

5.9.6.8 SOLID_TORUS

```
ENTITY SOLID_TORUS = STRUCTURE
                  origin       : ANY(POINT(D3));
                  dir_z        : ANY(DIRECTION(D3));
                radius_large : ANY(REAL);
                radius_small : ANY(REAL);
                 END;

<solid_torus> ::= SOLID_TORUS ( name : <any(point(d3))> ,
                  <any(direction(d3))> , <any(real)> , <any(real)> ) ;
```

The SOLID_TORUS (see Figure 22 on page 125) is a construct primitive. It is created by revolving a circular disc lying in the xz-plane about the z-axis. The circular disc is assumed to be disjoint and coplanar to the z-axis. The shape description consists of "radius_large" i.e. the distance from the axis to the center of the defining disc and of "radius_small" i.e.

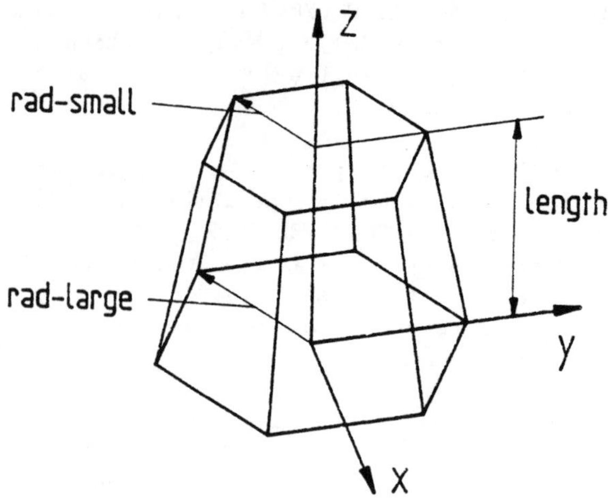

Figure 21. The TRUNCATED_PYRAMID primitive

the rádius of the defining disc. The axis of the SOLID_TORUS is colinear with the z-axis, its center lies in the **origin**.

The placement information of the SOLID_TORUS consists of the local **origin** and the local z-axis.

Material is assumed to be inside the SOLID_TORUS.

5.9.6.9 SWEEP

```
ENTITY SWEEP = CLASS( LINEAR_SWEEP, ROTATIONAL_SWEEP );

<sweep> ::= <linear_sweep> | <rotational_sweep>
```

The entity SWEEP consists of a class containing the entities LINEAR_SWEEP and ROTATIONAL_SWEEP.

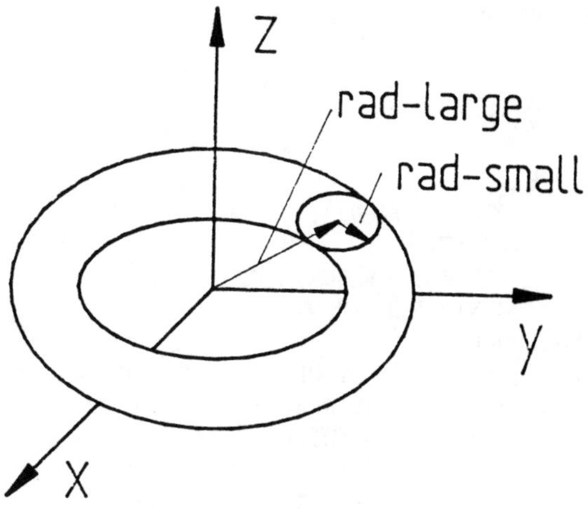

Figure 22. The SOLID_TORUS primitive

5.9.6.10 CONTOUR_ELEMENT

```
ENTITY CONTOUR_ELEMENT =
                STRUCTURE
                  curve      : REF_ONLY(ELEMENTARY_CURVE(D2));
                  startpoint : ANY(POINT(D2));
                  endpoint   : ANY(POINT(D2));
                END;

<contour_element> ::= CONTOUR_ELEMENT ( name :  name ,
                       <any(point(d2))> , <any(point(d2))> ) ;
```

A CONTOUR_ELEMENT is used in the scope of a CSG SWEEP. It defines start and end point of an elementary curve to which it refers. The sense of the curve is from start to the end point (e.g. to construct a circular arc the two points define the part of a circle that is used and together with the center of the circle they define the arc itself).

5.9.6.11 LINEAR_SWEEP

```
ENTITY LINEAR_SWEEP =
    STRUCTURE
           SCOPE;
                 DIRECTION(D2);
                 POINT(D2);
                 ELEMENTARY_CURVE(D2);
                 CONTOUR_ELEMENT;
           END_SCOPE;
      contour_sequence : LIST OF LIST OF REF_ONLY(CONTOUR_ELEMENT);
      shift_length     : ANY(REAL);
      shift_direction  : ANY(DIRECTION(D3));
      origin           : ANY(POINT(D3));
      dir_x            : ANY(DIRECTION(D3));
      dir_xz           : ANY(DIRECTION(D3));
    END;

<linear_sweep> ::=  LINEAR_SWEEP ( name : OPEN ) ;
           SCOPE;
               [<direction(d2)> | <point(d2)> |
               <elementary_curve(d2)> | <contour_element>]*
           END_SCOPE;
                  LINEAR_SWEEP_RESULT ( ( [ <name_list>
                      [ , <name_list> ]* ] ) ,
                      <any(real)> , <any(direction(d3))> ,
                      <any(point(d3))> , <any(direction(d3))> ,
                      <any(direction(d3))> ) ;
                  LINEAR_SWEEP ( name , CLOSE ) ;
```

A LINEAR_SWEEP (see Figure 23 on page 127) is a construct primitive. Its shape is defined by the swept area, a shift_length and a shift_direction. The swept area is composed of a list of ordered lists of CONTOUR_ELEMENT references. Every list of CONTOUR_ELEMENT references describes a closed contour that must not intersect itself. There must be at least one list of CONTOUR_ELEMENT references i.e. the outer bound of the swept area. Subsequent lists indicate inner bounds i.e. holes.

All the DIRECTION, POINT and ELEMENTARY_CURVE entities are located in the xy-plane. The z-value of the shift direction must not be zero. The shift length must be greater than zero.

The placement information consists of the attributes

- **origin** to indicate the origin of the local coordinate system,
- **dir_x** to define the local x-axis and
- **dir_xz** lying in the local xz-plane

The local y-axis is calculated by **dir_y** = **dir_xz** * **dir_x** and subsequently the local z-axis by **dir_z** = **dir_x** * **dir_y**. Material is assumed to be inside the LINEAR_SWEEP. Figure 23.

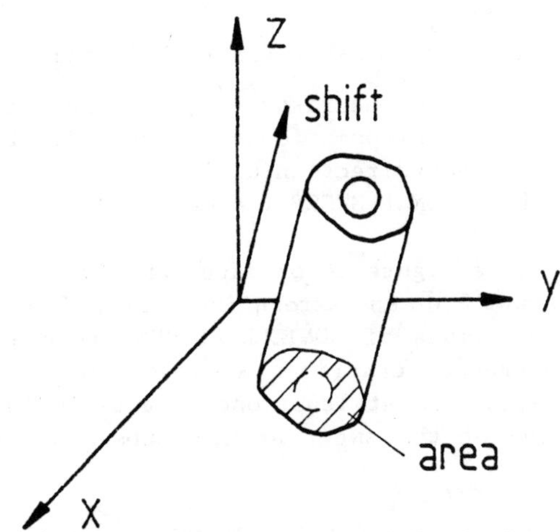

Figure 23. Example of a LINEAR_SWEEP primitive

5.9.6.12 ROTATIONAL_SWEEP

```
ENTITY ROTATIONAL_SWEEP =
     STRUCTURE
          SCOPE;
               DIRECTION(D2);
               POINT(D2);
               ELEMENTARY_CURVE(D2);
               CONTOUR_ELEMENT;
          END_SCOPE;
      contour_sequence : LIST OF LIST OF REF_ONLY(CONTOUR_ELEMENT);
      angle            : ANY(REAL);
      origin           : ANY(POINT(D3));
      dir_x            : ANY(DIRECTION(D3));
      dir_xz           : ANY(DIRECTION(D3));
     END;

<rotational_sweep> ::=
           ROTATIONAL_SWEEP ( name : OPEN ) ;
          SCOPE;
              [<direction(d2)> |
               <point(d2)> |
               <elementary_curve(d2)> |
                                      *
               <contour_element>]
          END_SCOPE;
             ROTATIONAL_SWEEP_RESULT ( [ <name_list>  ,
                                 *
               [ , <name_list> ]  ] ) , <any(real)>
               , <any(point(d3))> , <any(direction(d3))> ,
               <any(direction(d3))> ) ;
             ROTATIONAL_SWEEP ( name , CLOSE ) ;
```

A ROTATIONAL_SWEEP (see Figure 24 on page 129) is a construct primitive. It is defined by the swept area and a rotation angle. The swept area is composed of a list of ordered lists of CONTOUR_ELEMENT references. Every list of CONTOUR_ELEMENT references describes a closed contour that must not intersect itself. There must be at least one list of CONTOUR_ELEMENT references i.e. the outer bound of the swept area. Subsequent lists indicate inner bounds i.e. holes.

All the DIRECTION, POINT and ELEMENTARY_CURVE entities are located in the xy-plane. The rotation axis is defined by the positive x-axis. The y-values must be greater or equal zero. The rotation angle must be greater than zero and less or equal 2π.

The placement information consists of the attributes

- **origin** to indicate the origin of the local coordinate system,
- **dir_x** to define the local x-axis and
- **dir_xz** lying in the local xz-plane

The local y-axis is calculated by **dir_y = dir_xz * dir_x** and subsequently the local z-axis by **dir_z = dir_x * dir_y**. Material is assumed to be inside the ROTATIONAL_SWEEP.

5.10 HYBRID_SOLID

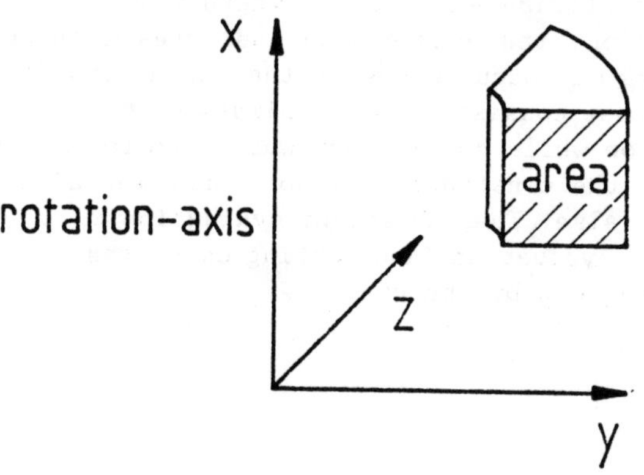

Figure 24. The ROTATIONAL_SWEEP primitive

```
ENTITY HYBRID_SOLID = STRUCTURE
            SCOPE;
                  CONSTRUCT;
                  B_REP;
            END_SCOPE;
                        consistency : LOGICAL;
                        update_mode : UPDATE;
                        expression  : REFERENCE(CONSTRUCT);
                        value       : LIST OF REFERENCE(B_REP);
                      END;
```

```
<hybrid_solid> ::=  HYBRID_SOLID ( name : OPEN ) ;
            SCOPE;
                 [<construct> |
                                *
                  <b_rep>]
            END_SCOPE;
                HYBRID_SOLID_RESULT ( logical , name, <name_list> ) ;
                     HYBRID_SOLID ( name , CLOSE ) ;
```

The HYBRID_SOLID entity corresponds in the field of solids to what the REAL and INTEGER entities are in the field of arithmetics. A hybrid solid consists of a functional description of a solids model in the form of a CONSTRUCT (referenced by the attribute expression) and its evaluated value in the form of a list of B_REP models (referenced by the attribute value). Both the value and the expression must refer to entities that are inside the scope of the hybrid solid.

The consistency attribute .indicates whether value is consistent with the present expression; the update_mode indicates when updating of value is to occur: Updating may occur whenever the expression (the construct) is modified (in which case consistency will always be true). When the entity is used in an application while consistency was found to be false (in which case any modification of the construct will not cause reevaluation but will just set consistency to false. The subsequent evaluation will set consistency to true again); or else, evaluation (and setting consistency to true) will occur only upon explicit request by the user.

5.11 GENERAL GROUPING MECHANISM

5.11.1 ASPECT

```
ENTITY ASPECT =  STRUCTURE
                   meaning : STRING;
                   type    : TYPE_ID;
                 END;

<aspect> ::=ASPECT ( name : string , <type_id> ) ;
```

An aspect is an entity that allows to group geometric information according to some arbitrary criteria. Many CAD systems provide such a grouping mechanism (often called layer or level). The user may activate or deactivate one or more aspects in his CAD system. Any operations performed on geometric information (display or other evaluations) will interpret only those geometric entities that are related to activated aspects. Any geometric entity not related to an aspect entity via a component_geometry_aspect relation is active by default (see "GEOMETRY_ASSOCIATION").

5.11.2 GEOMETRY_ASSOCIATION

```
PROPERTY GEOMETRY_ASSOCIATION =
                        STRUCTURE
                          object   : REFERENCE(COMPONENT);
                          geometry : REF_ONLY(GEOMETRIC_MODEL);
                          aspect   : [REF_ANY(ASPECT)] ;
                        END;
```

The geometry association relates geometry information to a component. This association is subject to the following rules:

1. Any geometric model may be related to one component only.
2. Any component may be associated to the same aspect entity only once. In other words, there must not be two geometry associations having the same entries for both the object and aspect attribute.
3. The missing aspect represents a default aspect that is always active (see "ASPECT").

5.12 PLACEMENT AND INSTANCING

5.12.1 GEOMETRIC

```
ENTITY GEOMETRIC = CLASS( POINT(DIM), CURVE(DIM), SURFACE,
                          EDGE_CURVE,WIREFRAME_MODEL(DIM),
                          SOLID_MODEL, COMPONENT, ASSEMBLY,
                          SURFACE_MODEL, INSTANCE(GEOMETRIC,DIM)) );

<geometric> ::= <point(dim)> | <curve(dim)> | <surface> |
                <edge_curve,> | <wireframe_model> |
                <solid_model> | <component> | <assembly> |
                <surface_model> | <instance>
```

GEOMETRIC entities represent the class of all geometric entities to which the CAD system user might apply operations like "translate", "rotate", or "scale".

5.12.2 INSTANCE

```
ENTITY INSTANCE = GENERIC (g: GEOMETRIC )
                  STRUCTURE
                   object    : REF_ANY(g);
                   placement : [ANY(PLACEMENT(DIMENSION(g))];
                  END;

<instance>   ::= INSTANCE( <ref_any> , [ <any(placement(dim))> ])
```

An instance is a reference to a geometric entity with an associated placement. The default value of the placement is "no rotation and no translation".

NOTE: An instance entity that either directly or indirectly (that is via other instance entities) refers to an entity of a certain geometric type is to be considered as being an entity of that type as far as the type restrictions in the HDSL are concerned.

Chained instancing (instances of instances of instances ...) is allowed up to an arbitrary length, but no cycles are allowed in such a data structure.

5.12.3 ROTATION

```
ENTITY ROTATION = GENERIC (d : DIM)
                    CLASS( ROT_MATRIX(d), ROT_GLOBAL(d),
                           ROT_AXIS );

<rotation(dim)> ::= <rotation(d2)> | <rotation(d3)>

<any(rotation(dim))> ::= <any(rotation(d2))> | <any(rotation(d3))>

<rotation(d2)> ::= <rot_matrix(d2)> | <rot_global(d2)> | <rot_axis>

<any(rotation(d2))> ::= <any(rot_matrix(d2))> |
                        <any(rot_global(d2))> |
                        <any(rot_axis)>

<rotation(d3)> ::= <rot_matrix(d3)> | <rot_global(d3)> | <rot_axis>

<any(rotation(d3))> ::= <any(rot_matrix(d3))> |
                        <any(rot_global(d3))> |
                        <any(rot_axis)>
```

This is a class of data types representing a rotation.

5.12.4 ROT_AXIS

```
ENTITY ROT_AXIS = STRUCTURE
                    point : ANY(POINT(D3));
                    axis  : ANY(DIRECTION(D3));
                    angle : ANY(REAL);
                  END;

<rot_axis> ::= ROT_AXIS ( name :  <any(point(d3))> ,
                 <any(direction(d3))> , <any(real)> ) ;
```

```
<any(rot_axis)> ::= <ref_any> |
                    ROT_AXIS ( <any(point(d3))> , <any(direction(d3))> ,
                               <any(real)> )
```

This entity type defines a rotation around an axis by a certain angle. The axis is described by a point and a direction. The angle is positive for clockwise rotation viewed in the direction of the vector.

5.12.5 ROT_GLOBAL

```
ENTITY ROT_GLOBAL = GENERIC (d : DIM)
                      STRUCTURE
                        CASE d OF
                          D2: (anglex : NIL;
                               angley : NIL);
                          D3: (anglex : ANY(REAL);
                               angley : ANY(REAL));
                        END;
                        anglez : ANY(REAL);
                      END;

<rot_global(dim)> ::= <rot_global(d2)> | <rot_global(d3)>

<any(rot_global(dim))> ::= <any(rot_global(d2))> |
                           <any(rot_global(d3))>

<rot_global(d2)> ::= ROT_GLOBAL ( name : <any(real)> ) ;

<any(rot_global(d2))> ::= <ref_any) |
                          ROT_GLOBAL ( any(real)> )

<rot_global(d3)> ::= ROT_GLOBAL ( name :  <any(real)> , <any(real)> ,
                        <any(real)> ) ;

<any(rot_global(d3))> ::= <ref_any) |
                          ROT_GLOBAL ( <any(real)> , <any(real)> ,
                                       <any(real)> )
```

This entity type defines a rotation around the global coordinate axes. The rotations about the x-, y-, and z-axes are to be performed in this sequence.

Rotation angles are positive for clockwise rotation viewed in the direction of the corresponding axis.

5.12.6 ROT_MATRIX

```
ENTITY ROT_MATRIX = GENERIC (d : DIM)
                      STRUCTURE
                        dir_x : ANY(DIRECTION(d));
                        CASE d OF
                          D3: (dir_xz : ANY(DIRECTION(d)));
                          D2: (dir_xz : NIL);
                        END;
                      END;

<rot_matrix(dim)> ::= <rot_matrix(d2)> | <rot_matrix(d3)>

<any(matrix(dim))> ::= <any(rot_matrix(d2))> |
                       <any(rot_matrix(d3))>

<rot_matrix(d2)> ::= ROT_MATRIX ( name : <any(direction(d2))> ) ;

<any(rot_matrix(d2))> ::= <ref_any> |
                          ROT_MATRIX ( <any(direction(d2))> )

<rot_matrix(d3)> ::= ROT_MATRIX ( name :  <any(direction(d3)> ,
                                  <any(direction(d3)> ) ;

<any(rot_matrix(d3))> ::= <ref_any> |
                          ROT_MATRIX ( <any(direction(d3))> ,
                                       <any(direction(d3))> )
```

This entity type defines a rotation by giving the 2 by 2 rotation matrix (for two-dimensional geometry) and by giving the 3 by 3 rotation matrix (for three-dimensional geometry).

1. In the three-dimensional case the rotation matrix is defined as

$$M = (\mathbf{n}_x, \mathbf{n}_y, \mathbf{n}_z)$$

where $\mathbf{n}_x$, $\mathbf{n}_y$, and $\mathbf{n}_z$ are the normalized direction vectors. Any point P in the local coordinate system of the entity to which the rotation is applied will have the coordinates

$$P' = M * P$$

in the local coordinate system from which this entity is being referred. The normalized direction vectors are obtained from the directions **dir_x** and **dir_xz** by the following algorithm

$$\mathbf{n}_x = \mathbf{dir\_x}$$
$$\mathbf{n}_y = \mathbf{dir\_xz*dir\_x}$$
$$\mathbf{n}_z = \mathbf{n}_y\mathbf{*dir\_x}$$
$$\mathbf{n}_x = \mathbf{n}_x/\mathrm{length}(\mathbf{n}_x)$$
$$\mathbf{n}_y = \mathbf{n}_y/\mathrm{length}(\mathbf{n}_y)$$
$$\mathbf{n}_z = \mathbf{n}_z/\mathrm{length}(\mathbf{n}_z)$$

2. In the two-dimensional case the rotation matrix is defined as

$$M = (\mathbf{n}_x, \mathbf{n}_y)$$

where $\mathbf{n}_x$, and $\mathbf{n}_y$ are the normalized direction vectors. Any point P in the local coordinate system of the entity to which the rotation is applied will have the coordinates

$$P' = M * P$$

in the local coordinate system from which this entity is being referred. The normalized direction vectors are obtained from the direction **dir_x** which is received on the neutral file by the following algorithm

$$\mathbf{n}_x = \mathbf{dir\_x}$$
$$\text{with } \mathbf{n}_x = (a_x, a_y)$$
$$\mathbf{n}_y = (-a_y, a_x)$$
$$\mathbf{n}_x = \mathbf{n}_x/\mathrm{length}(\mathbf{n}_x)$$
$$\mathbf{n}_y = \mathbf{n}_y/\mathrm{length}(\mathbf{n}_y)$$

5.12.7 PLACEMENT

```
ENTITY PLACEMENT = GENERIC (d : DIM)
                     STRUCTURE
                       rotation    : ANY(ROTATION(d));
                       translation : ANY(POINT(d));
                     END;

<placement(dim)> ::=  <placement(d2> | <placement(d3)>

<placement(d2)> ::=  PLACEMENT ( name :  <any(rotation(d2))> ,
                                         <any(point(d2))> ) ;

<any(placement(dim))> ::= <any(placement(d2))> | <any(placement(d3))>

<any(placement(d2))> ::= <ref_any> |
                     PLACEMENT ( <any(rotation(d2))> ,
                                 <any(point(d2))> )

<placement(d3)> ::=  PLACEMENT ( name :  <any(rotation(d3))> ,
                                         <any(<point(d3))> ) ;

<any(placement(d3))> ::= <ref_any> |
                     PLACEMENT ( <any(rotation(d3))> ,
                                 <any(point(d3))> )
```

The placement consists of a rotation followed by a translation. Various forms of specifying the rotation are possible. See ROTATION.

5.13 TEST DATA ELEMENTS

5.13.1 TEST_RELATION_FOR_D2_WIREFRAME

```
PROPERTY TEST_RELATION_FOR_D2_WIREFRAME=
              STRUCTURE
                geometry  : REFERENCE(WIREFRAME_MODEL(D2));
                test_line : REFERENCE(LINE(D2));
                results   : LIST OF REFERENCE(POINT(D2));
              END;

<test_relation_for_d2_wireframe> ::=
      TEST_RELATION_FOR_D2_WIREFRAME ( name , name , <name_list> ) ;
```

This relation expresses the fact that the points referenced by the results attribute have been produced in the sending CAD system by intersecting the two-dimensional wireframe model referenced by the geometry attribute with the test line. The CAD system user in the receiving environment may use this information to test the accuracy of the transmitted geometry by repeating this intersection operation.

5.13.2 TEST_RELATION_FOR_D3_WIREFRAME

```
PROPERTY TEST_RELATION_FOR_D3_WIREFRAME=
              STRUCTURE
                geometry   : REFERENCE(WIREFRAME_MODEL(D3));
                test_plane : REFERENCE(PLANAR_SURFACE));
                results    : LIST OF REFERENCE(POINT(D3));
              END;

<test_relation_for_d3_wireframe> ::=
      TEST_RELATION_FOR_D3_WIREFRAME ( name , name , <name_list> ) ;
```

This relation expresses the fact that the points referenced by the results attribute have been produced in the sending CAD system by intersecting the three-dimensional wireframe model referenced by the geometry attribute with the test plane. The CAD system user in the receiving environment may use this information to test the accuracy of the transmitted geometry by repeating this intersection operation.

5.13.3 TEST_RELATION_FOR_SURFACE_MODEL

```
PROPERTY TEST_RELATION_FOR_SURFACE_MODEL=
                STRUCTURE
                  geometry  : REFERENCE(SURFACE_MODEL);
                  test_line : REFERENCE(LINE(D3));
                  results   : LIST OF REFERENCE(POINT(D3));
                END;

<test_relation_for_surface_model> ::=
      TEST_RELATION_FOR_SURFACE_MODEL ( name , name , <name_list> ) ;
```

This relation expresses the fact that the points referenced by the results attribute have been produced in the sending CAD system by intersecting the surface model referenced by the geometry attribute with the test line. The CAD system user in the receiving environment may use this information to test the accuracy of the transmitted geometry by repeating this intersection operation.

5.13.4 TEST_RELATION_FOR_SOLID_MODEL

```
PROPERTY TEST_RELATION_FOR_SOLID =
            STRUCTURE
              geometry  : REFERENCE(SOLID);
              test_line : REFERENCE(LINE(D3));
              results   : LIST OF REFERENCE(POINT(D3));
            END;

<test_relation_for_solid> ::=
     TEST_RELATION_FOR_SOLID ( name , name , <name_list> ) ;
```

This relation expresses the fact that the points referenced by the results attribute have been produced in the sending CAD system by intersecting the surfaces of the solid model referenced by the geometry attribute with the test line. The CAD system user in the receiving environment may use this information to test the accuracy of the transmitted geometry by repeating this intersection operation.

5.14 MISCELLANEOUS

5.14.1 MATERIAL

```
PROPERTY MATERIAL = STRUCTURE
                      material_data : INTEGER;
                      associated_to : LIST OF REF_ONLY(
                                            CLASS( ASSEMBLY,
                                                   REGION,
                                                   COMPONENT) );
                    END;

<material> ::= MATERIAL ( integer , <name_list> ) ;
```

This is a preliminary definition of material properties that may be associated with geometric entities. The following priority rule applies: Material information associated with SHELL overrides SOLID_MODEL, SOLID_MODEL overrides COMPONENT, COMPONENT overrides ASSEMBLY, such that material information associated with ASSEMBLY provides default for contained COMPONENTS.

5.14.2 Private record structures attached to CAD data

5.14.2.1 RECORD

```
PROPERTY RECORD = STRUCTURE
                   associated_to : REFERENCE(GEOMETRIC);
                   record        : LIST OF PREDEFINED;
                   record_type   : [REFERENCE(RECORD_TYPE)];
                  END;
```

```
<record> ::=  RECORD ( name , [<predefined>
                                          *
                      [, <predefined>]  ] , [name] ) ;
```

The RECORD property allows the association of arbitrary data records to entities. The only restriction is that the elements in these records have to be of type PREDEFINED. Such records may be interrogated by special application programs. Records may be subject to a record type restriction given by a by a reference to a RECORD_TYPE entity. The entries in record must then correspond in sequence with the corresponding type identification in the RECORD_TYPE identified by the attribute ident. If no RECORD_TYPE reference is given then the RECORD entity must be referenced by an INDEX_ENTRY so that application programs can distinguish between different types of associated records.

5.14.2.2 RECORD_TYPE

```
ENTITY RECORD_TYPE = STRUCTURE
                      (* must be referenced by an INDEX_ENTRY *)
                      descriptor : LIST OF TYPE_ID;
                     END;
```

```
                                                              *
<record_type> ::=  RECORD_TYPE ( name : [<type_id> [, <type_id>]  ] );
```

A RECORD_TYPE entity may impose type restrictions on Records. An entity of this type must be referenced by an INDEX_ENTRY so that application programs can distinguish between different types of records.

5.14.3 Interfacing with other data bases (not CAD data bases)

5.14.3.1 DATA_BASE_BRIDGE

```
ENTITY DATA_BASE_BRIDGE = STRUCTURE
                            description : STRING;
                            (* when in use the DATA_BASE_BRIDGE
                               will be bound to a data base that is
                               a CAD data base according to this
                               reference model, but rather a general
                               purpose data base *)
                          END;

<data_base_bridge> ::=  DATA_BASE_BRIDGE ( name : string ) ;
```

A data base bridge allows to allocate general purpose data bases in which administrative data, organisational data, or any other data related to CAD entities may be stored.

5.14.3.2 DATA_BASE_LINK

```
ENTITY DATA_BASE_LINK =
              STRUCTURE
                object          : REFERENCE(GEOMETRIC);
                data_base       : REFERENCE(DATA_BASE_BRIDGE);
                additional_data : LIST OF USER_DEFINED_NAME;
                aspect          : [REF_ANY(ASPECT)] ;
              END;

<data_base_link> ::=  DATA_BASE_LINK ( name :  name , name ,
                        <user_defined_name_list> , [name])  ;
```

A data base link establishes a relation between a geometric object in the CAD data base and some information in the referenced data base. The information in the data base is identified by a list of user-defined names, but the type of information is not specified. Special programs or a human user may imply the type of information from the aspect.

5.15 PARAMETRIC MODELING

5.15.1 PREDEFINED

```
ENTITY PREDEFINED_ENTITY = CLASS( REAL,INTEGER );

<predefined_entity> ::= <real> | <integer>

<predefined> ::= real | integer | string | user_def | logical
```

PREDEFINED is the class of predefined data types: REAL, INTEGER, STRING (of arbitrary, possibly implementation dependent, maximum length), USER_DEFINED_NAME (with arbitrary length), and LOGICAL.

In this specification, only REAL and INTEGER data may appear as entities.

The USER_DEFINED_NAME is similar to a string except that it does not allow blank, delimiters, or escape sequences (only upper case and lower case letters and digits are allowed.

5.15.2 INTEGER

```
ENTITY INTEGER = STRUCTURE
                   value : INTEGER;
                 END;

<integer> ::= INTEGER ( name : integer ) ;
```

A INTEGER entity represents an integer value in the form of an entity: It may be referenced from other entities, it may have an index entry and an integer expression associated.

5.15.3 INTEGER_EXPRESSION

```
PROPERTY INTEGER_EXPRESSION =
           STRUCTURE
             value       : REF_ONLY(INTEGER);
             consistency : LOGICAL;
             update_mode : UPDATE;
             expression  : ARITHMETIC_EXPRESSION;
           END;
```

```
<integer_expression> ::= INTEGER_EXPRESSION ( name , logical ,
                             <update> , <arith_expression> ) ;
```

An INTEGER_EXPRESSION property indicates that the referenced real entity is in fact the value of an arithmetic expression.

The consistency attribute indicates whether that value is consistent with the present expression; the update_mode indicates when updating of value is to occur: Updating may occur whenever the expression (the construct) is modified (in which case consistency will always be true); or when the entity is used in an application while consistency was found to be false (in which case any modification of the construct will not cause reevaluation but will just set consistency to false. The subsequent evaluation will set consistency to true again); or else, evaluation (and setting consistency to true) will occur only upon explicit request by the user). The expression contains an ARITHMETIC_EXPRESSION (see "Arithmetic expressions" on page 162 for the syntax) which represents an arithmetic expression consistent with FORTRAN77 notation except that FORTRAN variables are replaced by references to INTEGER entities.

5.15.4 REAL

```
ENTITY REAL = STRUCTURE
                value : REAL;
              END;

<real> ::= REAL ( name : real ) ;
```

A REAL entity represents a real value in the form of an entity: It may be referenced from other entities, it may have an index entry and a real expression associated.

5.15.5 REAL_EXPRESSION

```
PROPERTY REAL_EXPRESSION =  STRUCTURE
                              value       : REF_ONLY(REAL);
                              consistency : LOGICAL;
                              update_mode : UPDATE;
                              expression  : ARITHMETIC_EXPRESSION;
                            END;
```

```
<real_expression> ::= REAL_EXPRESSION ( name , logical , <update> ,
                      <arith_expression> ) ;
```

A REAL_EXPRESSION property indicates that the referenced real entity is in fact the value of an arithmetic expression.

The consistency attribute indicates whether that value is consistent with the present expression; the update_mode indicates when updating of value is to occur: Updating may occur whenever the expression (the construct) is modified (in which case consistency will always be true); or when the entity is used in an application while consistency was found to be false (in which case any modification of the construct will not cause reevaluation but will just set consistency to false. The subsequent evaluation will set consistency to true again); or else, evaluation (and setting consistency to true) will occur only upon explicit request by the user. The expression contains an ARITHMETIC_EXPRESSION (see "Arithmetic expressions" on page 162 for the syntax) which represents an arithmetic expression consistent with FORTRAN77 notation except that FORTRAN variables are replaced by references to REAL entities.

5.15.6 MACRO

```
ENTITY MACRO = GENERIC (d : GEOMETRIC)
                STRUCTURE
                (*must be referenced by an INDEX_ENTRY*)
          SCOPE;
                FORMAL_PARAMETER;
                INTEGER;
                REAL;
                POINT(DIM);
                DIRECTION(DIM);
                PLACEMENT(DIM);
                CURVE(DIM);
                SURFACE;
                SOLID_MODEL;
                COMPONENT;
                ROUTINE;
                ASSEMBLY;
                RECORD_TYPE;
                RECORD;
                INDEX_ENTRY;
                MATERIAL;
          END_SCOPE;
                  result       : REF_ONLY(d);
                END;
```

```
<macro> ::= MACRO ( name : OPEN ) ;
          SCOPE;
               [<formal_parameter> | <real> | <point(dim)> |
                <direction(dim)> | <placement(dim)> | <curve(dim)> |
                <surface> | <solid_model> | <component> | <routine> |
                <assembly> | <record_type> | <record> | <index_entry> |
                <material>]*
          END_SCOPE;
             MACRO_RESULT ( name ) ;
           MACRO ( name , CLOSE ) ;
```

A macro is a special entity that can be used only for producing new geometric entities in an application of the CAD system. For this purpose the user will have to invoke the macro and associate actually existing entities to the formal parameter entities. The CAD system will then produce as a result a geometric entity which will be stored as the application desires. The algorithm that produces the result is stored in the macro in the form of a data structure (not as a sequence of commands). A typical application of the MACRO facility would be the generation of a pattern of holes which could be circular or rectangular depending on the actual parameter passed during invocation.

All macros need a user-defined name to be associated with them. The result must refer to an entity in the macro scope. References in macros and only in macros may be to FORMAL_PARAMETER entities.

5.15.7 ROUTINE

```
ENTITY ROUTINE = STRUCTURE
                     (* must be referenced by an INDEX_ENTRY*)
          SCOPE;
               FORMAL_PARAMETER;
          END_SCOPE;
                     library      : REFERENCE(ROUTINE_LIBRARY);
                     descriptor   : TYPE_ID;
               END;

<routine> ::= ROUTINE ( name : OPEN ) ;
          SCOPE;
               [<formal_parameter>]*
          END_SCOPE;
               ROUTINE_RESULT ( name , <type_id> ) ;
             ROUTINE ( name , CLOSE ) ;
```

See ROUTINE_LIBRARY. A routine is characterized by its formal parameters which will be substituted by entities of the proper type when the routine is invoked during an application. Furthermore, the routine has as attribute a reference to the routine library in which it is to be searched for, and it carries the type identification of the result in order to guarantee that the result type is correct. The name of the routine inside the library is stored as a user_defined_name in an index_entry referring to this entity. Results of the routines may be of type real or geometric.

5.15.8 FORMAL_PARAMETER

```
ENTITY FORMAL_PARAMETER = STRUCTURE
                            user_defined_name : USER_DEFINED_NAME;
                            descriptor        : TYPE_ID;
                          END;

<formal_parameter> ::=  FORMAL_PARAMETER  ( name :
                          user_defined_name , <type_id> ) ;
```

See MACRO and ROUTINE. Formal parameters are characterized by a user-defined name and a type to facilitate proper binding of actual entities to these formal parameters when the MACRO or ROUTINE is invoked in an application.

5.16 EXTENSIONS OF THE REFERENCE MODEL UNDER CONSIDERATION

5.16.1 POLY_CURVE

```
ENTITY POLY_CURVE = GENERIC (d : DIM)
              STRUCTURE
                degree   : INTEGER;
                rational : LOGICAL;
                x_coeff  : LIST OF REAL; (* 1..degree *)
                y_coeff  : LIST OF REAL; (* 1..degree *)
                CASE d OF
                  D3: (z_coeff : LIST OF REAL); (* 1..degree *)
                  D2: (z_coeff : NIL);
                END;
                weights  : LIST OF REAL;  (* 1..degree *)
               END;
```

```
<poly_curve(dim)> ::= <poly_curve(d2)> | <poly_curve(d3)>

<poly_curve(d2)> ::= POLY_CURVE ( name :  integer, logical ,
                     <real_list> , <real_list> , <real_list> ) ;

<poly_curve(d3)> ::= POLY_CURVE ( name :  integer, logical ,
                     <real_list> , <real_list> , <real_list> ,
                     <real_list> ) ;
```

The attribute degree has the value K.
The attribute x_coeff contains the K+1 x-coefficients for i = 0..K.
The attribute y_coeff contains the K+1 y-coefficients for i = 0..K.
The attribute z_coeff contains the K+1 z-coefficients for i = 0..K.
The attribute weights contains the w_i i = 0..K.

1. If rational=.T. then the curve is given by:

$$\mathbf{r}(u) = \frac{\sum_{i=0}^{K} w_i \mathbf{r}_i u^i}{\sum_{i=0}^{K} w_i u^i}$$

2. If rational = .F. then the denominator is one and so:

$$\mathbf{r}(u) = \sum_{i=0}^{K} \mathbf{r}_i u^i$$

5.16.2 POLY_SURFACE

```
ENTITY POLY_SURFACE =
          STRUCTURE
           rational : LOGICAL;
           u_degree : INTEGER;
           v_degree : INTEGER;
           x_coeff  : LIST OF REAL;(* 0..u_degree,
                                      0..v_degree  *)
           y_coeff  : LIST OF REAL;(* 0..u_degree,
                                      0..v_degree  *)
           z_coeff  : LIST OF REAL;(* 0..u_degree,
                                      0..v_degree  *)
           weights  : LIST OF REAL;(* 0..u_degree,
                                      0..v_degree  *)
          END;

<poly_surface> ::= POLY_SURFACE ( name : logical ,
                                  integer , integer ,
                                  <real_list> , <real_list> ,
                                  <real_list> , <real_list> ,  ) ;
```

The attribute u_degree has the value K1
The attribute v_degree has the value K2
The attribute x_coeff contains the (K1+1)(K2+1) x-coefficients for i = 0..K1 and j =0..K2 with the i-index changing first.
The attribute y_coeff contains the (K1+1)(K2+1) y-coefficients for i = 0..K1 and j =0..K2 with the i-index changing first.
The attribute z_coeff contains the (K1+1)(K2+1) z-coefficients for i = 0..K1 and j =0..K2 with the i-index changing first.
The attribute x_coeff contains the (K1+1)(K2+1) weights $w_{i,j}$ for i = 0..K1 and j =0..K1 with the i-index changing first.

1. If rational=.T. then the curve is given by:

$$\mathbf{r}(u,v) = \frac{\sum_{i=0}^{K1} \sum_{j=0}^{K2} w_{i,j} \mathbf{r}_{i,j} u^i v^j}{\sum_{i=0}^{K1} \sum_{j=0}^{K2} w_{i,j} u^i v^j} \qquad \text{with } 0 \le u,v \le 1$$

2. If rational = .F. then the surface is given by:

$$\mathbf{r}(u,v) = \sum_{i=0}^{K1} \sum_{j=0}^{K2} \mathbf{r}_{i,j} u^i v^j$$

3. This surface type corresponds to the POLY_CURVE and may be deleted at a later date)

5.16.3 Presentation of line geometry

The following entities and properties for specifying the display of line representations are based on a DIN proposal for the STEP standard presented in June 1987. The specification cannot be considered as complete; e.g. the colour tables are not included yet. Furthermore, the description of the meaning of all the attributes is not given. Nothing is said so far how entities in the scope of other entities inherit rendering properties or associations to rendering bundles. Hence, the reader should take this information merely as an indication of the method to be used for including rendering information in the model.

```
PROPERTY RENDER_POLYLINE = STRUCTURE
  object                      : REF_ONLY( GEOMETRIC );
  linetype                    : INTEGER;
  linewidth_scale_factor      : REAL;
  polyline_colour_index       : INTEGER;
  colour_table                : REF_ANY( RENDER_COLOUR_TABLE );
                              END;

ENTITY  RENDER_POLYLINE_BUNDLE  = STRUCTURE
  linetype                    : INTEGER;
  linewidth_scale_factor      : REAL;
  polyline_colour_index       : INTEGER;
  colour_table                : REF_ANY( RENDER_COLOUR_TABLE );
                              END;

PROPERTY RENDER_POLYMARKER = STRUCTURE
  object                      : REF_ONLY( GEOMETRIC );
  polymarker_index            : REF_ANY( RENDER_POLYMARKER_BUNDLE );
  marker_type                 : INTEGER;
  marker_size_scale_factor    : REAL;
  colour_table                : REF_ANY( RENDER_COLOUR_TABLE );
                              END;

ENTITY  RENDER_POLYMARKER_BUNDLE  = STRUCTURE
  polymarker_index            : REF_ANY( RENDER_POLYMARKER_BUNDLE );
  marker_type                 : INTEGER;
  marker_size_scale_factor    : REAL;
  colour_table                : REF_ANY( RENDER_COLOUR_TABLE );
                              END;
```

```
PROPERTY RENDER_SEGMENT = STRUCTURE
  object                     : REF_ONLY( GEOMETRIC );
  highlighting               : LOGICAL;
  detectability              : LOGICAL;
  visibility                 : LOGICAL;
  priority                   : INTEGER:
                           END;

ENTITY ONE_VIEW         = STRUCTURE
  window_in_world            : LIST OF POINT(D3); (* 4 points*)
  eye_point                  : POINT(D3);
  u_vector                   : POINT(D3);
  v_vector                   : POINT(D3);
  front_clipp_plane          : REAL;
  back_clipp_plane           : REAL;
  projected_origin           : POINT(D2);
                           END;

PROPERTY RENDER_ASSOCIATION =
              STRUCTURE
         object          : REFERENCE( GEOMETRIC );
         display_markers : REF_ONLY ( RENDER_POLYMARKER_BUNDLE);
         display_lines   : REF_ONLY ( RENDER_POLYLINE_BUNDLE);
         aspect          : [REF_ANY(ASPECT)] ;
              END;
```

6. LEVELS OF SCHEMA IMPLEMENTATIONS

As CAD systems provide different levels of capabilities one cannot expect all systems to support the full schema in their pre- and post-processors. On the other hand, it must not be left to the choice of the implementer of processors which subset of entities and attribute he wants to support. Thus, this specification includes a definition of allowable subsets of the complete schema. These allowable subsets are characterized by a set of numbers, called levels. Such levels are used to identify

1. the geometric modeling capabilities (l_g),
2. the capabilities of defining assembly structures (l_a),
3. the capabilities for parametric models and macros (l_p),
4. the capabilities for references (l_r).

6.1 THE GEOMETRIC MODELING LEVELS

6.1.1 Two-dimensional wireframes

On this level, no entities of type SOLID_MODEL, SURFACE, and D3 are available. Also, entities which can occur only within the scope of these entities are not available. DIM is restricted to D2 only.
This level is identified by $l_g = 0$.

6.1.2 Three-dimensional wireframes

On this level, no entities of type SOLID_MODEL and SURFACE are available. Also, entities which can occur only within the scope of these entities are not available.
This level is identified by $l_g = 1$.

6.1.3 Surface models

On this level, no entities of type SOLID_MODEL are available. Also, entities which can occur only within the scope of SOLID_MODEL entities are not available.
This level is identified by $l_g = 2$.

6.1.4 Single modeling type solids

Level $l_g = 3$ indicates solid modelers that do not support all modeling techniques. We distinguish between

a) pure CSG modelers,
b) polyhedron modelers, and
c) B-rep systems with exact surface treatment.

6.1.4.1 Pure CSG models

On this level, no entities of type B_REP and POLY_HEDRON are available.
This level is identified by $l_g = 3a$.

6.1.4.2 Pure POLY_HEDRON models

On this level, no entities of type B_REP and CONSTRUCT are available.
This level is identified by $l_g = 3b$.

6.1.4.3 Pure boundary representation models

On this level, no entities of type CONSTRUCT are available. Also, entities which can occur only within the scope of CONSTRUCT entities (such as BOX) are not available.
This level is identified by $l_g = 3c$.

6.1.5 Hybrid models

On this level, all capabilities provided by B_REP entities, POLY_HEDRON entities, and CONSTRUCT entities are available.
This level is identified by $l_g = 4$.

6.1.6 Full geometric capabilities

The full capabilities, including the COMPOUND_B_REP, are characterized by $l_g = 5$.

6.2 THE ASSEMBLY STRUCTURE

6.2.1 No assembly structure

On this level, no entities of type ASSEMBLY and COMPONENT are available. This level is identified by $l_a = 0$.

6.2.2 Assembly structure with three levels

Entities of type ASSEMBLY may not be nested. The only hierarchy allowed is

1. world,
2. assembly,
3. component.

This level is identified by $l_a = 3$.

6.2.3 Full assembly structure

In a full implementation, the nesting of levels of assemblies is restricted such that (including world and component) the maximum nesting level is eight. A possible but not necessary interpretation corresponds to the following hierarchy:

1. world,
2. product family
   Assemblies in the world scope are to be interpreted as representations different product families
3. product
   Assemblies in the first assembly level scope are to be interpreted as representations different products within a product family.

4. design version
   Assemblies in the second assembly level scope are to be interpreted as representations of different (optional) design versions of a product.
5. assembly group
   Assemblies in the next assembly level scope are to be interpreted as representations of different "assemblies" (in a mechanical engineering sense) that constitute an operational group within the whole product.
6. assembly
   The next level is the "assembly" as an engineer would interpret the term.
7. subassembly
   The next level is group of components that belongs together.
8. component.
   This is the level where geometry is defined.

The ASSEMBLY entity is used to represent levels 2 to 7 of this hierarchy. This level is identified by $l_a = 8$.

6.3 PARAMETRIC MODELS AND MACROS

6.3.1 No parametric models, no macros

On this level, the specification of the attribute type ANY must be replaced by the type TYPE itself. Hence, the specification of the attribute type ANY as given in the reference schema must be replaced by:

```
ATTRIBUTE ANY = GENERIC (type: PREDEFINED )
          CLASS( type, REF_ANY(type) );
```

On this level, no entities of type PREDEFINED are available.
On this level, no entities of type MACRO or FORMAL_PARAMETER are available.
This level is identified by $l_p = 0$.

6.3.2 Only one parametric capability

This level is indicated by l_p = 1a and 1b.

6.3.2.1 Parametric models only

On this level, no entities of type MACRO or FORMAL_PARAMETER and ROUTINE are available.
This level is identified by $l_p = 1a$.

6.3.2.2 Macro capabilities only

On this level, no entities of type PREDEFINED and ROUTINE are available.
This level is identified by $l_p = 1b$.

6.3.3 Full parametric capabilities

The full capabilities (entities of type PREDEFINED, MACRO, and ROUTINE) as described by the reference schema are characterized by the level $l_p = 2$.

6.4 REFERENCES

6.4.1 No external references, no library references

On this level, no attributes of type REF_EXTERNAL and REF_PART_LIBRARY are available.
This level is identified by $l_r = 0$.

6.4.2 No external references

On this level, no attribute of type REF_EXTERNAL are available.
This level is identified by $l_r = 1$.

6.4.3 No library references

On this level, no attribute of type REF_PART_LIBRARY is available.
This level is identified by $l_r = 2$.

6.4.4 Full referencing capabilities

The full capabilities as described by the reference schema are characterized by the level $l_r = 3$.

7. THE PHYSICAL LAYER

The physical layer of the CAD*I neutral file for solids describes how the CAD system data structures are mapped onto a sequential file. There are several levels of regarding the same sequential file:

1. the physical level,
2. the metafile level,
3. the alphabet level,
4. the token level,
5. the statement level, and
6. the file structure level.

7.1 THE PHYSICAL LEVEL

On the physical level we are concerned with the exchange of sequential files between computers. The content of the sequential files is irrelevant on this level.

7.1.1 Tape characteristics

If a magnetic tape is used for transferring the file, it has to have the following characteristics:

- 9 tracks,
- 1600 bits per inch,
- industry standard, no label,
- fixed logical records with a length of 80 bytes grouped into
- fixed physical blocks of 800 bytes length.

The last block on the file has to be padded with space characters if needed.

7.1.2 File transfer via computer networks

Any protocol that allows the transfer of sequential files may be used to communicate a CAD*I neutral file from one computer to another. No restrictions are made with respect to block lengths.

7.2 THE METAFILE LEVEL

According to the CAD*I project conventions, all neutral files consist of card image format sequential files. This means that they may be considered as a sequence of logical records of 80 bytes length where each byte contains the binary representation of the decimal coded alphabet. All CAD*I metafiles have a common format.

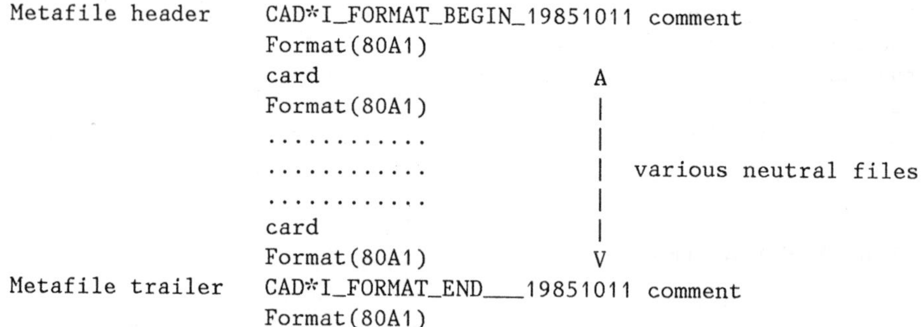

```
Metafile header    CAD*I_FORMAT_BEGIN_19851011 comment
                   Format(80A1)
                   card                       A
                   Format(80A1)               |
                   ............               |
                   ............               | various neutral files
                   ............               |
                   card                       |
                   Format(80A1)               V
Metafile trailer   CAD*I_FORMAT_END___19851011 comment
                   Format(80A1)
```

The first and the last card of the file are called the header and the trailer. Together, they constitute an *envelope* for the neutral file which they contain. Thus, a CAD*I metafile can contain any number of similar or different neutral files. It is, thus, possible to transmit on a single CAD*I metafile neutral files that were written according to different formats (such as IGES, SET, or VDA-FS), but also computer graphics files and text files, in addition to neutral files for solids. It is even possible that these different files carry information regarding the same technical product. Post-processors can then combine the information from the different files into the same data base provided that these files and the processors support the external referencing feature (see "Libraries and External References" on page 14) and user-defined names (see "User-defined name" on page 13) in a consistent way.

The neutral file specified in this document has the following general format:

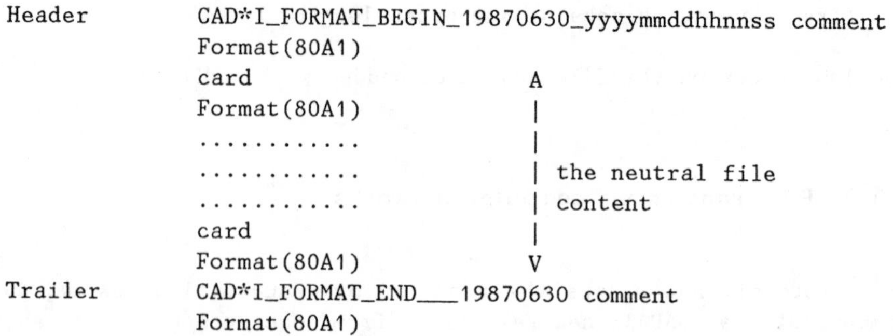

```
Header     CAD*I_FORMAT_BEGIN_19870630_yyyymmddhhnnss comment
           Format(80A1)
           card                       A
           Format(80A1)               |
           ............               |
           ............               | the neutral file
           ............               | content
           card                       |
           Format(80A1)               V
Trailer    CAD*I_FORMAT_END___19870630 comment
           Format(80A1)
```

where

- versdate. is the year, month, and day of registration of the neutral format specification at the CAD*I project management.
- yyyy is the year,
- mm is the month,
- dd is the day,
- hh is the hour,
- nn is the minute, and
- ss is the second of the local calendar time when the pre-processor began to write this particular record.
- comment is an arbitrary text which should, at least, indicate the organisation where the neutral file was generated.

Another useful neutral file that may be used in connection with the one defined in this document is the neutral file for fixed format letters. This file has been defined previously in the CAD*I project and is described in "Appendix D. A neutral file for fixed format letters" on page 225.

A description of a letter to precede a neutral file you find in " 13. Comments on pre-processors" on page 195.

7.3 THE ALPHABET LEVEL

On the alphabet level, the neutral file may be considered as a continuous stream of symbols from the basic alphabet.

The alphabet of the CAD*I/WG2 neutral file language, is defined as a set of bytes with integer values from 32 to 126. The standard "ISO 6937/2 1983(E)" defines the correspondence of the neutral file alphabet onto graphical representation on paper and terminals as far as hardware can accommodate such transformation from code to graphics. In this document the correspondence will be according to "Appendix A. The graphical alphabet" on page 213. To define the syntax of the neutral file language, only the graphical representation is used, where G(i) denotes the graphical representation of the byte with the decimal value i.
The symbol pair {{ }} denotes a set consisting of the elements listed inside this pair of double curly brackets.

```
space     =   {{ SPACE }}
digit     =   {{ 0 1 2 3 4 5 6 7 8 9 }}
lower     =   {{ a b c d e f g h i j k l m n o p q r s t u v w x y z
                 \ G(94) { G(96) } | [ ] ~ }}
upper     =   {{ A B C D E F G H I J K L M N O P Q R S T U V W X Y Z _ }}
special   =   {{ ! " # ¤ % & ' ( ) * + , . / :  ; < = > ? }}
```

Besides G(96) and G(94) denote the graphical representation of 'grave accent' and 'circumflex accent'. The graphical alphabet G denotes the union of the five sets defined above:

G = space + digit + lower + upper + special

7.4 TOKENS OF THE NEUTRAL FILE LANGUAGE

On the token level, the neutral file is considered as a sequence of tokens. The tokens can be formally defined by a regular set R(G) over the graphical alphabet. Besides, a regular set over the set G is defined as follows:

- each finite subset (especially the empty set) of the alphabet is in R(G)
- with the empty word e the set {{e}} is in R(G)
- if X,Y in R(G) then X+Y in R(G), where X+Y is defined as follows: X + Y = {{ z| z in X OR z in Y }}
- if X,Y in R(G) then XY in R(G), where XY is defined as follows: X & Y = XY = {{xy| x in X AND y in Y }} the set X & Y is denoted as the concatenation of X and Y.
- if X in R(G) then $[X]^*$ in R(G) where $[X]^*$ is defined as follows: $[X]^*$ = {{e}} + X + XX + XXX +.......
- if X in R(G) then [X] in R(G) where [X] is defined as follows: [X] = {{e}} + X
- if X in R(G) then $[X]^+$ in R(G) where $[X]^+$ is defined as follows: $[X]^+ = X(X^*)$

The precedence of the operations is (in decreasing order):

$[...]^*$ for arbitrary (including zero) repetition
$[...]^+$ for repetition with at least one occurrence
\+ for union
& for concatenation

Brackets are used in the usual way.
So, with (X,Y in R(G)), (X + Y) & Y is also a regular set.

In the following token definition all sets with only one element are denoted by this element. For example, if X is regular over the alphabet, and the character "a" is an element of the alphabet, then Xa and (X & a) (or aX and (a & X), respectively) denote the set resulting from concatenating an element from X with "a" (or "a" with an element from X, respectively).

It is easy to check that all the sets defined below are regular over the graphical alphabet G, where G is defined above.

Prior to the formal definition of tokens we specify:

- The space character delimits tokens except in strings where it is treated as a significant character. In other words, no token except the string may contain space characters.

```
comment       = (* a sequence over the graphical alphabet,
                   but the subsequence *) may not occur
                   in this character sequence  *)

delimiter     = {{ !: :! }} + special + keyword

keyword       = OPEN + CLOSE + SCOPE + END_SCOPE +
                {{ all keywords indicating attribute,
                   property, and entity types, also
                   the enumeration data type values and
                   the keywords indicating the header and
                   result section of entities with scope } }

sign          = {{ + }} + {{ - }}

integer       = [sign ][digit]+

real          = [digit]*.[digit]*[E integer]

number        = integer + real

letter        = upper + lower

alpha_num     = [ letter + digit ]+

name          = #alpha_num

user_def_name = "alpha_num"

char_set_sel  = {{ ISO6937 + GREEK + KANJI }}

esc_code      = integer + char_set_sel

esc_string    = esc_code [, esc_code ]*

esc_seq       = !: esc_string :! + !:!:

character     = letter + digit + special

string_char   = character \{{ ' !: }}

string_seq    = [ string_char + esc_seq ]+

string        = '[string_seq]*[''[string_seq]]*'
```

```
logical         =  .T. + .F.

token           =  name + user_def_name + number + string + logical +
                   delimiter + (comment & token)
```

Note, that the present neutral file specification could have been formulated without including a facility for escape sequences. However, if at any time in the future escape sequences are required it is necessary to take this possible extension into account at this time. Otherwise, upward compatibility of the previously written files could not be guaranteed. The consequence of this is that in a string the character sequence !: must be expressed by an escape sequence. The standard escape sequence for this is !:!:.

It is anticipated that future specification may require more powerful referencing mechanisms in the sense that user-defined names may have to be qualified. This could be achieved by replacing the above definition of the user-defined name token by

```
upper_scope     = {{ * }}
world_scope     = {{ ** }}
                                  *
scope_select    = [upper_scope.]  upper_scope + world_scope
                              +
qualifier       = [alpha_num.]
user_def_name   = "[scope_select] [qualifier] alpha_num"
```

Here,

1. "*" indicates the enclosing scope. This is the entity in whose scope the entity which contains this token is embedded.
2. "**" indicates the outermost scope: the world which contains this token.

Another extension of the tokens may be required when in later version of the specification more general (qualified) referencing may become necessary. In anticipation of such needs we define the token

```
                              +
qualified_name     = [ name . ]  name
```

7.4.1 Arithmetic expressions

The syntax of arithmetic expressions is as in FORTRAN77. However, the "variables" of a FORTRAN arithmetic expression are replaced by references to entities of type REAL or INTEGER.

The semantics of the arithmetic expressions is as in FORTRAN77.

```
<arithmetic_expression>  ::= [<sign>]number | [<sign>]name |
                             [<sign>]<ref_external>      |
                             [<sign>]( <sum> )           |
                             [<sign>]<function>

   <sum>                 ::= <term>[<sign><term>]*

   <sign>                ::= + | -

   <term>                ::= <factor>[<times_by><factor>]*

   <times_by>            ::= * | /

   <factor>              ::= <arithmetic_expression>
                              [**<arithmetic_expression>]

   <function>            ::= <function_1>(<sum>)         |
                             <function_2>(<sum>,<sum>) |
                             <function_n>(<sum>,<sum>[,<sum>]*)

   <function_1>          ::= INT   | REAL  | AINT  | ABS   | SQRT  |
                             EXP   | EXP2  | EXP10 | LOG   | LOG10 |
                             LOG2  | SIN   | COS   | TAN   | COTAN |
                             ASIN  | ACOS  | ATAN  | SINH  | COSH  | TANH

   <function_2>          ::= MOD   | SIGN  | DIM

   <function_n>          ::= MAX   | MIN
```

7.5 THE STATEMENT LEVEL

7.5.1 Basic statement productions

The neutral file content may be regarded as a sequence of "statements". Each statement is identified by a mnemonic keyword and may be followed by an argument list in parentheses. Statements are separated by the ";" delimiter. Arguments are enclosed in parentheses and separated from each other by the "," separator. Space characters and comments are not significant between tokens and are to be ignored. Hence, on this level, the neutral file may be defined as follows:

```
<neutral_file_content> ::= [<statement>]*
```

```
<statement>            ::= <entity_statement> | <property_statement>

<entity_statement>     ::= keyword(name :<argument_list>);

<property_statement>   ::= keyword(      <argument_list>);

<argument_list>        ::= [<argument>] [,[<argument>] ]*

<argument>             ::= OPEN | CLOSE | number  | string | name |
                           user_defined_name | <named_attribute> |
                           <structured_attribute> | <attribute_list>

<named_attribute>      ::= keyword <structured_attribute>

<structured_attribute> ::= ( <argument_list> )

<attribute_list>       ::= ( [ <argument> [ , <argument> ]* ] )
```

The purpose of introducing this statement level is the following:

1. Each statement on the file may be considered as a complete piece of information to be treated by the post-processor as one unit. After processing of a statement, the post-processor must return to a state that is consistent with the state list description in " 9. State lists" on page 181.

2. The formal transformation from the data structure layer to the physical layer will be described such that the fundamental concept of an entity will map onto one or more statements. In particular, if an entity has no scope it will be represented as a single statement on the neutral file (see "Rules for translating from the HDSL into BNF").

7.6 RULES FOR TRANSLATING FROM THE HDSL INTO BNF

The file structure specification is split into two parts: The overall file syntax is defined in "Structure of the neutral file language" on page 168, while the detailed syntax of all the entity and property records is given together with the data structure specification in " 5. The CAD*I reference model specification" on page 43 starting with the <world> as the target symbol.

The translation from a data specification into the corresponding BNF production set following these general rules:

1. Simple structure attribute definitions:

A structure attribute definition is called simple, if the corresponding attribute type is not a composite type (see "Fixed structure type" on page 25). Each simple structure attribute definition

```
attr : ATTRIBUTE_TYPE
```

where ATTRIBUTE_TYPE is either a type name, or a type_instance is translated into the nonterminal

```
<attribute_type>
```

The nonterminal <attribute_type> is derived from ATTRIBUTE_TYPE as follows:

> if ATTRIBUTE_TYPE is not a predefined type name then each capital letter of ATTRIBUTE_TYPE is replaced by the corresponding lower letter, and finally this new name will be enclosed by the characters '<' and '>'. For example, the type POINT(D2) (see "POINT" on page 58) is translated in <point(d2)>. If ATTRIBUTE_TYPE denotes one of the predefined types INTEGER, REAL, USER_DEFINED_NAME, STRING or LOGICAL, then ATTRIBUTE_TYPE is translated into the corresponding tokens. If ATTRIBUTE_TYPE denotes the predefined type ARITHMETIC_EXPRESSION, then ATTRIBUTE_TYPE is translated into <arithmetic_expression> (see "Arithmetic expressions" on page 162).

2. References:
   The type binding of references is ignored in the translation from HDSL to the file syntax. Hence, REFERENCE(A), REFERENCE(B), but also CLASS(REFERENCE(C), REFERENCE(D)) are translated into the same syntactical form: the token "name". Both REF_ONLY and REFERENCE become "name". The syntax (as opposed to the HDSL specification) no longer carries the information about the type of the referenced entity.

3. Composite attribute definitions:
   The structure attribute definition of attr0, with

```
attr0 : STRUCTURE
        attr1 : A;
        attr2 : [B];
        attr3 : C;
        attr4 : [D];
        END;
```

is translated into (<a> , [<b>] , <c> , [<d>]) .

Trailing commas without attribute values in between them may be dropped. Hence, (<a> , , <c> ,) and (<a> , , <c>) are all valid representations of the same structured attribute.

The attribute definition of attr1, with

```
attr1 : CLASS( A , B , C );
```

is translated into the nonterminal <attr1> and the production <attr1> ::= <a> | <b> | <c> .

The attribute definition of attr2, with

```
attr2 : LIST OF A;
```

is translated into the nonterminal <attr2> and the production
<attr2> ::= [<a>]*.

4. Productions for properties and unscoped entities

```
ENTITY A = STRUCTURE
             attr1 : A;
             attr2 : [B];
             attr3 : C;
             attr4 : [D];
             END;
```

is translated into the production

```
<a> ::= A ( name : <a> , [<b>] , <c> [, <d>] ) ;  |
        A ( name : <a> , [<b>] , <c> ) ;
```

```
ATTRIBUTE P = ENUM(s1,s2);

ENTITY A    = GENERIC (x:P)
                 STRUCTURE
                   attr1 : A(s1);
                   CASE x OF
                    s1 : (attr21 : B);
                    s2 : (attr22 : C);
                   END;
                 END;
```

is translated into the productions

```
<a(p)>  ::=  <a(s1)> | <a(s2)>
<a(s1)> ::=  A ( name: <a(s1)> , <b> ) ;
<a(s2)> ::=  A ( name: <a(s1)> , <c> ) ;
```

```
PROPERTY A = STRUCTURE
                attr1 : A;
                attr2 : [B];
                attr3 : C;
                attr4 : [D];
             END;
```

is translated into the production

```
<a> ::= A ( <a> , [<b>] , <c> [, <d>] ) ; |
        A ( <a> , [<b>] , <c> ) ;
```

```
ATTRIBUTE P = CLASS(INTEGER,REAL);

PROPERTY A  = GENERIC (x:P)
                STRUCTURE
                  attr1 : A;
                  attr2 : x;
                  attr3 : C;
                END;
```

is translated into the productions

```
<a(p)>       ::=  <a(integer)> | <a(real)>
<a(integer)> ::=  A ( <a> , integer ) ;
<a(real)>    ::=  A ( <a> , real ) ;
```

5. Productions for entities containing a scope section:

   Such entities are translated into the productions

```
<keyword> ::=
      keyword ( name : OPEN ) ;
         [<header_section>]
         SCOPE ;
           list of productions for the contained
           entities and properties
           in arbitrary sequence except that they
           must obey the rule of backward referencing.
         END_SCOPE ;
         [<result_section>]
      keyword ( name , CLOSE ) ;

<header_section> ::= keyword_HEADER ( <argument_list> ) ;

<result_section> ::= keyword_RESULT ( <argument_list> ) ;
```

6. Productions for named attributes:

```
ATTR  AT = STRUCTURE
             attr1 : A;
             attr2 : [B];
             attr3 : C;
           END;
```

is translated into <at> ::= AT (<a> , [<b>] , <c>) ;

7. Productions for entities which appear in the ANY clause

   Some unscoped entities (like POINT) appear in the definition of the ANY attribute of the HDSL. These entities are implicitly defined as structured attributes. The translation is as follows: If A is specified as an unscoped entity which appears in the ANY clause, and if <a> is the corresponding production for the structured attribute A (not the entity!) then

   ANY(A) is translated into:

   <any(a)> ::= <ref_any> | a

8. Classes of entities, properties, or attributes:

   A CLASS type specification is translated into the alternative representation. Hence, if A and B are translated into <a> and <b>, then CLASS(A,B) is translated into <a>|<b>.

7.7 STRUCTURE OF THE NEUTRAL FILE LANGUAGE

The structure of the neutral file language is formal described by a context-free grammar G(N,T,P,Z), where N denotes the set of the non-terminal characters and T the set of the terminal characters. The start character Z is defined as follows:

Z = <neutral_file>

The symbols constituting the set of terminals T is defined in more detail in "Appendix A. The graphical alphabet" on page 213 and "Tokens of the neutral file language" on page 160. One can prove that the language, specified by the grammar G(N,T,P,Z) (where P is defined below) is not regular. Therefore, the treatment of this language is more complicated than in the case of the token language.

The complete syntax definition of the neutral file in BNF notation is given by the productions defined below and those which have been documented together with the reference model specification in " 5. The CAD*I reference model specification" on page 43. The BNF representation was produced from the HDSL definition by applying the rules set forth in "Rules for translating from the HDSL into BNF" on page 164. In case of conflict between the BNF representation and the HDSL representation the HDSL representation has always higher priority. The BNF representation is included in this document only for the sake of speeding up the development of processors.

```
<neutral_file>        ::= <header> <world>

<header>            ::=  HEADER(string,string,string,string,string,
                          string,[string],
                          string,string,string,string,
                          integer,integer,integer);
```

where <world> is the non-terminal defined in "WORLD" on page 46 and the meaning of the HEADER argument list is specified in "Interpreter" on page 173.

IMPLEMENTATION GUIDELINES

8. DEFINITION OF THE FINITE STATE MACHINE POST-PROCESSOR

This chapter defines the neutral file semantics by defining the effect of each statement on the file in terms of the changes which will result in the post-processor data structure. This technique is borrowed from the GKS standard. The post-processor data structure consists of a number of "state lists" defined more precisely in " 9. State lists" on page 181.

8.1 THE FINITE STATE MACHINE APPROACH

The underlying concept, based on a finite state machine, is illustrated in Figure 25 on page 174.

The components of such a machine are

- the input,
- the output, and
- the state.

Any input item entering the machine has the effect of producing

1. a change in the state of the machine and/or

2. a number (possibly zero) of output items depending on the input item and the state of the machine prior to interpreting the input item.

The semantics of an input item is defined as the effect which it will produce when received by the finite state machine.

Figure 25 on page 174 shows (in addition to the underlying concept) three different processor types:

1. the pre-processor which converts CAD data base contents into a neutral file,
2. the post-processor which converts neutral files into CAD data base content,
3. the converter which processes a neutral file and converts it into another neutral file while performing some transformation (such as elimination of certain entities).

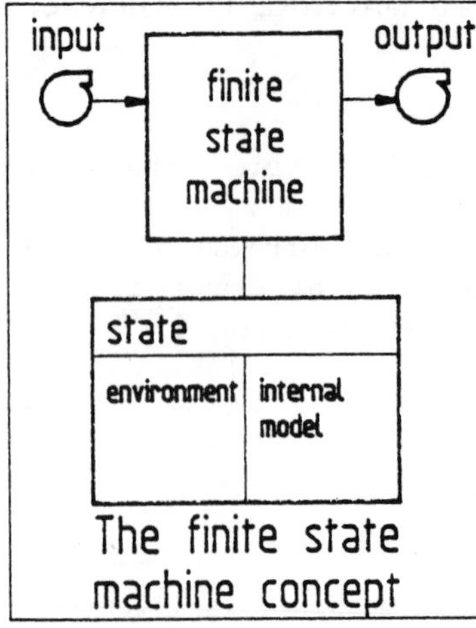

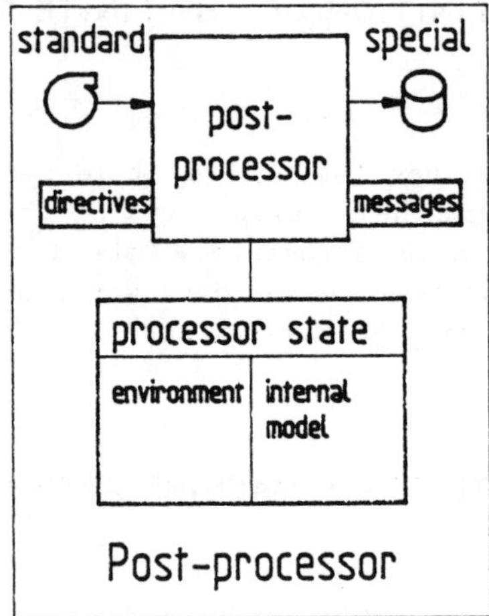

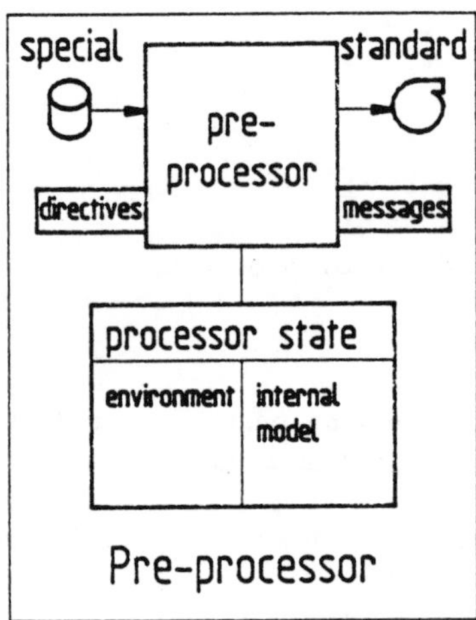

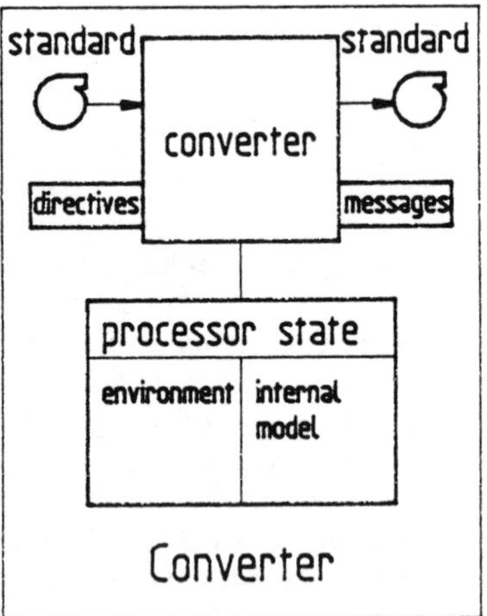

Figure 25. The finite state machine concept

8.2 INTERPRETER

8.2.1 Begin interpretation of the neutral file

```
statement: HEADER(string,string,string,string,string,
                  string,[string],
                  string,string,string,string,
```

integer,integer,integer);

state: UNDEFINED
parameters:

1 author, the person who generated the file
2 company, the full address
3 computer hardware on which the file was generated
4 operating system, full identification
5 pre-processor identification including release number
6 date and time of pre-processing,
format 'yyyymmddhhnnss' (e.g.:'19850501143601')
7 disclaimer (optional, the null string is assumed as default)
minimum schema levels required for post-processor
(see " 6. Levels of schema implementations" on page 151):
8 geometry, allowed values: '0','1','2','3a','3b,'3c','4','5'
9 assembly, allowed values: '0','3','8'
10 parametric, allowed values: '0','1a','1b','2'
11 referencing, allowed values: '0','1','2','3'
12 maximum number of digits for integers on the file
13 maximum number of significant digits in real mantissa
14 maximum number of digits for exponents

obtain directives:
- mapping rules for neutral file entities onto the receiving CAD system in cases where there is a conflict between the reference schema and the facilities provided by the receiving CAD system.

effect:
- set state to READY_FOR_INTERPRETATION
- initialize post-processor

8.3 WORLD

8.3.1 Open world

statement: WORLD(name:OPEN);

parameter: OPEN
state: READY_FOR_INTERPRETATION

obtain directives:

- identification of the receiving world in terms of the receiving operating systems' data set naming conventions
- selection of whether the receiving world exists already or has to be initialized.
- should the transferred world become a new assembly in the receiving world?

effect:
- set state WORLD_OPEN
- initialize OPEN_ENTITY(WORLD)
- if the receiving environment is not empty then copy its content into the OPEN_ENTITY(WORLD). Note, that this copying is of a conceptual nature only; in an implementation the copying process may be replaced by proper referencing of the receiving data base.
- set mode to NO_SCOPE

8.3.2 Close world

statement: WORLD(name,CLOSE);

parameter: CLOSE
state: WORLD_OPEN
mode: NO_SCOPE

effect:
- set state to READY_FOR_INTERPRETATION
- store the transferred world in the receiving data base as a new world or an assembly depending on the directive obtained when the world was opened (and stored in the post_processor_state list).

8.4 ENTITY WITH SCOPE (EXCEPT WORLD)

8.4.1 Open entity

statement: keyword (name: OPEN);

parameter: name
OPEN
state: entity_OPEN where entity is one of the entities

```
                in whose scope this new entity may exist
mode:           SCOPE
effect:         - allocate and initialize corresponding
                  open_entity_list
                - set name in open_entity_list
                - set operating state to new operating state
                  (e.g. ASSEMBLY_OPEN)
                - set mode to NO_SCOPE
                - if MACRO set macro_mode ON
```

8.4.2 Begin scope definition

statement: SCOPE;

```
parameter:      -
state:          entity_OPEN
mode:           NO_SCOPE
effect:         - set mode in open_entity_list to SCOPE
```

8.4.3 End scope definition

statement: END_SCOPE;

```
parameter:      -
state:          entity_OPEN
mode:           SCOPE
effect:         - set mode in open_entity_list to NO_SCOPE
```

8.4.4 Close entity

statement: keyword (name, CLOSE);

```
parameter:      name
                CLOSE
state:          entity_OPEN
mode:           NO_SCOPE
effect:         - store entity in corresponding entity list
                  of the enclosing entity
                - restore operating state and mode of
```

```
                 enclosing open_entity_list
               - if MACRO set macro_mode OFF
```

8.5 ENTITY WITHOUT SCOPE

```
statement     ::=    keyword ( name: <argument_list> );
    state:         entity_OPEN where entity is one of the entities
                   in whose scope this new entity may exist
    mode:          SCOPE
    parameter:     name
                   <argument_list>

    effect:        - create an entity corresponding to type keyword
                     in the corresponding entity list of the
                     open_entity_list.
                   - set mode to NO_SCOPE
                     Evaluate the attributes as defined by the argument
                     list and store them in the sequence as given by the
                     HDSL schema specification
                   - set mode to SCOPE
```

8.6 PROPERTY DEFINITION

```
statement     ::=    keyword ( <argument_list> );
    mode:          SCOPE
    parameter:     <argument_list>
    effect:        - create a property corresponding to
                     type keyword in the corresponding property
                     list of the open_entity_list.
                   - set mode to NO_SCOPE
                     Evaluate the attributes as defined by the argument
                     list and store them in the sequence as given by the
                     HDSL schema specification
                     - set mode to SCOPE
```

8.7 INTERPRETATION OF ARGUMENT LISTS (EXCEPT REFERENCES)

```
    state:         entity_OPEN where entity is one of the entities
                   in whose argument list this new type of
```

attribute exists in the proper position

mode: NO_SCOPE

effect:
- store value in the proper attribute as given by the position of each argument in the argument list

8.8 REFERENCES

syntactical form:
name
<ref_part_library>
<ref_external>

mode: NO_SCOPE

effect:
if parameter type = name then do:
- search for the entity indicated by name in the open entity lists up to the world level
- store reference to the entity found

else if parameter type = <ref_part_library> then do:
- evaluate the library reference and store

else if parameter type = <ext_library> then do:
- search for the entity indicated by the user_defined_name in the receiving data base environment
- check type consistency
- store reference to the entity found

8.9 EXAMPLES OF ERROR MESSAGES

E00001 processor not in proper state
E00002 name already exists in the scope of the enclosing_entity
E00003 receiving world does not exist
E00004 receiving environment (world or assembly depending on the obtained directive) contains entity with a user_defined_name identical to the one of an entity
E00005 name in CLOSE not equal to corresponding OPEN
E00006 referred name not found
E00007 one or more names represent entity of incorrect type
E00008 referred user_defined_name not found
E00009 one or more user_defined_names represent entity of incorrect type
E00010 parameter reference allowed in MACRO state ON only
E00011 entity/property type .... must be defined within

the SCOPE/END_SCOPE brackets

E00101 not sufficient space for storing information

E00102 receiving world provides insufficient capabilities for ..... (print missing capability)

E00201 level of nesting too high (for assembly)

E00202 More than one reference of type REF_ONLY to entity

E00203 Entity of type ..... has no index entry associated

E00204 Incorrect attribute type .... in place where attribute type ..... was expected

E00301 post-processor implementation restriction (explain)

9. STATE LISTS

All state lists are divided into three sections:

1. control section

   The control section is a storage for information which is relevant only as long as an entity is open. This section will not survive when the list is closed. Essential items in this section are the enclosing entity and its state. Also the name which was used on the neutral file to identify the entity is part of this section.

2. directory section

   The directory section contains a directory of all named entities received within the open entity from the neutral file. The directory contains the names as given on the file together with references to the entities after the storage in the open entity.

3. value section

   The value section will store the result of actions which have been carried out to define the open entity. Upon closure of an open entity the value will become one entry in the enclosing_entity_list. When the open world is closed, its value is copied into the receiving CAD system data base (either on the world level or on an assembly level depending on the directives to the post-processor).

The general structure of open entities is:

```
--------------------+------------------------------+
control             + - enclosing entity           +
section             + - enclosing entity state     +
--------------------+------------------------------+
directory section   + - list of names and          +
                    +   references to the          +
                    +   entities                   +
--------------------+------------------------------+
value section       + - corresponds to HDSL entity +
--------------------+------------------------------+
```

which may be represented using the HDSL (see " 5. The CAD*I reference model specification" on page 43):

```
      TYPE OPEN_ENTITY = GENERIC( TYPE_ID )
         enclosing_entity       : REFERENCE(OPEN_ENTITY);
         enclosing_entity_state: STATE;
         directory              : LIST OF STRUCTURE
         name                   : INTEGER;
         entity                 : REFERENCE(ENTITY);
        END;
        value                   : TYPE_ID;
  (* The value will become an entry in the corresponding list of
     the enclosing entity upon closure of this open entity *)
       END;
```

with

```
   TYPE STATE = ( ASSEMBLY_OPEN, B_REP_OPEN, COMPOUND_B_REP_OPEN,
                  CONSTRUCT_OPEN, HYBRID_SOLID_OPEN, LINEAR_SWEEP_OPEN,
                  .. and so on for all entities with scope...
                  READY_FOR_INTERPRETATION, UNDEFINED );
```

The data structure representing the post-processor is the following:

```
  VAR post_processor_state = STRUCTURE
     header:
              STRUCTURE
     author                          : STRING;
     company                         : STRING;
     computer_hardware               : STRING;
     operating_system                : STRING;
     pre_processor_identification    : STRING;
     date_of_pre_processing          : STRING;
     disclaimer                      : STRING;
     geometry_level                  : STRING;
     assembly_level                  : STRING;
     parametric_level                : STRING;
     referencing_level               : STRING;
     maximum_number_of_digits_for_integers_on_the_file      : INTEGER;
     maximum_number_of_significant_digits_in_real_mantissa : INTEGER;
     maximum_number_of_digits_for_exponents                 : INTEGER;
    END;
     identification_of_receiving_world                      : STRING;
     identification_of_receiving_assembly (*if not world*) : STRING;
     is_this_an_update_of_existing_data                     : LOGICAL;
     national_character_set: (ISO6937,GREEK,KANJI);(*initial ISO6937*)
     operating_state: STATE;                       (*initial UNDEFINED*)
     macro_mode       : (ON,OFF);                  (*initial OFF*)
     mode             : (SCOPE,NO_SCOPE);
     open_world_list: OPEN_ENTITY(WORLD);
   END;
```

10. RELATIONSHIPS BETWEEN OPERATING SYSTEMS AND CAD

10.1 DATA BASES AND LIBRARIES

Figure 26 illustrates this correspondence.

CAD aspect	*operating system aspect*
universe	computing environment
world	data set or a set of consistently named data sets containing CAD data
part library	data set or a set of consistently named data sets containing CAD data
routine library	data set or a set of consistently named data sets containing executable programs that can be invoked from the CAD system and will produce data to be stored in the CAD system data base

Figure 26. The relationship between computing environment and CAD system

We define the correspondence between computer operating systems and CAD systems by introducing special terms for the CAD model and by defining their meaning in conventional operating system terminology. The terms to be discussed here are:

1. the universe:

   The "universe" is meant to comprise the entire "computing environment" available at a given CAD site.

2. the world:

   "Worlds" correspond either to a single data set or to a number of coherently named data sets which are used to store a set of CAD models that belong together. Worlds may be addressed (and deleted, e.g.) on the operating system level as a single unit.

3. the part library:

time	*action*
preparation of CAD system use in the sending universe	worlds which exist in the sending universe are allocated to the sending world to be used as libraries
modeling in the sending world with references to libraries in the sending universe	references to entities in libraries are resolved by temporarily binding these entities into the model
pre-processing time	only the names of the referred-to libraries are included on the neutral file
post-processing time	only the names of the referred-to libraries are transferred into the receiving CAD system
preparation of CAD system use in the receiving universe	worlds which exist already in the receiving universe are allocated to the receiving world to be used as libraries

Figure 27. Times and actions related to part library entities and their binding

A "part library" is a world in the sense described above. It becomes a a part library simply by being referred to in another world.

4. the routine library:

   A "routine library" is an operating system data set (or a list of them) that contains executable modules of routines. Such routines may be called or invoked from the CAD system during an application, and produce an entity, as a result which may be stored in the data base.

10.2 BINDING OF OBJECTS FROM THE RECEIVING WORLD AND PART LIBRARIES

Most references in a neutral file will be internal, that is to entities that are transferred on the same file. However, external references to entities not transferred on the file but assumed to reside already in the receiving environment are also supported. The post-processor will have to search for these entities on the basis of their external reference and resolve that reference.

Furthermore, references to entities in libraries are supported with the understanding that binding of these part library references will be be even further delayed until the model is evaluated by some processor (e.g., the display processor). Which libraries are to be used for resolving references, from the world to libraries is not fixed until the time of allocation of a part library reference to the actual data set containing the referred world. In general, this will occur when the CAD system operator starts working with this world. In order to allow different associations between references to libraries and their realizations, libraries are given names in the CAD model. When discussing the transfer of CAD models, it is important to distinguish between several different instances of time when different actions occur, as shown in Figure 27 on page 184. (On binding see J.H. Saltzer: Naming and Binding of Objects. In: Lect. Notes in Comp. Sc. 60, Springer, Heidelberg (1978) 99-208; see also J. Encarnacao, E.G. Schlechtendahl: Computer Aided Design, Springer, Heidelberg, 1983).

In order to provide the required flexibility, the CAD system must provide tables of part library references for each world as indicated in Figure 28 on page 186.

part library name list *always present*	*part library allocation list* *present only during use of the world*
first part library name	operating system name for the first data set representing this part library, operating system name for the second data set representing this part library, ...
second part library name	operating system name for the first data set representing this part library, operating system name for the second data set representing this part library, ...
. . . .	. . . .

Figure 28. The part library of a CAD world

11. PROGRAMMING RULES FOR CAD*I PROCESSORS

11.1 PROGRAMMING LANGUAGE

11.1.1 Determination of the programming language

The CAD*I environment consists of a set of internal CAD*I processing programs interfacing external products such as CAD systems, FEM computational programs. All internal CAD*I software should be written in a common FORTRAN 77 subset.

- Language : FORTRAN 77
- Standard : ANSI X 3.9, DIN 66027, ISO 1539

Other programming languages are permitted in the following cases:

1. Designing the last step of an interface for a specific product (CAD, FEM, DATA BASE etc.) in a local system language (PASCAL, PL1,etc.) depends on the following condition:

   - the local system language can be linked by the loader to the FORTRAN 77 programming language.

2. Other internal problems which can not be handled by FORTRAN 77:

   - dynamic memory management
   - advanced file handling
   - structured data types
   - recursive programming problems

11.1.2 Requirements of structured programming

1. COMMON

   - only named COMMON blocks
   - variable names in a COMMON statement are recommended to be the same in all program units

2. DATA- or PARAMETER

- constants must be defined by DATA- or PARAMETER statements
- mathematical constants should be defined in a statement function
- do not change the value of an argument initialized with a DATA statement
- no use of DATA for COMMON arguments, except in BLOCKDATA subprograms

3. DO

- every DO-loop of nested DO-loops should have an unambiguous terminal statement label
- loops must be realized only by DO statements

4. DIMENSION

- type statements should be preferred for dimension specification of arrays

5. ENTRY

- no entry statements allowed

6. EQUIVALENCE

- the EQUIVALENCE statement should not appear in a program unit

7. GOTO

- assigned GOTO should not appear in a program unit
- avoid uncontrolled application of GOTO statements
- going up GOTO statements should be avoided

8. IF

- use of arithmetic IF statements is not recommended
- FORTRAN77 does not allow to jump into a loop or a selection

9. RETURN

- subroutines should have only one RETURN statement as the last executable one

10. Sequence of statements

- SUBROUTINE or FUNCTION statement
- PARAMETER statement
- DIMENSION statement
- DATA statement
- type statements (REAL,INTEGER,...)

- named COMMON

11. Statement labels

    - must appear in an increasing order
    - beginning with 9 only for error detection
    - label 9999 for STOP and END

12. STOP

    - must be used only in the main program

13. SUBROUTINE

    - variable names and array names in a subroutine reference may be the same in all program units

14. type

    - every variable must be explicitly declared

11.2 SOFTWARE DESIGN

11.2.1 Organisation of the program

Every program must be divided into the following program parts:

- input processing
- check for restrictions
- error detection and output of errors
- processing part
- output of results

Care must be taken to ensure that individual program units should be able to run within the framework of other programs and other data processing systems.

Machine and operating system dependent features must be concentrated in specific identified subroutines and functions

Each program unit must document itself by structure program design.

All statements within one block must be indented and optical emphasis of diverse logic through indentations and paragraphs must be given.

Initialization of variables only by executable statements.

No blank lines may be included in the program.

The main program is to be restricted to control tasks

Specific subprograms should be reserved for problems of data organisation and data transfer input/output.

Comments should not repeat what the corresponding statement does, according to the rules of the program language standard.

The choice of the subprogram names should be based on a meaningful system.

11.2.2 Software commenting

The documentation of the CAD*I programs is divided as follows:

- rough program design (e.g. modularisation)
- fine program design (e.g. structogram)
- internal documentation (e.g. source code)
- external documentation (DIN 66230)

The internal documentation is based on the source code as documentation. Each program should have a standardized header of the following form:

```
C*****************************************************************************
C   VERSION:          DATE:            NAME:             ORG.:
C
C
C
C   MACHINE DEPENDENCY:
C
C
C   PURPOSE AND METHODS:
C
C   INPUT:
C
C   OUTPUT
C
C   EXTERNAL REFERENCES:
C       - SUBROUTINES :
```

```
C       - FUNCTIONS    :
C       - COMMONS      :
C
C   LOCAL VARIABLES: ( of general interest )
C
C
C   EXPLANATION OF TEST PARTS AND ERROR HANDLING:
C
C
C   AUTHOR:              DATE:                ORG.:
C
C**********************************************************************
```

12. PROGRAMMING INTERFACE

It is planned to define a FORTRAN subroutine package consistent with the schema defined in " 5. The CAD*I reference model specification" on page 43 This package should allow reading and writing from and to data bases as well as from and to neutral files. The GKS FORTRAN binding is to be used as a reference for this approach.

The following is a list of the necessary constituents of such a binding.

12.1 MAPPING OF HDSL DATA TYPES ONTO FORTRAN

The data types used in the reference schema definition have to be mapped onto FORTRAN capabilities. For example, the representation of STRUCTURE, LIST, IDENTIFIER, REFERENCE, and the others must be defined in terms of INTEGER, REAL, ARRAY etc..

12.2 APPLICATION PROGRAM INTERFACE ROUTINES

- Subroutines for interrogating a data base.
  - Subroutines for navigating in a data base. Such routines are required for writing a pre-processor.
  - Subroutines for reading a specific entity from the data base. Such routines are required for writing a pre-processor.
- Subroutines for writing entities into a data base. Such routines are required for writing a post-processor.
- Subroutines for writing entities onto the neutral file. In principle, these routines should be identical to the ones for writing into a data base as far as their interface to the application program is concerned.
- Subroutines for interrogating a neutral file.
  - Subroutines for interrogating the next entity on the neutral file. Such routines are required for writing a post-processor.
  - Subroutines for reading the next entity. Such routines are required for writing a post-processor.

13. COMMENTS ON PRE-PROCESSORS

The task of the pre-processor is to produce a neutral file from the information in a CAD system data base. The data base is assumed to be consistent with the schema described in " 5. The CAD*I reference model specification" on page 43 Even though the implementation of the pre-processor will have to depend significantly on the individual CAD system, a basic algorithm for the translation process from the CAD system data base to the neutral file can be formulated: The main purpose of this algorithm is to ensure the the neutral file is strictly sequential.

The processing occurs in at least two phases

Phase A This is the preparation of the pre-processing. The pre-processor expects from the operator at least the following directives:

- Is the "letter" file (see "Appendix D. A neutral file for fixed format letters" on page 225) which is to precede the neutral file to be typed in or is the text already available as a data set on the sending computer? Depending on the answer the letter text or the data set identification of the letter text is expected to be typed in.
- identification of the CAD data base to be processed,
- input of those header data which cannot be derived from the CAD data base,
- identification of the entities in the sending world to be transferred (unless the complete world is to be transferred),
- identification of the computer file which is to receive the neutral solids file,
- processing options which control the conversion from the CAD system data base onto the reference schema if the CAD system data structures do not map immediately onto the reference schema.

Phase B In the second phase the actual translation of the data structure into a sequential form (the neutral file) takes place. This requires extensive navigation in and inspection of the data base of the sending system. References from entities which are to be transferred to other entities also transferred will be written to the neutral file as using the internal names on the file. Entities which are not transferred on the file will be referenced using their user-defined names. Corresponding entities are expected to exist already in the receiving environment. More details are given below in "Implementation of level 1 and level 2 pre-processor routines" on page 197.

> Each entity when written onto the neutral file is assigned a unique positive integer as name. Uniqueness must be guaranteed in any given environment. However, names may be used (but it is not recommanded to use this technique) repeatedly in scopes which do not overlap. E.g., the same name may be used for entities inside any two assemblies contained in the scope of the world.

For the process of transforming the data structure into a sequential representation in phase B following rules apply:

1. Inspect the world scope first
2. Inspect the scope of all enclosed scoped entities. Do this recursively as required by the schema.
3. Convert the data attributes into the specified neutral file format and write them to the neutral file.

Phase B of the pre-processor consists of the following main modules:

1. scanning the sending data base (or a sequential file representing that data base in some native format),
2. parsing,
3. semantic analysis,
4. error and message handling.
5. code generation by writing the neutral file.

While the first four modules have to be developed for each CAD system individually, the code generation routines are common to all pre-processors. Five levels of code generation routines have been identified and developed:

- *Level 5* routines are interface routines which take data from the system-dependant part of the pre-processor and make the necessary adjustment to level 4 routines.

- *Level 4* routines primarily employ level 3 routines to build up entity and property lists.

- *Level 3* routines employ lower level routines to build up a complete entity, property, or attribute definition.

- *Level 2* routines use level 1 routines to build complete sequences of tokens separated by delimiters.

- *Level 1* routines are a few basic routines that manage an 80 character internal buffer which, when necessary, is written to the file. Level 1 routines add simple tokens (real, integer, etc.) to the buffer.

Since the level 1 and level 2 routines are elementary building blocks for all pre-processor development they are described in somewhat more detail below.

13.1.1 Implementation of level 1 and level 2 pre-processor routines

The implementation is in FORTRAN77 and the following chapters use the concepts and notions of this programming language. The pre-processor operates on six logical units for input and output:

- LUI - The logical unit associated with the native data base or native sequential file.
- LUE - The logical unit associated with the error and log file.
- LUO - The logical unit associated with the neutral file to be generated.
- LTI - The logical unit associated with the user directives.
- LTO - The logical unit associated with the system prompts.
- LST - The logical unit associated with the statistics output.

These are collected in the COMMON area /IOFILS/ as follows:

```
COMMON /IOFILS/ LUI, LUE, LUO, LTI, LTO, LST
INTEGER         LUI, LUE, LUO, LTI, LTO, LST
```

This COMMON area must be initialized in the initialization module and the files must be opened for READ (LUI and LTI) and WRITE operations (LUE, LUO, LTO, and LST). With the possible exception of LUI (which is not used by the standardized code generator routines) all files are SEQUENTIAL and FORMATTED.

In the following we describe the low level and utility routines that manage the actual printing to the neutral file. We will distinguish between input parameters in normal text and *output parameters* in italics as indicated here.

13.1.1.1 Level 1 routines

These routines are intended to add integers, reals, and strings to an 80-character buffer which is automatically written to unit LUO and reset when necessary. The buffer is managed by the COMMON areas

```
COMMON /BUFFR1/ USED
INTEGER         USED
COMMON /BUFFR2/ CARD
CHARACTER*80    CARD
```

USED indicates the last occupied position in CARD and is initialized to zero. CARD is initialized to blanks. The routines are:

```
ADDINT( IVAL, ISTAT ) Add an integer value to the buffer
ADDREA( RVAL, ISTAT ) Add a real value to the buffer
ADDSTR( TEXT, ILEN, MODE, ISTAT ) Add a string of length ILEN
                                  to the buffer. Mode indicates whethe
                                  the buffer is previously to be writt
                                  to the file and reset.
```

A COMMON area

```
COMMON / HOWTPR/ PRETTY, DPI, DPM
INTEGER                  DPI, DPM
LOGICAL          PRETTY
```

controls the formatting. The format into which real values are converted is defined by this COMMON area as 1PEw.d where d=DPM and w=DPM+7. The LOGICAL PRETTY controls whether the file is to be formatted for easy readability by humans or to be compressed to the most compact form. With PRETTY = .TRUE. the variable DPI controls the printing of integer values in format Iw with w=DPI.

Another COMMON area controls the statistics:

```
COMMON / STTICS/ NLINES, .......
INTEGER          NLINES
```

where NLINES indicates the number of 80-character records actually written to the neutral file.

13.1.1.2 Level 2 routines

The most important routines for level 2 are:

```
NAMINT ( IVAL, ISTAT ) output a name (#integer)
REFANY ( IVAL, ISTAT ) output a reference (#integer)
READIM ( RARR, IDIM, ISTAT ) output IDIM reals (with separators)
REFDIM ( IARR, IDIM, ISTAT ) output IDIM references (with separators)
SCOPE  ( MODE, ISTAT ) output SCOPE; or END_SCOPE;
WRCMNT ( TEXT, ISTAT ) output a comment
OPCLEN ( KEYWRD, INAM, MODE, ISTAT ) output
                       KEYWRD(#INAM:OPEN); or KEYWRD(#INAM,CLOSE);
MFBGEN ( MODE, TEXT, ISTAT ) output the CAD*I metafile
                                    header or trailer
NFBGEN ( MODE, TEXT, ISTAT ) output the neutral file
                                    header or trailer
LTBGEN ( MODE, TEXT, ISTAT ) output the letter file
                                    header or trailer
```

13.1.1.3 An example of a level 3 routine

In order to illustrate how level 1 and level 2 routines are combined to implement higher level routines we add the routine POINT as an example.

```
      SUBROUTINE POINT (MODE, INAM, COOR,   ISTAT)
      INTEGER             MODE, INAM,        ISTAT
      REAL                            COOR(3)
C     -------------------------------------------------------
C PURPOSE: TO ADD A POINT ENTITY TO THE NEUTRAL FILE
C
C INPUT  : MODE - 0 FIRST AND ONLY POINT IN A LIST
C                 1 FIRST IN LONGER LIST
C                 2 INTERMEDIATE POINT IN LIST
C                 3 LAST POINT IN LIST
C          INAM - INTEGER TELLING THE POINTS NAME
C          COOR - ARRAY OF COORDINATE VALUES
C OUTPUT : ISTAT- STATUS FLAG, 0 IF OK, -1 IF AN ERROR OCCURRED
C     -------------------------------------------------------
      COMMON / HOWTPR/ PRETTY, DPI, DPM
      INTEGER                  DPI, DPM
      LOGICAL          PRETTY
C
      INTEGER          PRMOD
C- CHECK INPUT
      IF(MODE.LT.0.OR.MODE.GT.3.OR.INAM.LT.1)GO TO 91
C- SET PRINT MODE
      PRMOD=0
      IF(PRETTY)PRMOD=-1
C- FOR MODE=0 or 1 WRITE KEYWORD POINT
      IF(MODE.GT.1)GOTO 10
      CALL ADDSTR('POINT(',6,PRMOD,ISTAT)
      IF(ISTAT.NE.0)GOTO 99
      GOTO 20
C- INTERMEDIATE OR LAST POINT
   10 CONTINUE
      IF(PRETTY)THEN
C-START NEW LINE WITH SOME MARGIN
         CALL ADDSTR('     ',6,-1,ISTAT)
         IF(ISTAT.NE.0)GOTO 99
      ENDIF
C-ADD NAME AND COORDINATES
   20 CALL NAMINT(INAM,ISTAT)
      IF(ISTAT.NE.0)GOTO 99
      CALL READIM(COOR,3,ISTAT)
      IF(ISTAT.NE.0)GOTO 99
```

```
C-IF ONLY OR LAST POINT ADD RIGHT PARANTHESIS AND SEMICOLON
C-ELSE ONLY SEMICOLON
      IF(MODE.EQ.0.OR.MODE.EQ.3)THEN
         CALL ADDSTR(');',2,0,ISTAT)
      ELSE
         CALL ADDSTR(';',1,0,ISTAT)
      ENDIF
C-RETURN WITH RESULTING STATUS INDICATOR
      GO TO 99
C-ERROR IN INPUT TO THIS ROUTINE
   91 CALL ERROUT('POINT - CALLED WITH WRONG INPUT PARAMETERS',2)
      ISTAT=-1
   99 RETURN
      END
```

14. COMMENTS ON POST-PROCESSORS

The post-processor has the task to interpret the neutral file and to build an internal representation of the transferred model in the receiving CAD system. The post-processor consists of the following modules:

1. scanner,
2. parser,
3. semantics analysis and data structure generation.

For the for two phases, the CAD*I project has developed a general scanner/parser generator (valid for a large class of neutral file languages) from which a special scanner/parser for the physical file format defined in this document was derived. The interphase between the scanner/parser and the subsequent steps is described in " 15. The interface of the CAD*I parser" on page 203.

The semantic processing of the post-processor is determined by the directives of the operator, by the actual interpretation and, in case of errors by the error handling.

A) Directives from the operator

The post-processor expects at least the following directives from the operator:

- identification of the target CAD data base which is to receive the transferred model,
- selection of whether the transferred model is to create a new data base or whether the receiving data base exists already,
- identification of the target assembly if the transferred model is to become an assembly in an already existing data base,
- identification of the computer file containing the neutral file,
- processing options such as level of error tracing, destination and amount of control output,
- processing options which control the conversion into the CAD system data base from the reference schema if the CAD system data structures do not map immediately onto the reference schema.

B) Interpretation

- The neutral file is read only once sequentially from the beginning to the end. The post-processor is controlled by the statements on the neutral file: The effect of these statements is described in " 8. Definition of the finite state machine post-processor" on page 173.

C) Error handling

While parsing the file the post-processor has to check both the semantics and the syntax and react on errors with error messages and actions.

Possible actions could be:

- In case of a syntax error the post-processor attempts to recover.
- In case of a semantic error the post-processor attempts to find the next valid statement and continues interpretation
- If a certain number of errors had occurred the interpretation should be canceled
- The data stream to the data base will either be continued or stopped and also the already written data will be either kept or deleted, depending on directives from the operator.

D) Resolving internal and external references

If an entity is identified by its name, the name is searched for in the directories of the open entities.

If an entity is referred to by an external name the entity is searched for in the receiving data base environment (assembly or world).

15. THE INTERFACE OF THE CAD*I PARSER

The CAD*I project has developed a scanner/parser which is suitable for post-processing the neutral file language. This software was developed for speeding up the generation of post-processors for different systems. The advantage of using this scanner/parser is that post-processor development for another CAD system can now be restricted to the analysis of semantics and building up the data structure. This chapter describes the theoretical basis for the parser and its interface to later phases of post-processing.

15.1 PARSE TREE

A context free grammar **G** is defined by the **4-Tuple (N,T,Z,R)** where **N** denotes the non-terminal set, **T** denotes the terminal set, **Z** denotes the start character (**Z** is an element of **N**) and **R** denotes the set of context free productions. The elements of **R** are called the **R-productions** of **G** and the union of the sets **N,T** is called the vocabulary V of G.

Non-terminal characters have to occur on the left-hand side of at least one production. Terminal characters do not occur on the left-hand side of any production.

Besides, a context free production is a replacement rule for a non-terminal character. Context free productions are denoted by

P: X ::= v1 v2 ..... vK

where **P** is the name of the production, **X** is a non-terminal character (i.e. **X** is an element of **N**), **v1v2..vK** is the corresponding vocabulary sequence to **P** (**vj** is an element of **V** (j=1..N)) and **K** denotes the length of the production **P**. One calls **X** the left-hand side and **v1v2..vK** the right-hand side of **P** and applies **P** to a sequence **VS** of vocabulary elements by replacing the leftmost non-terminal character **X** occurring in **VS** by the right-hand side of **P**. The new sequence is denoted by **P(VS)**. The right-hand side **v1v2..vK** of **P**, which now appears as a subsequence of P(VS), is called the **P-part** of P(VS). If and only if **X** does not occur in **VS** then **P** is not applicable to **VS**.

```
****************************************************************************
*                                                                          *
*   EXAMPLE:  N =  (<a>,<c>)    T =  (a,b,d)    R =  (P,Q)                 *
*                                                                          *
*                    R :  <c> ::= c <a> b                                  *
*                    Q :  <a> ::= a <c> a                                  *
*                                                                          *
*                                                                          *
*              If VS = <a>aabb<c>d<c>bbbb then the equations               *
*                                                                          *
*                         R(VS) = <a>aabbc<a>bd<c>bbbb                     *
*                      Q(R(VS)) = a<c>aaabbc<a>bd<c>bbbb                   *
*                      R(Q(VS)) = ac<a>baaabb<c>d<c>bbbb                   *
*                      R(R(VS)) = <a>aabbc<a>bdc<a>bbbbb                   *
*                                                                          *
*              are valid. The production R is not applicable              *
*              to the sequence R(R(VS)) because the left-hand             *
*              side <c> of R does not occur in R(R(VS)).                  *
*                                                                          *
****************************************************************************
```

Instead of P1(P2...Pn(VS)...) one writes (P1•P2•..•Pn)(VS) and calls (P1•P2•..•Pn) the **n-composition** of the productions Pj (j=1..n). In the example above, one sees that the order of the productions Pj (j=1..n) in (P1•P2•..•Pn) is significant for the value of (P1•P2•..•Pn)(VS) (R(Q(VS) ≠ Q(R(VS)).

If one applies the n-composition (P1•P2•...•Pn) to a sequence VS one applies at first P1 to VS, then P2 to P1(VS), then P3 to P1(P2(VS)) and so on, i.e. the application of the productions P1,P2,...Pn to VS is sequential. But for the description of the **parse tree**, it is useful to define the concurrent application of the productions P1,P2,....Pn to VS. The following example shows the difference between a sequential application and a concurrent application of two productions P,Q to a vocabulary sequence VS.

```
*****************************************************************************
*                                                                           *
*   EXAMPLE:  N =  (<a>,<c>)   T =  (a,b,d)   R =  (R,Q)                    *
*                                                                           *
*                      P  :  <c> ::= c <a> b                                *
*                      Q  :  <a> ::= a <c> a                                *
*                                                                           *
*                                                                           *
*              if VS = <c>aabb<a> then the result of the                    *
*              sequential application of the productions                    *
*              P and Q (i.e. at first P than Q) is:                         *
*                                                                           *
*                 (Q•P)(VS) =  ca<c>abaabb<a>                               *
*                                                                           *
*              but the result of the concurrent application                 *
*              of the productions P and Q is:                               *
*                                                                           *
*                 (P|Q)(VS) = c<a>baabba<c>a                                *
*                                                                           *
*              where (P|Q) indicates that P,Q are applied                   *
*              at the same time to VS. ( (P|Q) is called                    *
*              the 2-independant composition of P and Q.                    *
*                                                                           *
*****************************************************************************
```

In case of the **sequential** application of P and Q, the leftmost non-terminal character <a>, **occurring in P(VS)** is replaced by the right-hand side of the production Q, but in case of the **concurrent application** of P and Q, the leftmost <a>, **occurring in VS** is replaced by the right-hand side of Q.

Definition: If P,Q are context free productions, then the application of the *2-independant composition (P|Q)* to the sequence *VS* is described by the following sequential procedure:

> One applies at first P to VS as described above, and than replaces the leftmost X in P(VS), (X denotes the left-hand side of Q) that does not belong to the P-part of P(VS), by the right-hand side of Q. The (P|Q)-part of (P|Q)(VS) is the set consisting of the P-part of P(VS) and the right-hand side of the production Q. If and only if there is no X in P(VS) with the condition described above or P is not applicable to VS then (P|Q) is not applicable to the sequence VS.

Definition: If P,Q,R are context free productions then the application of the *3-independant composition (P|Q|R)* to the sequence *VS* is described by the following sequential procedure:

One applies at first the 2-independant composition (P|Q) to VS as described above, and than replaces the leftmost X in (P|Q)(VS), (X denotes the left-hand side of R) that does not belong to one of the elements of the (P|Q)-part of (P|Q)(VS), by the right-hand side of R. The (P|Q|R)-part of (P|R|Q)(VS) is the set extension of the (P|Q)-part of (P|Q)(VS) by the right-hand side of the production R. if and only If there is no X in (P|Q)(VS) with the condition described above or (P|Q) is not applicable to VS then (P|Q|R) is not applicable to the sequence VS.

From these definitions, one can easily derive the application of a *n-independant composition (P1|P2|...|Pn)* to VS.

Definition: The length of (P1|P2|...|Pn) is the maximal length of the productions Pj (j=1..n).

Theorem (without proof): If there is an index j (j=1..n) so that the left-hand side of Pj does not occur in VS, then (P1|P2|...|Pn) is not applicable to VS.

```
*****************************************************************************
*                                                                           *
*   EXAMPLE:  N =  (<a>,<c>)    T =  (a,b,d)    P =  (R,Q)                  *
*                                                                           *
*                       R  :  <c> ::= c <a> b                               *
*                       Q  :  <a> ::= a <c> a                               *
*                                                                           *
*                                                                           *
*             if VS = <a>aabb<c>d<c>bbbb then the equations                 *
*                                                                           *
*                (Q|R)(VS)     =  a<c>aaabbc<a>bd<c>bbbb                    *
*                (Q|R|R)(VS)   =  a<c>aaabbc<a>bdc<a>bbbbb                  *
*                                                                           *
*             are valid. The composition (Q|R|R|R) is not                   *
*             applicable to VS, because there was no third                  *
*             appearance of the non-terminal character <c>      *           
*             in the sequence VS.                                           *
*                                                                           *
*****************************************************************************
```

Now we can get a short definition of the notion **syntax derivation**, that is the base for the definition of the **parse tree**.

Definition: Let G=(N,T,Z,R) be a context free grammar, and let Sj (j=1..k) be a R-production or a n-independant composition of n R-productions, then **S=(S1,...Sn-1,Sn)** is the syntax derivation of the statement **ST** if and only if **S** generates **ST** i.e. if and only if the equation **ST=Sn(Sn-1(..S1(Z)..))**, is valid. Besides, n is called the length of the derivation **S**.

Then **S=(S1,....Sn-1,Sn)** can be represented by a **K-ary** tree **T(K)**, where **K** is the maximal length of the elements **Sj** (j=1..n) of **S**. The depth of the tree (i.e. the number of tree levels) is equal to the length of the derivation **S** and on each (tree-) level j (the root of the tree is on level 0), the successor relation of **T(K)** is (are) defined as follows:

The character A denotes a non-terminal character, and v denotes a vocabulary element.

v suc(j) A : 1) **Sj is an independant composition**:
there is a production PR in the independent composition Sj so that the left-hand side of PR is equal to A and v occurs in the right-hand side of PR.

2) **Sj is a production**:
the left-hand side of Sj is equal to A and v occurs in the right-hand side of Sj.

In case 1) and 2) v is called the *successor of A on level j*.

Definition: SUC(A,j) is called the *successor set of the non-terminal node A on level j* and is defined by the equation SUC(A,j) = (v | (v suc(j) A) is valid),

Definition: A parse tree of a statement ST is the **K-ary** tree that represents the syntax derivation S=(S1,....Sn) of ST.

```
**********************************************************************************
*                                                                                *
*  EXAMPLE:                                                                      *
*                                                                                *
*     V=N+T  N=(<Z>,<b>,<d>)  T=(a,b,c,d)                                        *
*                                                                                *
*     P1: <Z> ::= <b>                                                            *
*     P2: <Z> ::= a c                                                            *
*     P3: <b> ::= a <b> c                                                        *
*     P4: <b> ::= b <d>                                                          *
*     P5: <d> ::= d <d> <d>                                                      *
*     P6: <d> ::= d                                                              *
*                                                                                *
*     ST: aabdddcc                                                               *
*                                                                                *
*     Then ST=(P6|P6)(P5(P4(P3(P3(P1(Z)))))) is valid and the                    *
*     sequence that generates ST is S=(P1,P3,P3,P4,P5,(P6|P6)).                  *
*                                                                                *
*     Graphical representation of the parse tree of ST:                          *
*                                                                                *
*                          <Z>              start   | P1                         *
*   **************************|******************************************        *
*                             |                     |                            *
*     +---------------<b----------+         level 1 | P3                         *
*     |                       |           |         |                            *
*     a    +------------<b>----+           c  level 2 | P3                       *
*          |                  |     |               |                            *
*          a    +--------<b>    c            level 3 | P4                        *
*               |              |                    |                            *
*               b    +----<d>------+         level 4 | P5                        *
*                    |    |        |                |                            *
*                    d    <d>      <d>       level 5 | (P6|P6)                   *
*                          |        |               |                            *
*                          d        d        level 6 |                           *
*                                                                                *
*   The successor relation (N1 suc(J) N2) between two nodes                      *
*   N1, N2 is characterized by an arrow from N2 to N1.                           *
*   For example, the successor set of node <b> on level 2                        *
*   is (a,<b>,c) and the successor set of node <b> on                            *
*   level 3 is (b,<d>).                                                          *
*                                                                                *
**********************************************************************************
```

15.2 EXAMPLE

For this example, the structure of the solid sphere[1] is formally defined by the grammar S=(N,T,<Z>,P):

```
N:  {{ <any_real> <ref_any> <place>
       <rotation>  <point>  <any_dir>
       <any_poi>  <Z> }}

T:  {{ real name PLACEMENT ROT_AXIS POINT : , ( ) ; }}


P:  {{ P1 P2 P3 P4 P5 P6 P7 }}

P1: <Z>        ::= SOLID_SPHERE ( name : real , <place> ) ;
P2: <place>    ::= PLACEMENT ( <rot> , <point> ) ;
P3: <rot>      ::= ROT_AXIS ( <any_poi> , <any_dir> , <any_rea> ) ;
P4: <point>    ::= POINT ( real , real , real ) ;
P5: <any_rea> ::= name
P6: <any_dir> ::= name
P7: <any_poi> ::= name
```

The statement ST is defined as follows:

```
ST = SOLID_SPHERE
        (#4: 10.5 , PLACEMENT(
                        ROT_AXIS( #1, #2, #3 ),
                        POINT( 15.0 , 45.0 , -30.0 )) );
```

The corresponding derivation is defined by the sequence S:

```
S   = (P1, P2, IC1, IC2)
IC1 = (P3|P4)
IC2 = (P5|P6|P7)
```

Delimiters are only used to show the PARSER where a symbol (token) begins and where a symbol terminates. Delimiters do not denote any CAD specific

---

[1] Note that this example grammar is similar but not identical to the CAD*I specification. It has been simplified for the sake of illustration.

informations that have to be translated by the code generation of the post processor. So one can reduce the parse tree, that is the interface data structure between the ANALYSE module and the code generation, by all TERMINAL NODES that denote any DELIMITERS. After this reduction one eliminates all useless non-terminal nodes. Figure 29 on page 211 shows the reduced CAD*I parse tree of the statement ST. where the node names (non-terminal names and terminal names) are INTEGER coded as follows:

0 : NON-TERMINAL NODE
1 : DELIMITER (does not occur in the reduced parse tree)
2 : STRING
3 : REAL
4 : INTEGER
5 : NAME
6 : KEYWORD
7 : USER DEFINED NAME
8 : LOGICAL

The parser analyses statement by statement and writes the interface data structures onto the parse tree file.

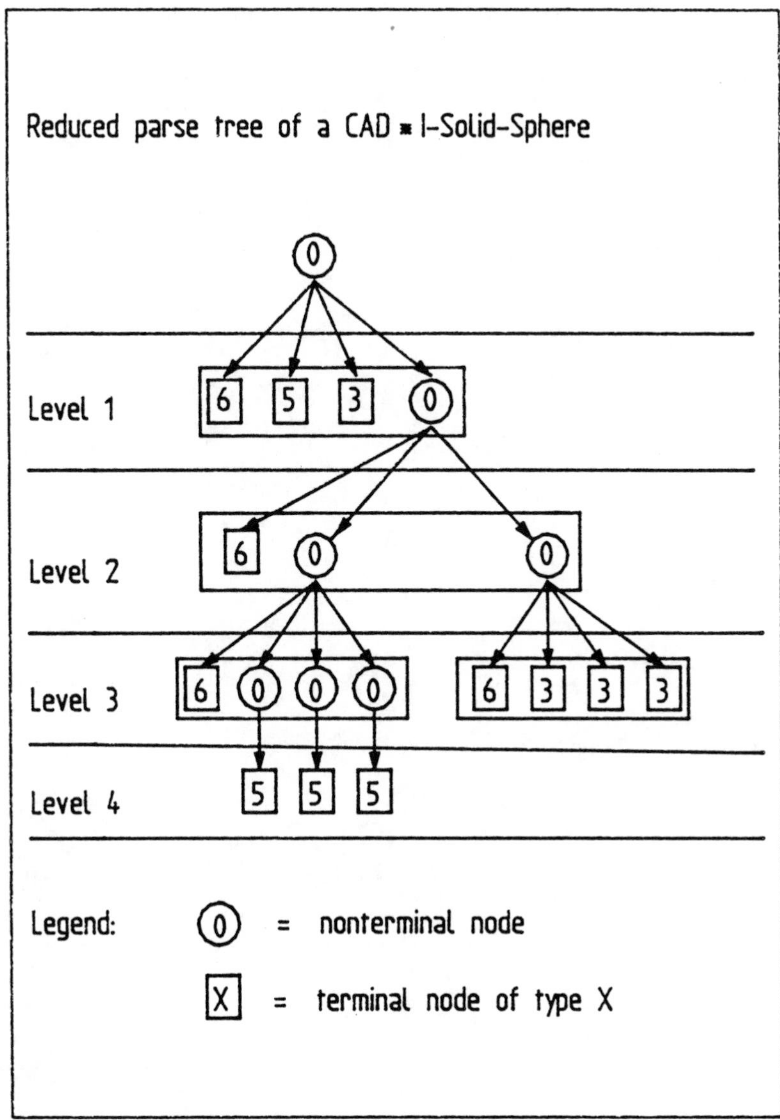

Figure 29. The graphical representation of the reduced parse tree

The decimal value of the alphabet elements stands in the first line and their graphical representation in the second one, where G(i) denotes the graphical representation of the decimal i. The representation is not complete because the graphics G(94) and G(96) cannot be printed by the text system, that generates this report. G(94) and G(96) indicates the graphical representation of 'circumflex accent' and 'grave accent'.

<table>
<tr><td>32</td><td>33</td><td>34</td><td>35</td><td>36</td><td>37</td><td>38</td><td>39</td><td>40</td><td>41</td><td>42</td><td>43</td><td>44</td></tr>
<tr><td>SPACE</td><td>!</td><td>"</td><td>#</td><td>¤</td><td>%</td><td>&</td><td>'</td><td>(</td><td>)</td><td>*</td><td>+</td><td>,</td></tr>
<tr><td>45</td><td>46</td><td>47</td><td>48</td><td>49</td><td>50</td><td>51</td><td>52</td><td>53</td><td>54</td><td>55</td><td>56</td><td>57</td></tr>
<tr><td>-</td><td>.</td><td>/</td><td>0</td><td>1</td><td>2</td><td>3</td><td>4</td><td>5</td><td>6</td><td>7</td><td>8</td><td>9</td></tr>
<tr><td>58</td><td>59</td><td>60</td><td>61</td><td>62</td><td>63</td><td>64</td><td>65</td><td>66</td><td>67</td><td>68</td><td>69</td><td>70</td></tr>
<tr><td>:</td><td>;</td><td><</td><td>=</td><td>></td><td>?</td><td>@</td><td>A</td><td>B</td><td>C</td><td>D</td><td>E</td><td>F</td></tr>
<tr><td>71</td><td>72</td><td>73</td><td>74</td><td>75</td><td>76</td><td>77</td><td>78</td><td>79</td><td>80</td><td>81</td><td>82</td><td>83</td></tr>
<tr><td>G</td><td>H</td><td>I</td><td>J</td><td>K</td><td>L</td><td>M</td><td>N</td><td>O</td><td>P</td><td>Q</td><td>R</td><td>S</td></tr>
<tr><td>84</td><td>85</td><td>86</td><td>87</td><td>88</td><td>89</td><td>90</td><td>91</td><td>92</td><td>93</td><td>94</td><td>95</td><td>96</td></tr>
<tr><td>T</td><td>U</td><td>V</td><td>W</td><td>X</td><td>Y</td><td>Z</td><td>[</td><td>\</td><td>]</td><td></td><td>_</td><td></td></tr>
<tr><td>97</td><td>98</td><td>99</td><td>100</td><td>101</td><td>102</td><td>103</td><td>104</td><td>105</td><td>106</td><td>107</td><td>108</td><td>109</td></tr>
<tr><td>a</td><td>b</td><td>c</td><td>d</td><td>e</td><td>f</td><td>g</td><td>h</td><td>i</td><td>j</td><td>k</td><td>l</td><td>m</td></tr>
<tr><td>110</td><td>111</td><td>112</td><td>113</td><td>114</td><td>115</td><td>116</td><td>117</td><td>118</td><td>119</td><td>120</td><td>121</td><td>122</td></tr>
<tr><td>n</td><td>o</td><td>p</td><td>q</td><td>r</td><td>s</td><td>t</td><td>u</td><td>v</td><td>w</td><td>x</td><td>y</td><td>z</td></tr>
<tr><td>123</td><td>124</td><td>125</td><td>126</td><td></td><td></td><td></td><td></td><td></td><td></td><td></td><td></td><td></td></tr>
<tr><td>{</td><td>|</td><td>}</td><td>~</td><td></td><td></td><td></td><td></td><td></td><td></td><td></td><td></td><td></td></tr>
</table>

APPENDIX B. THE ESCAPE SEQUENCES

Escape codes are to be used for symbols which cannot be represented by the basic alphabet defined in "The alphabet level" on page 159. The escape codes together with the normal alphabet constitute the "extended alphabet". Several extend alphabets are available. They are selected and unselected by alphabetical escape codes:

1. escape code !:ISO6937:! selects the extended character set as documented in "The Latin alphabet (ISO6937)".

2. escape code !:GREEK:! selects the extended character set as documented in "The Greek alphabet" on page 216.

3. escape code !:KANJI:! selects the extended character set of Kanji characters which have sequence codes between 0 and 9999.

B.1 THE LATIN ALPHABET (ISO6937)

ISO6937/2 is used as a basis for coding the "decimal coded character" representations (DCC) of Latin characters. The coding method B of the ISO standard is used. According to this method, Latin characters are coded by one or two pairs of integers:

(1)	n_4/n_3	n_2/n_1
(2)	n_4/n_3	-
(3)	-	n_2/n_1

where $8 \le n_4 \le 15$

$0 \le n_3 \le 7$

$0 \le n_2 \le 7$

$0 \le n_1 \le 7$

Syntactically the three forms are distinguished as

```
<one_to_seven>       ::=  1 | 2 | 3 | 4 | 5 | 6 | 7
<eight_to_fifteen>   ::=  8 | 9 | 10 | 11 | 12 | 13 | 14 | 15
<form1>              ::=  <form2> <form3>
<form2>              ::=  <eight_to_fifteen> | <one_to_seven>
<form3>              ::=  <one_to_seven> | <one_to_seven>
```

The second form defines implicitly $n_2 = n_1 = 0$.

The third form defines implicitly $n_4 = 8$, $n_3 = 0$.

From this representation method the DCC is definded as follows:

$$DCC = 16*(8*(16*(n_4-8) + n_3) + n_2) + n_1$$

The algorithm (formulated in FORTRAN77) to derive the 4 numbers n_1-n_4 from a DCC is as follows:

```
subroutine tran(dcc,n1,n2,n3,n4)
integer dcc,var1,var2,n1,n2,n3,n4
var1=dcc
var2=var1/16
n1=var1-(16*var2)
var1=var2
var2=var1/8
n2=var1-(8*var2)
var1=var2
var2=var1/16
n3=var1-(16*var2)
n4=var2+8
return
end
```

As an example, the character sequence 'äß !' contains Latin characters with the ISO method B code representations 12/8 6/1, 15/11, 2/0, 2/1, and would be represented on the neutral file by the string '!:ISO6937,9313,15744,32,33:!'

B.2 THE GREEK ALPHABET

This table of decimal coded characters for escape sequences is to be replaced when an ISO standard for Greek character symbols becomes available.

!:1:!	for α	!:25:!	for A (capital α)
!:2:!	for β	!:26:!	for B (capital β)
!:3:!	for γ	!:27:!	for Γ
!:4:!	for δ	!:28:!	for Δ
!:5:!	for ε	!:29:!	for E (capital ε)
!:6:!	for ζ	!:30:!	for Z (capital ζ)
!:7:!	for η	!:31:!	for H (capital η)
!:8:!	for ϑ	!:32:!	for Θ
!:9:!	for ι	!:33:!	for I (capital ι)
!:10:!	for κ	!:34:!	for K (capital κ)

```
!:11:!  for λ        !:35:!  for Λ
!:12:!  for μ        !:36:!  for M (capital μ)
!:13:!  for ν        !:37:!  for N (capital ν)
!:14:!  for ξ        !:38:!  for Ξ
!:15:!  for ο        !:39:!  for O (capital ο)

!:16:!  for π        !:40:!  for Π
!:17:!  for ρ        !:41:!  for P (capital ρ)
!:18:!  for σ        !:42:!  for Σ

!:19:!  for τ        !:43:!  for T (capital τ)
!:20:!  for υ        !:44:!  for Y (capital υ)
!:21:!  for ϕ        !:45:!  for Φ
!:22:!  for χ        !:46:!  for X (capital χ)
!:23:!  for ψ        !:47:!  for Ψ
!:24:!  for ω        !:48:!  for Ω
```

B.3 THE KANJI ALPHABET

A Japanese standard for defining integer coding of the Kanji characters is available.

APPENDIX C. ALPHABET TRANSLATION INTO A PRIVATE ALPHABET

In order to allow the implementation of pre- and post-processors on computers that use different character representations, translation tables for conversion into and from such "private" alphabets may be defined. Exchanging neutral files with others using private alphabet coding is a matter of agreement between the exchanging partners. Files coded in a private alphabet are *not* considered as conforming to this specification!

As an example of a private alphabet coding we give the mapping from the neutral file alphabet as defined in "Appendix A. The graphical alphabet" on page 213 into a subset of the EBCDIC code. With this translation neutral files may be printed in an EBCDIC environment. The decimal value of the alphabet elements according to "Appendix A. The graphical alphabet" on page 213 stands in the first line, the decimal representation of the corresponding EBCDIC character stands in the second line, and their graphical representation in the third one. The representation is not complete because the EBCDIC graphics G'(94) and G'(96) cannot be printed by the text system, that generates this report. G'(94) and G'(96) indicates the graphical representation of 'separated vertical bar' and 'grave accent'.

32	33	34	35	36	37	38	39	40	41	42	43	44
64	90	127	123	91	108	80	125	77	93	92	78	107
SPACE	!	"	#	$	%	&	'	(	)	*	+	,

45	46	47	48	49	50	51	52	53	54	55	56	57
96	75	97	240	241	242	243	244	245	246	247	248	249
-	.	/	0	1	2	3	4	5	6	7	8	9

58	59	60	61	62	63	64	65	66	67	68	69	70
122	94	76	126	110	111	124	193	194	195	196	197	198
:	;	<	=	>	?	@	A	B	C	D	E	F

71	72	73	74	75	76	77	78	79	80	81	82	83
199	200	201	209	210	211	212	213	214	215	216	217	226
G	H	I	J	K	L	M	N	O	P	Q	R	S

84	85	86	87	88	89	90	91	92	93	94	95	96
227	228	229	230	231	232	233	99	224	100	95	109	121
T	U	V	W	X	Y	Z	¢	\	¬		_	

97	98	99	100	101	102	103	104	105	106	107	108	109
129	130	131	132	133	134	135	136	137	145	146	147	148
a	b	c	d	e	f	g	h	i	j	k	l	m

110	111	112	113	114	115	116	117	118	119	120	121	122
149	150	151	152	153	162	163	164	165	166	167	168	169
n	o	p	q	r	s	t	u	v	w	x	y	z

123	124	125	126
192	106	208	161
{	|	}	~

The graphic representation of most alphabet decimal codes is the same according to "Appendix A. The graphical alphabet" on page 213 and the above EBCDIC table. Only the representations for codes 36, 91, 93, 94 are different. As in "Appendix A. The graphical alphabet" on page 213, the graphical representation of code 94 and 96 (EBCDIC codes 95 and 121) which indicate the 'vertical broken bar' and the 'grave accent' could not be printed by the text processing system used.

The following two FORTRAN77 subroutines perform the translation between the standard alphabet and the private alphabet defined in this chapter. These routines may be used as a reference for writing similar converters for other private alphabets.

```
      SUBROUTINE ISOEBC (LEN,IN,OUT)
C
C*******************************************************************************
C
C  VERSION             : 1.0;  1986.10.3
C
C  MASCHINE DEPENDENCY : NONE
C
C  PURPOSE AND METHODS : THIS SUBROUTINE TRANSLATES THE ISO - CODED
C                        INPUT STRING 'IN' INTO AN EBCDIC - CODED OUTPUT
C                        STRING 'OUT'.
C                        THE METHOD IS LIKE AS THE DIRECT INDEX TRANS-
C                        LATION TECHNIQUE, OFTEN USED IN AN ASSEMBLER
C                        ENVIROMENT. A PATICULAR LETTER FROM THE INPUT
C                        STRING IS USED AS AN INDEX BY THE TRANSLATION
C                        TABLE. ACCORDING TO THIS VALUE, THE CONTENT
C                        OF THE TABLE VALUE IS RETURNED IN THE OUTPUT
C                        STRING.
C                        NOTE :
C                        THERE IS NO CHECK FOR THE LENGTH OF THE OUTPUT
C                        STRING. IF THE OUTPUT STRING IS LESS THAN THE
C                        INPUT STRING, THE PROGRAM CODE WILL BE
C                        DESTROYED.
C
C  INPUT               : LEN INTEGER*4 LENGTH OF STRING 'IN' (BYTES)
C                        IN  CHARACTER STRING (CONTAINS ISO STRING)
C
```

```
C  OUTPUT                : OUT CHARACTER STRING
C
C  EXTERNAL REFERENCES : NONE
C
C  LOCAL VARIABLES      : TRANSLATION TABLE 'TRTAB'
C
C  AUTHOR               : W.OLBRICH, KERNFORSCHUNGSZENTRUM KARLSRUHE
C                                    INSTITUT FUER REAKTORENTWICKLUNG
C
C*******************************************************************************
C
C
      INTEGER         LEN, I, ILETT
      CHARACTER       IN*(*), OUT*(*)
      INTEGER         TRTAB(0:127)
C
      DATA     TRTAB /
     &   0,  0,  0,  0,  0,  0,  0,  0,  0,  0,  0,  0,  0,  0,  0,  0,
     &   0,  0,  0,  0,  0,  0,  0,  0,  0,  0,  0,  0,  0,  0,  0,  0,
     &  64, 90,127,123, 91,108, 80,125, 77, 93, 92, 78,107, 96, 75, 97,
     & 240,241,242,243,244,245,246,247,248,249,122, 94, 76,126,110,111,
     & 124,193,194,195,196,197,198,199,200,201,209,210,211,212,213,214,
     & 215,216,217,226,227,228,229,230,231,232,233, 99,224,100, 95,109,
     & 121,129,130,131,132,133,134,135,136,137,145,146,147,148,149,150,
     & 151,152,153,162,163,164,165,166,167,168,169,192,106,208,161,  0/
C
C
      DO 10 I=1,LEN
         ILETT = ICHAR(IN(I:I))
         OUT(I:I) = CHAR(TRTAB(ILETT))
   10 CONTINUE
C
      RETURN
      END
      SUBROUTINE EBCISO (LEN,IN,OUT)
C
C*******************************************************************************
C
C  VERSION              : 1.0;  1986.10.3
C
C  MASCHINE DEPENDENCY : NONE
C
C  PURPOSE AND METHODS : THIS SUBROUTINE TRANSLATED THE EBCDIC - CODED
C                        INPUT STRING 'IN' INTO AN ISO - CODED OUTPUT
C                        STRING 'OUT'.
C                        THE METHOD IS LIKE AS THE DIRECT INDEX TRANS-
C                        LATION TECHNIQUE, OFTEN USED IN AN ASSEMBLER
C                        ENVIROMENT. A PATICULAR LETTER FROM THE INPUT
```

```
C                           STRING IS USED AS AN INDEX BY THE TRANSLATION
C                           TABLE. ACCORDING TO THIS VALUE, THE CONTENT
C                           OF THE TABLE VALUE IS RETURNED IN THE OUTPUT
C                           STRING.
C                           NOTE :
C                           THERE IS NO CHECK FOR THE LENGTH OF OUTPUT
C                           STRING. IF THE OUTPUT STRING IS LESS THAN THE
C                           INPUT STRING, THE PROGRAM CODE WILL BE
C                           DESTROYED.
C
C  INPUT                  : LEN INTEGER*4 LENGTH OF STRING 'IN' (BYTES)
C                           IN  CHARACTER STRING (CONTAINS EBCDIC STRING)
C
C  OUTPUT                 : OUT CHARACTER STRING
C
C  EXTERNAL REFERENCES : NONE
C
C  LOCAL VARIABLES        : TRANSLATION TABLE 'TRTAB'
C
C  AUTHOR                 : W.OLBRICH, KERNFORSCHUNGSZENTRUM KARLSRUHE,
C                                       INSTITUT FUER REAKTORENTWICKLUNG
C
C*******************************************************************************
C
C
      INTEGER          LEN, I, ILETT
      CHARACTER        IN*(*), OUT*(*)
      INTEGER          TRTAB(0:255)
C
      DATA     TRTAB /
     &   0,  0,  0,  0,  0,  0,  0,  0,  0,  0,  0,  0,  0,  0,  0,  0,
     &   0,  0,  0,  0,  0,  0,  0,  0,  0,  0,  0,  0,  0,  0,  0,  0,
     &   0,  0,  0,  0,  0,  0,  0,  0,  0,  0,  0,  0,  0,  0,  0,  0,
     &   0,  0,  0,  0,  0,  0,  0,  0,  0,  0,  0,  0,  0,  0,  0,  0,
     &  32,  0,  0,  0,  0,  0,  0,  0,  0,  0,  0, 46, 60, 40, 43,  0,
     &  38,  0,  0,  0,  0,  0,  0,  0,  0,  0, 33, 36, 42, 41, 59, 94,
     &  45, 47,  0, 91, 93,  0,  0,  0,  0,  0,124, 44, 37, 95, 62, 63,
     &   0,  0,  0,  0,  0,  0,  0,  0,  0, 96, 58, 35, 64, 39, 61, 34,
     &   0, 97, 98, 99,100,101,102,103,104,105,  0,  0,  0,  0,  0,  0,
     &   0,106,107,108,109,110,111,112,113,114,  0,  0,  0,  0,  0,  0,
     &   0,126,115,116,117,118,119,120,121,122,  0,  0,  0,  0,  0,  0,
     &   0,  0,  0,  0,  0,  0,  0,  0,  0,  0,  0,  0,  0,  0,  0,  0,
     & 123, 65, 66, 67, 68, 69, 70, 71, 72, 73,  0,  0,  0,  0,  0,  0,
     & 125, 74, 75, 76, 77, 78, 79, 80, 81, 82,  0,  0,  0,  0,  0,  0,
     &  92,  0, 83, 84, 85, 86, 87, 88, 89, 90,  0,  0,  0,  0,  0,  0,
     &  48, 49, 50, 51, 52, 53, 54, 55, 56, 57,  0,  0,  0,  0,  0,  0/
C
C
```

```
      DO 10 I=1,LEN
         ILETT = ICHAR(IN(I:I))
         OUT(I:I) = CHAR(TRTAB(ILETT))
   10 CONTINUE
C
      RETURN
      END
```

APPENDIX D. A NEUTRAL FILE FOR FIXED FORMAT LETTERS

Information transferred via CAD*I neutral files will normally contain not only data for post-processors, but also information which is directed to the responsible person on the receiving side. Such information will be called a letter.

This document describes a fixed format (card image) letter

The card image letter is restricted to characters of the basic alphabet defined in "Appendix A. The graphical alphabet" on page 213 and does not allow escape sequences for national symbols (such as Greek letters). Each line in the letter corresponds to an 80-character block on the file ("card image").

```
<header>         ::= CAD*I_FORMAT_BEGIN_19851109 <any text>
                 format: 80A1
<text_line>      ::= <any text except the trailer>
                 format: 80A1
<trailer>        ::= CAD*I_FORMAT_END___19851109 <any text>
                 format: 80A1
```

Each 80-byte record (card) is to be interpreted as follows:

effect: display or print card

error: E0001 character not included in the alphabet
E0002 end of file encountered

Note that this neutral file may be used not only for letters but also for transmitting the source code of routines (see "ROUTINE" on page 145) that are to be compiled and linked into the receiving CAD environment.

APPENDIX E. EXAMPLES OF CAD*I NEUTRAL FILES

The following is an example of a CAD*I metafile containing four neutral files: different ways:

1. The first one is a letter file describing the content of the second file.
2. The second file represents a CSG model and the corresponding polyhedron model (see Figure 30 on page 228) according to the previous CAD*I specification version 2.1 in a compact form.
3. The third file is again a letter file describing the content of the fourth file.
4. The fourth file represents the same CSG and polyhedron model as the second file according to the previous CAD*I specification version 2.1 in an expanded ("pretty print") form.
5. The fifth file is again a letter file describing the content of the sixth file.
6. The sixth file represents another CSG model according to the present CAD*I specification version 3.1.
7. The seventh file is again a letter file describing the content of the sixth file.
8. The eighth file represents a B-rep model according to the present CAD*I specification version 3.1.

```
  CAD*I_FORMAT_BEGIN_19851011 METAFILE
  CAD*I_FORMAT_BEGIN_19851109 start letter describing next file

  File 1 and 2
  ------------
  This example contains the CAD*I representation of the first test part
  which was exchanged between the EUCLID system and the Bravo3 system.
  The test part is a simple spinning top which was created in the EUCLID
  system by boolean operations applied on CSG primitives. The neutral
  file contains both the CSG tree and the polyhedron representation which
  corresponds to the EUCLID data structure.

  The following neutral file is in compact form

CAD*I_FORMAT_END___19851109 end of letter describing next file
CAD*I_FORMAT_BEGIN_19860611 EUCLID PREPROZESSOR
HEADER('GENGENBACH/REICHERT','Kernforschungszentrum Karlsruhe','Micro-VAX II','V
MS_4.2','EUCLID-Preprocessor 1.0','15-APR-1987','??disclaimer??','4','3','0','0'
,10,5,5);WORLD(OPEN);WORLD_HEADER(+1.00000E-03,+1.00000E+00,+2.00000E+03,+1.0000
0E-04);SCOPE;HYBRID_SOLID(#1:OPEN);SCOPE;CONSTRUCT(#2:OPEN);SCOPE;SOLID_SPHERE(#
6:+1.50000E+02,PLACEMENT(:ROT_MATRIX(:DIRECTION(:+1.00000E+00,+0.00000E+00,+0.00
```

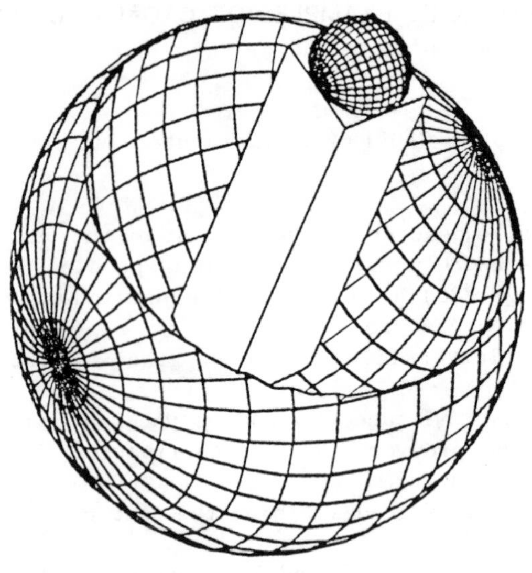

Figure 30. CSG and Polyhedron test part

```
000E+00:),DIRECTION(:+0.00000E+00,+1.00000E+00,+0.00000E+00:),DIRECTION(:+0.0000
0E+00,+0.00000E+00,+1.00000E+00:):),POINT_CONSTANT(:+1.00000E+02,+1.00000E+02,+1
.00000E+02:):));SOLID_SPHERE(#7:+1.30000E+02,PLACEMENT(:ROT_MATRIX(:DIRECTION(:+
1.00000E+00,+0.00000E+00,+0.00000E+00:),DIRECTION(:+0.00000E+00,+1.00000E+00,+0.
00000E+00:),DIRECTION(:+0.00000E+00,+0.00000E+00,+1.00000E+00:):),POINT_CONSTANT
(:+1.00000E+02,+1.00000E+02,+1.70000E+02:):));BOX(#8:+6.00000E+01,+6.00000E+01,+
3.00000E+02,PLACEMENT(:ROT_MATRIX(:DIRECTION(:+1.00000E+00,+0.00000E+00,+0.00000
E+00:),DIRECTION(:+0.00000E+00,+1.00000E+00,+0.00000E+00:),DIRECTION(:+0.00000E+
00,+0.00000E+00,+1.00000E+00:):),POINT_CONSTANT(:+7.00000E+01,+7.00000E+01,+0.00
000E+00:):));SOLID_SPHERE(#9:+3.00000E+01,PLACEMENT(:ROT_MATRIX(:DIRECTION(:+1.0
0000E+00,+0.00000E+00,+0.00000E+00:),DIRECTION(:+0.00000E+00,+1.00000E+00,+0.000
00E+00:),DIRECTION(:+0.00000E+00,+0.00000E+00,+1.00000E+00:):),POINT_CONSTANT(:+
1.00000E+02,+1.00000E+02,+3.00000E+02:):));BOOLEAN(#5:UNION,#8,#9);BOOLEAN(#4:DI
FFERENCE,#6,#7);BOOLEAN(#3:UNION,#4,#5);END_SCOPE;CONSTR_RESULT(#3);CONSTRUCT(#2
:CLOSE);POLY_HEDRON(#225:OPEN);SCOPE;POINT_CONSTANT(#12:+2.50000E+02,+1.00000E+0
2,+1.00000E+02);POINT_CONSTANT(#13:+2.06066E+02,+1.66131E+02,+1.70743E+01);POINT
_CONSTANT(#14:+2.06066E+02,+2.06066E+02,+1.00000E+02);POINT_CONSTANT(#17:+1.0000
0E+02,+2.50000E+02,+1.00000E+02);POINT_CONSTANT(#18:+1.00000E+02,+1.93523E+02,-1
.72747E+01);POINT_CONSTANT(#21:-6.06599E+00,+2.06066E+02,+1.00000E+02);POINT_CON
STANT(#22:-6.06599E+00,+1.66131E+02,+1.70743E+01);POINT_CONSTANT(#25:-5.00000E+0
```

```
1,+1.00000E+02,+1.00000E+02);POINT_CONSTANT(#28:+2.06066E+02,+7.63981E+01,-3.406
72E+00);POINT_CONSTANT(#31:+1.00000E+02,+6.66219E+01,-4.62392E+01);POINT_CONSTAN
T(#34:-6.06599E+00,+7.63981E+01,-3.40669E+00);POINT_CONSTANT(#39:+2.06066E+02,+4
.43782E+00,+5.39797E+01);POINT_CONSTANT(#42:+1.00000E+02,-3.51453E+01,+3.49174E+
01);POINT_CONSTANT(#45:-6.06599E+00,+4.43785E+00,+5.39797E+01);POINT_CONSTANT(#5
0:+2.06066E+02,+4.43780E+00,+1.46020E+02);POINT_CONSTANT(#53:+1.00000E+02,-3.514
53E+01,+1.65083E+02);POINT_CONSTANT(#56:-6.06599E+00,+4.43783E+00,+1.46020E+02);
POINT_CONSTANT(#61:+2.06066E+02,+4.79405E+01,+1.80713E+02);POINT_CONSTANT(#62:+2
.23146E+02,+8.50926E+01,+1.62821E+02);POINT_CONSTANT(#63:+2.23310E+02,+8.56615E+
01,+1.62821E+02);POINT_CONSTANT(#66:+1.00000E+02,-1.71259E+01,+1.79453E+02);POIN
T_CONSTANT(#67:+1.91924E+02,+1.71795E+01,+1.62932E+02);POINT_CONSTANT(#70:-6.065
99E+00,+4.79404E+01,+1.80712E+02);POINT_CONSTANT(#71:+8.07614E+00,+1.71795E+01,+
1.62932E+02);POINT_CONSTANT(#74:-2.33095E+01,+8.56615E+01,+1.62821E+02);POINT_CO
NSTANT(#75:-2.31464E+01,+8.50926E+01,+1.62821E+02);POINT_CONSTANT(#78:+2.24609E+
02,+9.71037E+01,+1.57311E+02);POINT_CONSTANT(#79:+2.23277E+02,+1.10119E+02,+1.57
311E+02);POINT_CONSTANT(#80:+2.14894E+02,+1.36469E+02,+1.70000E+02);POINT_CONSTA
NT(#81:+2.06066E+02,+1.49757E+02,+1.86663E+02);POINT_CONSTANT(#82:+2.06066E+02,+
1.66131E+02,+1.82926E+02);POINT_CONSTANT(#85:+1.98779E+02,+1.68013E+02,+1.85286E
+02);POINT_CONSTANT(#88:-6.06599E+00,+1.49757E+02,+1.86663E+02);POINT_CONSTANT(#
89:-6.06599E+00,+1.66131E+02,+1.82926E+02);POINT_CONSTANT(#90:+1.22104E+00,+1.68
013E+02,+1.85286E+02);POINT_CONSTANT(#93:-1.48940E+01,+1.36469E+02,+1.70000E+02)
;POINT_CONSTANT(#94:-2.32772E+01,+1.10119E+02,+1.57311E+02);POINT_CONSTANT(#95:-
2.46087E+01,+9.71037E+01,+1.57311E+02);POINT_CONSTANT(#100:+1.98779E+02,+1.75374
E+02,+1.70000E+02);POINT_CONSTANT(#101:+1.91924E+02,+1.85069E+02,+1.55765E+02);P
OINT_CONSTANT(#102:+1.00000E+02,+2.23145E+02,+1.55765E+02);POINT_CONSTANT(#105:+
8.07614E+00,+1.85069E+02,+1.55765E+02);POINT_CONSTANT(#106:+1.22103E+00,+1.75374
E+02,+1.70000E+02);POINT_CONSTANT(#111:+1.91924E+02,+1.57314E+02,+9.81310E+01);P
OINT_CONSTANT(#114:+1.00000E+02,+1.81054E+02,+6.83619E+01);POINT_CONSTANT(#117:+
8.07614E+00,+1.57314E+02,+9.81311E+01);POINT_CONSTANT(#122:+1.91924E+02,+7.95450
E+01,+8.03809E+01);POINT_CONSTANT(#125:+1.30000E+02,+7.38374E+01,+5.53743E+01);P
OINT_CONSTANT(#126:+1.30000E+02,+1.30000E+02,+6.81930E+01);POINT_CONSTANT(#127:+
1.00000E+02,+1.30000E+02,+5.67093E+01);POINT_CONSTANT(#130:+7.00000E+01,+1.30000
E+02,+6.81930E+01);POINT_CONSTANT(#131:+7.00000E+01,+7.38374E+01,+5.53743E+01);P
OINT_CONSTANT(#132:+8.07614E+00,+7.95450E+01,+8.03809E+01);POINT_CONSTANT(#137:+
1.91924E+02,+1.71795E+01,+1.30116E+02);POINT_CONSTANT(#140:+1.00000E+02,-1.71259
E+01,+1.13595E+02);POINT_CONSTANT(#141:+1.00000E+02,+7.00000E+01,+4.41145E+01);P
OINT_CONSTANT(#142:+1.30000E+02,+7.00000E+01,+5.84345E+01);POINT_CONSTANT(#145:+
8.07614E+00,+1.71795E+01,+1.30116E+02);POINT_CONSTANT(#146:+7.00000E+01,+7.00000
E+01,+5.84345E+01);POINT_CONSTANT(#163:+7.00000E+01,+7.00000E+01,+3.00000E+02);P
OINT_CONSTANT(#164:+1.30000E+02,+7.00000E+01,+3.00000E+02);POINT_CONSTANT(#167:+
1.30000E+02,+1.00000E+02,+3.00000E+02);POINT_CONSTANT(#168:+1.30000E+02,+1.30000
E+02,+3.00000E+02);POINT_CONSTANT(#171:+1.00000E+02,+1.30000E+02,+3.00000E+02);P
OINT_CONSTANT(#172:+7.00000E+01,+1.30000E+02,+3.00000E+02);POINT_CONSTANT(#175:+
7.00000E+01,+1.00000E+02,+3.00000E+02);POINT_CONSTANT(#179:+1.21213E+02,+8.08875
E+01,+3.00000E+02);POINT_CONSTANT(#180:+1.21213E+02,+1.21213E+02,+3.00000E+02);P
OINT_CONSTANT(#181:+7.87868E+01,+1.21213E+02,+3.00000E+02);POINT_CONSTANT(#182:+
7.87868E+01,+8.08875E+01,+3.00000E+02);POINT_CONSTANT(#183:+1.00000E+02,+7.29709
E+01,+3.00000E+02);POINT_CONSTANT(#186:+1.21213E+02,+8.08875E+01,+3.09204E+02);P
```

OINT_CONSTANT(#189:+1.00000E+02,+7.29709E+01,+3.13017E+02);POINT_CONSTANT(#192:+
7.87868E+01,+8.08875E+01,+3.09204E+02);POINT_CONSTANT(#197:+1.21213E+02,+9.52796
E+01,+3.20681E+02);POINT_CONSTANT(#200:+1.00000E+02,+9.33244E+01,+3.29248E+02);P
OINT_CONSTANT(#203:+7.87868E+01,+9.52796E+01,+3.20681E+02);POINT_CONSTANT(#208:+
1.21213E+02,+1.13226E+02,+3.16585E+02);POINT_CONSTANT(#211:+1.00000E+02,+1.18705
E+02,+3.23455E+02);POINT_CONSTANT(#214:+7.87868E+01,+1.13226E+02,+3.16585E+02);P
OLY_LOOP(#11:(/#12,#13,#14/));POLY_LOOP(#16:(/#14,#17,#18,#13/));POLY_LOOP(#20:(
/ #17,#21,#22,#18/));POLY_LOOP(#24:(/#21,#25,#22/));POLY_LOOP(#27:(/#12,#13,#28/
);POLY_LOOP(#30:(/#13,#18,#31,#28/));POLY_LOOP(#33:(/#18,#22,#34,#31/));POLY_LOO
P(#36:(/#22,#25,#34/));POLY_LOOP(#38:(/#12,#28,#39/));POLY_LOOP(#41:(/#28,#31,#4
2,#39/));POLY_LOOP(#44:(/#31,#34,#45,#42/));POLY_LOOP(#47:(/#34,#25,#45/));POLY_
LOOP(#49:(/#12,#39,#50/));POLY_LOOP(#52:(/#39,#42,#53,#50/));POLY_LOOP(#55:(/#42
,#45,#56,#53/));POLY_LOOP(#58:(/#45,#25,#56/));POLY_LOOP(#60:(/#12,#50,#61,#62,#
63/));POLY_LOOP(#65:(/#50,#53,#66,#67,#61/));POLY_LOOP(#69:(/#53,#56,#70,#71,#66
/));POLY_LOOP(#73:(/#56,#25,#74,#75,#70/));POLY_LOOP(#77:(/#12,#63,#78,#79,#80,#
81,#82/));POLY_LOOP(#84:(/#85,#82,#81/));POLY_LOOP(#87:(/#88,#89,#90/));POLY_LOO
P(#92:(/#74,#25,#89,#88,#93,#94,#95/));POLY_LOOP(#97:(/#12,#82,#14/));POLY_LOOP(
#99:(/#82,#85,#100,#101,#102,#17,#14/));POLY_LOOP(#104:(/#90,#89,#21,#17,#102,#1
05,#106/));POLY_LOOP(#108:(/#89,#25,#21/));POLY_LOOP(#110:(/#80,#79,#111,#101,#1
00/));POLY_LOOP(#113:(/#102,#101,#111,#114/));POLY_LOOP(#116:(/#105,#102,#114,#1
17/));POLY_LOOP(#119:(/#106,#105,#117,#94,#93/));POLY_LOOP(#121:(/#79,#78,#122,#
111/));POLY_LOOP(#124:(/#111,#122,#125,#126,#127,#114/));POLY_LOOP(#129:(/#114,#
127,#130,#131,#132,#117/));POLY_LOOP(#134:(/#117,#132,#95,#94/));POLY_LOOP(#136:
(/#78,#63,#62,#137,#122/));POLY_LOOP(#139:(/#122,#137,#140,#141,#142,#125/));POL
Y_LOOP(#144:(/#141,#140,#145,#132,#131,#146/));POLY_LOOP(#148:(/#132,#145,#75,#7
4,#95/));POLY_LOOP(#150:(/#62,#61,#67,#137/));POLY_LOOP(#152:(/#137,#67,#66,#140
/));POLY_LOOP(#154:(/#140,#66,#71,#145/));POLY_LOOP(#156:(/#145,#71,#70,#75/));P
OLY_LOOP(#158:(/#100,#85,#81,#80/));POLY_LOOP(#160:(/#93,#88,#90,#106/));POLY_LO
OP(#162:(/#142,#141,#146,#163,#164/));POLY_LOOP(#166:(/#126,#125,#142,#164,#167,
#168/));POLY_LOOP(#170:(/#130,#127,#126,#168,#171,#172/));POLY_LOOP(#174:(/#146,
#131,#130,#172,#175,#163/));POLY_LOOP(#177:(/#163,#175,#172,#171,#168,#167,#164/
));POLY_LOOP(#178:(/#179,#167,#180,#171,#181,#175,#182,#183/));POLY_LOOP(#185:(/
#179,#186,#167/));POLY_LOOP(#188:(/#183,#189,#186,#179/));POLY_LOOP(#191:(/#182,
#192,#189,#183/));POLY_LOOP(#194:(/#175,#192,#182/));POLY_LOOP(#196:(/#167,#186,
#197/));POLY_LOOP(#199:(/#186,#189,#200,#197/));POLY_LOOP(#202:(/#189,#192,#203,
#200/));POLY_LOOP(#205:(/#192,#175,#203/));POLY_LOOP(#207:(/#167,#197,#208/));PO
LY_LOOP(#210:(/#197,#200,#211,#208/));POLY_LOOP(#213:(/#200,#203,#214,#211/));PO
LY_LOOP(#216:(/#203,#175,#214/));POLY_LOOP(#218:(/#167,#208,#180/));POLY_LOOP(#2
20:(/#208,#211,#171,#180/));POLY_LOOP(#222:(/#211,#214,#181,#171/));POLY_LOOP(#2
24:(/#214,#175,#181/));POLY_FACE(#10:(/#11/));POLY_FACE(#15:(/#16/));POLY_FACE(#
19:(/#20/));POLY_FACE(#23:(/#24/));POLY_FACE(#26:(/#27/));POLY_FACE(#29:(/#30/))
;POLY_FACE(#32:(/#33/));POLY_FACE(#35:(/#36/));POLY_FACE(#37:(/#38/));POLY_FACE(
#40:(/#41/));POLY_FACE(#43:(/#44/));POLY_FACE(#46:(/#47/));POLY_FACE(#48:(/#49/)
);POLY_FACE(#51:(/#52/));POLY_FACE(#54:(/#55/));POLY_FACE(#57:(/#58/));POLY_FACE
(#59:(/#60/));POLY_FACE(#64:(/#65/));POLY_FACE(#68:(/#69/));POLY_FACE(#72:(/#73/
));POLY_FACE(#76:(/#77/));POLY_FACE(#83:(/#84/));POLY_FACE(#86:(/#87/));POLY_FAC
E(#91:(/#92/));POLY_FACE(#96:(/#97/));POLY_FACE(#98:(/#99/));POLY_FACE(#103:(/#1
04/));POLY_FACE(#107:(/#108/));POLY_FACE(#109:(/#110/));POLY_FACE(#112:(/#113/))

```
;POLY_FACE(#115:(/#116/));POLY_FACE(#118:(/#119/));POLY_FACE(#120:(/#121/));POLY
_FACE(#123:(/#124/));POLY_FACE(#128:(/#129/));POLY_FACE(#133:(/#134/));POLY_FACE
(#135:(/#136/));POLY_FACE(#138:(/#139/));POLY_FACE(#143:(/#144/));POLY_FACE(#147
:(/#148/));POLY_FACE(#149:(/#150/));POLY_FACE(#151:(/#152/));POLY_FACE(#153:(/#1
54/));POLY_FACE(#155:(/#156/));POLY_FACE(#157:(/#158/));POLY_FACE(#159:(/#160/))
;POLY_FACE(#161:(/#162/));POLY_FACE(#165:(/#166/));POLY_FACE(#169:(/#170/));POLY
_FACE(#173:(/#174/));POLY_FACE(#176:(/#177,#178/));POLY_FACE(#184:(/#185/));POLY
_FACE(#187:(/#188/));POLY_FACE(#190:(/#191/));POLY_FACE(#193:(/#194/));POLY_FACE
(#195:(/#196/));POLY_FACE(#198:(/#199/));POLY_FACE(#201:(/#202/));POLY_FACE(#204
:(/#205/));POLY_FACE(#206:(/#207/));POLY_FACE(#209:(/#210/));POLY_FACE(#212:(/#2
13/));POLY_FACE(#215:(/#216/));POLY_FACE(#217:(/#218/));POLY_FACE(#219:(/#220/))
;POLY_FACE(#221:(/#222/));POLY_FACE(#223:(/#224/));POLY_SHELL(#226:(/#10,#15,#19
,#23,#26,#29,#32,#35,#37,#40,#43,#46,#48,#51,#54,#57,#59,#64,#68,#72,#76,#83,#86
,#91,#96,#98,#103,#107,#109,#112,#115,#118,#120,#123,#128,#133,#135,#138,#143,#1
47,#149,#151,#153,#155,#157,#159,#161,#165,#169,#173,#176,#184,#187,#190,#193,#1
95,#198,#201,#204,#206,#209,#212,#215,#217,#219,#221,#223/));END_SCOPE;POLY_HEDR
ON(#225:CLOSE);END_SCOPE;HYBRID_SOLID_RESULT(.T.,UPON_MODIFICATION,#2,#225);HYBR
ID_SOLID(#1:CLOSE);END_SCOPE;WORLD(CLOSE);
CAD*I_FORMAT___END 19860611 EUCLID PREPROCESSOR
CAD*I_FORMAT_BEGIN_19851109 start letter describing next file

    File 3 and 4
    ------------
    This example contains the CAD*I representation of the first test part
    which was exchanged between the EUCLID system and the Bravo3 system.
    The test part is a simple spinning top which was created in the EUCLID
    system by boolean operations applied on CSG primitives. The neutral
    file corresponds to the specification version 2.1 and contains both
    the CSG tree and the polyhedron representation which corresponds to
    the EUCLID data structure.

    The following neutral file is in pretty print form.

   CAD*I_FORMAT_END___19851109 end of letter describing next file
   CAD*I_FORMAT_BEGIN_19860611 EUCLID PREPROZESSOR
   HEADER(
           'GENGENBACH/REICHERT',
           'Kernforschungszentrum Karlsruhe',
           'Micro-VAX II',
           'VMS_4.2',
           'EUCLID-Preprocessor 1.0',
           '15-APR-1987',
           '??disclaimer??',
           '4',
           '3',
           '0',
           '0',
           '0',10,5,5);
   WORLD(OPEN);
```

```
WORLD_HEADER(+1.00000E-03,+1.00000E+00,+2.00000E+03,+1.00000E-04);
SCOPE;
HYBRID_SOLID(#1:OPEN);
SCOPE;
CONSTRUCT(#2:OPEN);
SCOPE;
SOLID_SPHERE(#6:+1.50000E+02,
                PLACEMENT(:ROT_MATRIX(:DIRECTION(:+1.00000E+00,
                                                  +0.00000E+00,
                                                  +0.00000E+00:),
                                       DIRECTION(:+0.00000E+00,
                                                  +1.00000E+00,
                                                  +0.00000E+00:),
                                       DIRECTION(:+0.00000E+00,
                                                  +0.00000E+00,
                                                  +1.00000E+00:):),
                           POINT_CONSTANT(:+1.00000E+02,
                                           +1.00000E+02,
                                           +1.00000E+02:):));
SOLID_SPHERE(#7:+1.30000E+02,
                PLACEMENT(:ROT_MATRIX(:DIRECTION(:+1.00000E+00,
                                                  +0.00000E+00,
                                                  +0.00000E+00:),
                                       DIRECTION(:+0.00000E+00,
                                                  +1.00000E+00,
                                                  +0.00000E+00:),
                                       DIRECTION(:+0.00000E+00,
                                                  +0.00000E+00,
                                                  +1.00000E+00:):),
                           POINT_CONSTANT(:+1.00000E+02,
                                           +1.00000E+02,
                                           +1.70000E+02:):));
BOX(#8:+6.00000E+01,
       +6.00000E+01,
       +3.00000E+02,
       PLACEMENT(:ROT_MATRIX(:DIRECTION(:+1.00000E+00,
                                         +0.00000E+00,
                                         +0.00000E+00:),
                              DIRECTION(:+0.00000E+00,
                                         +1.00000E+00,
                                         +0.00000E+00:),
                              DIRECTION(:+0.00000E+00,
                                         +0.00000E+00,
                                         +1.00000E+00:):),
                  POINT_CONSTANT(:+7.00000E+01,
                                  +7.00000E+01,
                                  +0.00000E+00:):));
SOLID_SPHERE(#9:+3.00000E+01,
```

```
               PLACEMENT(:ROT_MATRIX(:DIRECTION(:+1.00000E+00,
                                                 +0.00000E+00,
                                                 +0.00000E+00:),
                                      DIRECTION(:+0.00000E+00,
                                                 +1.00000E+00,
                                                 +0.00000E+00:),
                                      DIRECTION(:+0.00000E+00,
                                                 +0.00000E+00,
                                                 +1.00000E+00:):),
                         POINT_CONSTANT(:+1.00000E+02,
                                         +1.00000E+02,
                                         +3.00000E+02:):));
BOOLEAN(#5:UNION,#8,#9);
BOOLEAN(#4:DIFFERENCE,#6,#7);
BOOLEAN(#3:UNION,#4,#5);
END_SCOPE;
CONSTR_RESULT(#3);
CONSTRUCT(#2:CLOSE);
POLY_HEDRON(#225:OPEN);
SCOPE;
POINT_CONSTANT(#12:+2.50000E+02,
                   +1.00000E+02,
                   +1.00000E+02);
POINT_CONSTANT(#13:+2.06066E+02,
                   +1.66131E+02,
                   +1.70743E+01);
POINT_CONSTANT(#14:+2.06066E+02,
                   +2.06066E+02,
                   +1.00000E+02);
POINT_CONSTANT(#17:+1.00000E+02,
                   +2.50000E+02,
                   +1.00000E+02);
POINT_CONSTANT(#18:+1.00000E+02,
                   +1.93523E+02,
                   -1.72747E+01);
POINT_CONSTANT(#21:-6.06599E+00,
                   +2.06066E+02,
                   +1.00000E+02);
POINT_CONSTANT(#22:-6.06599E+00,
                   +1.66131E+02,
                   +1.70743E+01);
POINT_CONSTANT(#25:-5.00000E+01,
                   +1.00000E+02,
                   +1.00000E+02);
POINT_CONSTANT(#28:+2.06066E+02,
                   +7.63981E+01,
                   -3.40672E+00);
POINT_CONSTANT(#31:+1.00000E+02,
```

```
                    +6.66219E+01,
                    -4.62392E+01);
POINT_CONSTANT(#34:-6.06599E+00,
                    +7.63981E+01,
                    -3.40669E+00);
POINT_CONSTANT(#39:+2.06066E+02,
                    +4.43782E+00,
                    +5.39797E+01);
POINT_CONSTANT(#42:+1.00000E+02,
                    -3.51453E+01,
                    +3.49174E+01);
POINT_CONSTANT(#45:-6.06599E+00,
                    +4.43785E+00,
                    +5.39797E+01);
POINT_CONSTANT(#50:+2.06066E+02,
                    +4.43780E+00,
                    +1.46020E+02);
POINT_CONSTANT(#53:+1.00000E+02,
                    -3.51453E+01,
                    +1.65083E+02);
POINT_CONSTANT(#56:-6.06599E+00,
                    +4.43783E+00,
                    +1.46020E+02);
POINT_CONSTANT(#61:+2.06066E+02,
                    +4.79405E+01,
                    +1.80713E+02);
POINT_CONSTANT(#62:+2.23146E+02,
                    +8.50926E+01,
                    +1.62821E+02);
POINT_CONSTANT(#63:+2.23310E+02,
                    +8.56615E+01,
                    +1.62821E+02);
POINT_CONSTANT(#66:+1.00000E+02,
                    -1.71259E+01,
                    +1.79453E+02);
POINT_CONSTANT(#67:+1.91924E+02,
                    +1.71795E+01,
                    +1.62932E+02);
POINT_CONSTANT(#70:-6.06599E+00,
                    +4.79404E+01,
                    +1.80712E+02);
POINT_CONSTANT(#71:+8.07614E+00,
                    +1.71795E+01,
                    +1.62932E+02);
POINT_CONSTANT(#74:-2.33095E+01,
                    +8.56615E+01,
                    +1.62821E+02);
POINT_CONSTANT(#75:-2.31464E+01,
```

```
                +8.50926E+01,
                +1.62821E+02);
POINT_CONSTANT(#78:+2.24609E+02,
                +9.71037E+01,
                +1.57311E+02);
POINT_CONSTANT(#79:+2.23277E+02,
                +1.10119E+02,
                +1.57311E+02);
POINT_CONSTANT(#80:+2.14894E+02,
                +1.36469E+02,
                +1.70000E+02);
POINT_CONSTANT(#81:+2.06066E+02,
                +1.49757E+02,
                +1.86663E+02);
POINT_CONSTANT(#82:+2.06066E+02,
                +1.66131E+02,
                +1.82926E+02);
POINT_CONSTANT(#85:+1.98779E+02,
                +1.68013E+02,
                +1.85286E+02);
POINT_CONSTANT(#88:-6.06599E+00,
                +1.49757E+02,
                +1.86663E+02);
POINT_CONSTANT(#89:-6.06599E+00,
                +1.66131E+02,
                +1.82926E+02);
POINT_CONSTANT(#90:+1.22104E+00,
                +1.68013E+02,
                +1.85286E+02);
POINT_CONSTANT(#93:-1.48940E+01,
                +1.36469E+02,
                +1.70000E+02);
POINT_CONSTANT(#94:-2.32772E+01,
                +1.10119E+02,
                +1.57311E+02);
POINT_CONSTANT(#95:-2.46087E+01,
                +9.71037E+01,
                +1.57311E+02);
POINT_CONSTANT(#100:+1.98779E+02,
                 +1.75374E+02,
                 +1.70000E+02);
POINT_CONSTANT(#101:+1.91924E+02,
                 +1.85069E+02,
                 +1.55765E+02);
POINT_CONSTANT(#102:+1.00000E+02,
                 +2.23145E+02,
                 +1.55765E+02);
POINT_CONSTANT(#105:+8.07614E+00,
```

```
                     +1.85069E+02,
                     +1.55765E+02);
POINT_CONSTANT(#106:+1.22103E+00,
                     +1.75374E+02,
                     +1.70000E+02);
POINT_CONSTANT(#111:+1.91924E+02,
                     +1.57314E+02,
                     +9.81310E+01);
POINT_CONSTANT(#114:+1.00000E+02,
                     +1.81054E+02,
                     +6.83619E+01);
POINT_CONSTANT(#117:+8.07614E+00,
                     +1.57314E+02,
                     +9.81311E+01);
POINT_CONSTANT(#122:+1.91924E+02,
                     +7.95450E+01,
                     +8.03809E+01);
POINT_CONSTANT(#125:+1.30000E+02,
                     +7.38374E+01,
                     +5.53743E+01);
POINT_CONSTANT(#126:+1.30000E+02,
                     +1.30000E+02,
                     +6.81930E+01);
POINT_CONSTANT(#127:+1.00000E+02,
                     +1.30000E+02,
                     +5.67093E+01);
POINT_CONSTANT(#130:+7.00000E+01,
                     +1.30000E+02,
                     +6.81930E+01);
POINT_CONSTANT(#131:+7.00000E+01,
                     +7.38374E+01,
                     +5.53743E+01);
POINT_CONSTANT(#132:+8.07614E+00,
                     +7.95450E+01,
                     +8.03809E+01);
POINT_CONSTANT(#137:+1.91924E+02,
                     +1.71795E+01,
                     +1.30116E+02);
POINT_CONSTANT(#140:+1.00000E+02,
                     -1.71259E+01,
                     +1.13595E+02);
POINT_CONSTANT(#141:+1.00000E+02,
                     +7.00000E+01,
                     +4.41145E+01);
POINT_CONSTANT(#142:+1.30000E+02,
                     +7.00000E+01,
                     +5.84345E+01);
POINT_CONSTANT(#145:+8.07614E+00,
```

```
                     +1.71795E+01,
                     +1.30116E+02);
POINT_CONSTANT(#146:+7.00000E+01,
                     +7.00000E+01,
                     +5.84345E+01);
POINT_CONSTANT(#163:+7.00000E+01,
                     +7.00000E+01,
                     +3.00000E+02);
POINT_CONSTANT(#164:+1.30000E+02,
                     +7.00000E+01,
                     +3.00000E+02);
POINT_CONSTANT(#167:+1.30000E+02,
                     +1.00000E+02,
                     +3.00000E+02);
POINT_CONSTANT(#168:+1.30000E+02,
                     +1.30000E+02,
                     +3.00000E+02);
POINT_CONSTANT(#171:+1.00000E+02,
                     +1.30000E+02,
                     +3.00000E+02);
POINT_CONSTANT(#172:+7.00000E+01,
                     +1.30000E+02,
                     +3.00000E+02);
POINT_CONSTANT(#175:+7.00000E+01,
                     +1.00000E+02,
                     +3.00000E+02);
POINT_CONSTANT(#179:+1.21213E+02,
                     +8.08875E+01,
                     +3.00000E+02);
POINT_CONSTANT(#180:+1.21213E+02,
                     +1.21213E+02,
                     +3.00000E+02);
POINT_CONSTANT(#181:+7.87868E+01,
                     +1.21213E+02,
                     +3.00000E+02);
POINT_CONSTANT(#182:+7.87868E+01,
                     +8.08875E+01,
                     +3.00000E+02);
POINT_CONSTANT(#183:+1.00000E+02,
                     +7.29709E+01,
                     +3.00000E+02);
POINT_CONSTANT(#186:+1.21213E+02,
                     +8.08875E+01,
                     +3.09204E+02);
POINT_CONSTANT(#189:+1.00000E+02,
                     +7.29709E+01,
                     +3.13017E+02);
POINT_CONSTANT(#192:+7.87868E+01,
```

```
                    +8.08875E+01,
                    +3.09204E+02);
POINT_CONSTANT(#197:+1.21213E+02,
                    +9.52796E+01,
                    +3.20681E+02);
POINT_CONSTANT(#200:+1.00000E+02,
                    +9.33244E+01,
                    +3.29248E+02);
POINT_CONSTANT(#203:+7.87868E+01,
                    +9.52796E+01,
                    +3.20681E+02);
POINT_CONSTANT(#208:+1.21213E+02,
                    +1.13226E+02,
                    +3.16585E+02);
POINT_CONSTANT(#211:+1.00000E+02,
                    +1.18705E+02,
                    +3.23455E+02);
POINT_CONSTANT(#214:+7.87868E+01,
                    +1.13226E+02,
                    +3.16585E+02);
POLY_LOOP(#11:(/#12,#13,#14/));
POLY_LOOP(#16:(/#14,#17,#18,#13/));
POLY_LOOP(#20:(/#17,#21,#22,#18/));
POLY_LOOP(#24:(/#21,#25,#22/));
POLY_LOOP(#27:(/#12,#13,#28/));
POLY_LOOP(#30:(/#13,#18,#31,#28/));
POLY_LOOP(#33:(/#18,#22,#34,#31/));
POLY_LOOP(#36:(/#22,#25,#34/));
POLY_LOOP(#38:(/#12,#28,#39/));
POLY_LOOP(#41:(/#28,#31,#42,#39/));
POLY_LOOP(#44:(/#31,#34,#45,#42/));
POLY_LOOP(#47:(/#34,#25,#45/));
POLY_LOOP(#49:(/#12,#39,#50/));
POLY_LOOP(#52:(/#39,#42,#53,#50/));
POLY_LOOP(#55:(/#42,#45,#56,#53/));
POLY_LOOP(#58:(/#45,#25,#56/));
POLY_LOOP(#60:(/#12,#50,#61,#62,#63/));
POLY_LOOP(#65:(/#50,#53,#66,#67,#61/));
POLY_LOOP(#69:(/#53,#56,#70,#71,#66/));
POLY_LOOP(#73:(/#56,#25,#74,#75,#70/));
POLY_LOOP(#77:(/#12,#63,#78,#79,#80,#81,#82/));
POLY_LOOP(#84:(/#85,#82,#81/));
POLY_LOOP(#87:(/#88,#89,#90/));
POLY_LOOP(#92:(/#74,#25,#89,#88,#93,#94,#95/));
POLY_LOOP(#97:(/#12,#82,#14/));
POLY_LOOP(#99:(/#82,#85,#100,#101,#102,#17,#14/));
POLY_LOOP(#104:(/#90,#89,#21,#17,#102,#105,#106/));
POLY_LOOP(#108:(/#89,#25,#21/));
```

```
POLY_LOOP(#110:(/#80,#79,#111,#101,#100/));
POLY_LOOP(#113:(/#102,#101,#111,#114/));
POLY_LOOP(#116:(/#105,#102,#114,#117/));
POLY_LOOP(#119:(/#106,#105,#117,#94,#93/));
POLY_LOOP(#121:(/#79,#78,#122,#111/));
POLY_LOOP(#124:(/#111,#122,#125,#126,#127,#114/));
POLY_LOOP(#129:(/#114,#127,#130,#131,#132,#117/));
POLY_LOOP(#134:(/#117,#132,#95,#94/));
POLY_LOOP(#136:(/#78,#63,#62,#137,#122/));
POLY_LOOP(#139:(/#122,#137,#140,#141,#142,#125/));
POLY_LOOP(#144:(/#141,#140,#145,#132,#131,#146/));
POLY_LOOP(#148:(/#132,#145,#75,#74,#95/));
POLY_LOOP(#150:(/#62,#61,#67,#137/));
POLY_LOOP(#152:(/#137,#67,#66,#140/));
POLY_LOOP(#154:(/#140,#66,#71,#145/));
POLY_LOOP(#156:(/#145,#71,#70,#75/));
POLY_LOOP(#158:(/#100,#85,#81,#80/));
POLY_LOOP(#160:(/#93,#88,#90,#106/));
POLY_LOOP(#162:(/#142,#141,#146,#163,#164/));
POLY_LOOP(#166:(/#126,#125,#142,#164,#167,#168/));
POLY_LOOP(#170:(/#130,#127,#126,#168,#171,#172/));
POLY_LOOP(#174:(/#146,#131,#130,#172,#175,#163/));
POLY_LOOP(#177:(/#163,#175,#172,#171,#168,#167,#164/));
POLY_LOOP(#178:(/#179,#167,#180,#171,#181,#175,#182,#183/));
POLY_LOOP(#185:(/#179,#186,#167/));
POLY_LOOP(#188:(/#183,#189,#186,#179/));
POLY_LOOP(#191:(/#182,#192,#189,#183/));
POLY_LOOP(#194:(/#175,#192,#182/));
POLY_LOOP(#196:(/#167,#186,#197/));
POLY_LOOP(#199:(/#186,#189,#200,#197/));
POLY_LOOP(#202:(/#189,#192,#203,#200/));
POLY_LOOP(#205:(/#192,#175,#203/));
POLY_LOOP(#207:(/#167,#197,#208/));
POLY_LOOP(#210:(/#197,#200,#211,#208/));
POLY_LOOP(#213:(/#200,#203,#214,#211/));
POLY_LOOP(#216:(/#203,#175,#214/));
POLY_LOOP(#218:(/#167,#208,#180/));
POLY_LOOP(#220:(/#208,#211,#171,#180/));
POLY_LOOP(#222:(/#211,#214,#181,#171/));
POLY_LOOP(#224:(/#214,#175,#181/));
POLY_FACE(#10:(/#11/));
POLY_FACE(#15:(/#16/));
POLY_FACE(#19:(/#20/));
POLY_FACE(#23:(/#24/));
POLY_FACE(#26:(/#27/));
POLY_FACE(#29:(/#30/));
POLY_FACE(#32:(/#33/));
POLY_FACE(#35:(/#36/));
```

```
POLY_FACE(#37:(/#38/));
POLY_FACE(#40:(/#41/));
POLY_FACE(#43:(/#44/));
POLY_FACE(#46:(/#47/));
POLY_FACE(#48:(/#49/));
POLY_FACE(#51:(/#52/));
POLY_FACE(#54:(/#55/));
POLY_FACE(#57:(/#58/));
POLY_FACE(#59:(/#60/));
POLY_FACE(#64:(/#65/));
POLY_FACE(#68:(/#69/));
POLY_FACE(#72:(/#73/));
POLY_FACE(#76:(/#77/));
POLY_FACE(#83:(/#84/));
POLY_FACE(#86:(/#87/));
POLY_FACE(#91:(/#92/));
POLY_FACE(#96:(/#97/));
POLY_FACE(#98:(/#99/));
POLY_FACE(#103:(/#104/));
POLY_FACE(#107:(/#108/));
POLY_FACE(#109:(/#110/));
POLY_FACE(#112:(/#113/));
POLY_FACE(#115:(/#116/));
POLY_FACE(#118:(/#119/));
POLY_FACE(#120:(/#121/));
POLY_FACE(#123:(/#124/));
POLY_FACE(#128:(/#129/));
POLY_FACE(#133:(/#134/));
POLY_FACE(#135:(/#136/));
POLY_FACE(#138:(/#139/));
POLY_FACE(#143:(/#144/));
POLY_FACE(#147:(/#148/));
POLY_FACE(#149:(/#150/));
POLY_FACE(#151:(/#152/));
POLY_FACE(#153:(/#154/));
POLY_FACE(#155:(/#156/));
POLY_FACE(#157:(/#158/));
POLY_FACE(#159:(/#160/));
POLY_FACE(#161:(/#162/));
POLY_FACE(#165:(/#166/));
POLY_FACE(#169:(/#170/));
POLY_FACE(#173:(/#174/));
POLY_FACE(#176:(/#177,#178/));
POLY_FACE(#184:(/#185/));
POLY_FACE(#187:(/#188/));
POLY_FACE(#190:(/#191/));
POLY_FACE(#193:(/#194/));
POLY_FACE(#195:(/#196/));
```

```
POLY_FACE(#198:(/#199/));
POLY_FACE(#201:(/#202/));
POLY_FACE(#204:(/#205/));
POLY_FACE(#206:(/#207/));
POLY_FACE(#209:(/#210/));
POLY_FACE(#212:(/#213/));
POLY_FACE(#215:(/#216/));
POLY_FACE(#217:(/#218/));
POLY_FACE(#219:(/#220/));
POLY_FACE(#221:(/#222/));
POLY_FACE(#223:(/#224/));
POLY_SHELL(#226:(/#10,#15,#19,#23,#26,#29,#32,#35,#37,#40,#43,#46,#48,#51
                ,#54,#57,#59,#64,#68,#72,#76,#83,#86,#91,#96,#98,#103
                ,#107,#109,#112,#115,#118,#120,#123,#128,#133,#135,#138
                ,#143,#147,#149,#151,#153,#155,#157,#159,#161,#165,#169
                ,#173,#176,#184,#187,#190,#193,#195,#198,#201,#204,#206
                ,#209,#212,#215,#217,#219,#221,#223/));
END_SCOPE;
POLY_HEDRON(#225:CLOSE);
END_SCOPE;
HYBRID_SOLID_RESULT(.T.,UPON_MODIFICATION,#2,#225);
HYBRID_SOLID(#1:CLOSE);
END_SCOPE;
WORLD(CLOSE);
CAD*I_FORMAT___END 19860611 EUCLID PREPROCESSOR
CAD*I_FORMAT_BEGIN_19851109 start letter describing next file

 File 5 and 6
 ------------
 The following is an example of a CAD*I neutral file according to
 version 3.1 of the specification.  The test part is a LINEAR_SWEEP
 created with a contour containing lines and circles.

 The following neutral file is in pretty print form.

CAD*I_FORMAT_END___19851109 end of letter describing next file
CAD*I_FORMAT_BEGIN_19870630_19870505140528 Bravo3 PREPROZESSOR
    HEADER(
       (*  AUTHOR   :  *)   'F.KATZ',
       (*  ADDRESS  :  *)   'IRE/KFK',
       (*  HARDWARE:  *)   'IBM3090',
       (*  OP. SYS.:  *)   'IBM3090-MVS/XA',
       (*  PRE_PROC:  *)   'SYNTHAVISION 1.1',
       (*  DATE     :  *)   'MAY-5-1987',
       (*  DISCLAIM:  *)   'LINEAR_SWEEP',
       (*  LEV_GEOM:  *)   '3A',
       (*  LEV_ASSE:  *)   '3',
       (*  LEV_PARA:  *)   '1A',
```

```
   (*  LEV_REF :  *)    '1',
   (*  MAX_INT :  *)    3,
   (*  MANTISSE:  *)    4,
   (*  EXPONENT:  *)    2);
WORLD(OPEN);
   WORLD_HEADER(
   (*  LENG.UN.:  *)    +1.0000E-03,
   (*  ANGL.UN :  *)    +1.0000E+00,
   (*  WORLD.S.:  *)    +1.0000E+05,
   (*  MINDIST :  *)    +1.0000E-08);
   SCOPE;
CONSTRUCT( #1:OPEN);
   SCOPE;

   LINEAR_SWEEP( #2:OPEN);
   SCOPE;
   POINT( #3:                    +0.0,         +0.0,         +0.0);
   POINT( #4:+5.0000E+00,+5.0000E+00,                        +0.0);
   POINT( #5:+1.5000E+01,+5.0000E+00,                        +0.0);
   POINT( #6:+2.0000E+01,                      +0.0,         +0.0);
   POINT( #7:+2.0000E+01,-1.0000E+01,                        +0.0);
   POINT( #8:+1.5000E+01,-1.5000E+01,                        +0.0);
   POINT( #9:+5.0000E+00,-1.5000E+01,                        +0.0);
   POINT(#10:                    +0.0,-1.0000E+01,           +0.0);
   POINT(#11:                    +0.0,         +0.0,         +0.0);
   CIRCLE(#12:+5.0000E+00,+5.0000E+00,-9.5367E-07,         +0.0);
   CONTOUR_ELEMENT(#13:#12, #3, #4);
   DIRECTION(#14:+1.0000E+00,         +0.0,         +0.0);
   LINE(#15: #4,#14);
   CONTOUR_ELEMENT(#16:#15, #4, #5);
   CIRCLE(#17:+5.0000E+00,+2.0000E+01,+5.0000E+00,         +0.0);
   CONTOUR_ELEMENT(#18:#17, #5, #6);
   DIRECTION(#19:         +0.0,-1.0000E+00,         +0.0);
   LINE(#20: #6,#19);
   CONTOUR_ELEMENT(#21:#20, #6, #7);
   CIRCLE(#22:+5.0000E+00,+2.0000E+01,-1.5000E+01,         +0.0);
   CONTOUR_ELEMENT(#23:#22, #8, #7);
   DIRECTION(#24:-1.0000E+00,         +0.0,         +0.0);
   LINE(#25: #8,#24);
   CONTOUR_ELEMENT(#26:#25, #8, #9);
   CIRCLE(#27:+5.0000E+00,+5.0000E+00,-1.0000E+01,         +0.0);
   CONTOUR_ELEMENT(#28:#27,#10, #9);
   DIRECTION(#29:         +0.0,+1.0000E+00,         +0.0);
   LINE(#30:#10,#29);
   CONTOUR_ELEMENT(#31:#30,#10,#11);
   END_SCOPE;
   LINEAR_SWEEP_RESULT((/(/#13,#16,#18,#21,#23,#26,#28,#31/)/),
     +5.0000E+01,
```

```
          DIRECTION(:       +0.0,       +0.0,+1.0000E+00,
          POINT(:-1.5000E+01,-1.0000E+01,                 +0.0:),
          DIRECTION(:+1.0000E+00,       +0.0,       +0.0:),
          DIRECTION(:       +0.0,       +0.0,+1.0000E+00:));
        LINEAR_SWEEP(  #2:CLOSE);
        END_SCOPE;
        CONSTR_RESULT(INSTANCE(:  #2:) );
    CONSTRUCT(  #1:CLOSE);
    END_SCOPE;
    WORLD(CLOSE);
CAD*I_FORMAT_END___19870630_Bravo3 PREPROZESSOR
CAD*I_FORMAT_BEGIN_19851109 start letter describing next file
```

The following example shows a neutral file in a pretty print format written by the pre-processor of Proren. The model represents a simple box and includes therefore beside the topological elements only the geometrical elements point, direction, line and planar surface. The neutral file corresponds to the specification version 2.1.

```
CAD*I_FORMAT_END___19851109 end of letter describing next file
CAD*I_FORMAT_BEGIN_19860611  Proren Preprocessor
 HEADER('Weick/Mittelstaedt',
        'Kernforschungszentrum Karlsruhe',
        'MICRO-VAXII',
        'VMS_4.4',
        'Proren-Preprocessor 1.0',
        '1987-MAY-14 16:26:29',
        'Testversion',
        '3C',
        '0',
        '0',
        '0',10,5,3);
 WORLD(OPEN);
 WORLD_HEADER(+1.00000E+00,+1.00000E-25,+1.00000E+34,+1.00000E-34);
 SCOPE;
 B_REP(#1:OPEN);
 SCOPE;
 POINT_CONSTANT(#2:+0.00000E+00,+0.00000E+00,+0.00000E+00;
                #3:+0.00000E+00,+0.00000E+00,+5.00000E+01;
                #4:+0.00000E+00,+1.00000E+02,+5.00000E+01;
                #5:+0.00000E+00,+1.00000E+02,+0.00000E+00;
                #6:+2.00000E+02,+0.00000E+00,+0.00000E+00;
                #7:+2.00000E+02,+0.00000E+00,+5.00000E+01;
                #8:+2.00000E+02,+1.00000E+02,+5.00000E+01;
                #9:+2.00000E+02,+1.00000E+02,+0.00000E+00);
 LINE(#10:#2,#3;
      #11:#3,#4;
      #12:#4,#5;
```

```
      #13:#2,#5;
      #14:#6,#7;
      #15:#7,#8;
      #16:#8,#9;
      #17:#6,#9;
      #18:#3,#7;
      #19:#4,#8;
      #20:#5,#9;
      #21:#2,#6);
PLANE(#22:POINT_CONSTANT(:+0.00000E+00,
                          +0.00000E+00,
                          +0.00000E+00:),
          DIRECTION(:-1.00000E+00,
                     +0.00000E+00,
                     +0.00000E+00:);
      #23:POINT_CONSTANT(:+2.00000E+02,
                          +0.00000E+00,
                          +0.00000E+00:),
          DIRECTION(:+1.00000E+00,
                     +0.00000E+00,
                     +0.00000E+00:);
      #24:POINT_CONSTANT(:+0.00000E+00,
                          +0.00000E+00,
                          +5.00000E+01:),
          DIRECTION(:+0.00000E+00,
                     +0.00000E+00,
                     +1.00000E+00:);
      #25:POINT_CONSTANT(:+0.00000E+00,
                          +0.00000E+00,
                          +0.00000E+00:),
          DIRECTION(:+0.00000E+00,
                     +0.00000E+00,
                     -1.00000E+00:);
      #26:POINT_CONSTANT(:+0.00000E+00,
                          +1.00000E+02,
                          +0.00000E+00:),
          DIRECTION(:+0.00000E+00,
                     +1.00000E+00,
                     +0.00000E+00:);
      #27:POINT_CONSTANT(:+0.00000E+00,
                          +0.00000E+00,
                          +5.00000E+01:),
          DIRECTION(:+0.00000E+00,
                     -1.00000E+00,
                     +0.00000E+00:));
VERTEX(#28:#2;
       #29:#3;
       #30:#4;
```

```
         #31:#5;
         #32:#6;
         #33:#7;
         #34:#8;
         #35:#9);
EDGE(#36:#10,#28,#29;
      #37:#11,#29,#30;
      #38:#12,#30,#31;
      #39:#13,#28,#31;
      #40:#14,#32,#33;
      #41:#15,#33,#34;
      #42:#16,#34,#35;
      #43:#17,#32,#35;
      #44:#18,#29,#33;
      #45:#19,#30,#34;
      #46:#20,#31,#35;
      #47:#21,#28,#32);
LOOP(#48:(/(:#36,.T.:),
           (:#37,.T.:),
           (:#38,.T.:),
           (:#39,.F.:)/);
      #49:(/(:#40,.F.:),
           (:#41,.F.:),
           (:#42,.F.:),
           (:#43,.T.:)/);
      #50:(/(:#44,.T.:),
           (:#41,.T.:),
           (:#45,.F.:),
           (:#37,.F.:)/);
      #51:(/(:#39,.T.:),
           (:#46,.T.:),
           (:#43,.F.:),
           (:#47,.F.:)/);
      #52:(/(:#38,.F.:),
           (:#46,.F.:),
           (:#42,.T.:),
           (:#45,.T.:)/);
      #53:(/(:#47,.T.:),
           (:#40,.T.:),
           (:#44,.F.:),
           (:#36,.F.:)/));
FACE(#54:#22,(/#48/),.T.;
    #55:#23,(/#49/),.T.;
    #56:#24,(/#50/),.T.;
    #57:#25,(/#51/),.T.;
    #58:#26,(/#52/),.T.;
    #59:#27,(/#53/),.T.);
SHELL(#60:(/(:#54:),
```

```
              (:#55:),
              (:#56:),
              (:#57:),
              (:#58:),
              (:#59:)/));
 END_SCOPE;
 B_REP(#1:CLOSE);
 END_SCOPE;
 WORLD(CLOSE);
CAD*I_FORMAT_END___19860611  Proren Preprocessor
CAD*I_FORMAT_END___19851011  Metafile
```

INDEX

A

B

C

D

E

F

G

H

K

L

M

V

W